T0245725

The
Scandal
of
CAL

The
Scandal
of
CAL

LAND GRABS, WHITE SUPREMACY,
AND MISEDUCATION AT
UC BERKELEY

Tony Platt

HEYDAY
Berkeley, California

Copyright © 2023 by Anthony M. Platt

All rights reserved. No portion of this work may be reproduced or transmitted in any form or by any means, electronic or mechanical, including photocopying and recording, or by any information storage or retrieval system, without permission in writing from Heyday.

Library of Congress Cataloging-in-Publication Data
Names: Platt, Tony, 1942- author.
Title: The scandal of Cal : land grabs, white supremacy, and miseducation
    at UC Berkeley / Tony Platt.
Description: Berkeley, California : Heyday, 2023. | Includes
    bibliographical references and index.
Identifiers: LCCN 2023002975 (print) | LCCN 2023002976 (ebook) | ISBN
    9781597146210 (hardcover) | ISBN 9781597146227 (epub)
Subjects: LCSH: University of California, Berkeley--History. | Indian land
    transfers--California--History. | Indians of North
    America--Relocation--California--Berkeley--History. | Racism in higher
    education--California--Berkeley--History. | White
    supremacy--California--Berkeley--History.
Classification: LCC LD758 .P53 2023 (print) | LCC LD758 (ebook) | DDC
    378.794/67--dc23/eng/20230207
LC record available at https://lccn.loc.gov/2023002975
LC ebook record available at https://lccn.loc.gov/2023002976

Cover Art: Shutterstock composite
Cover Design: *the*BookDesigners
Interior Design/Typesetting: *the*BookDesigners

Published by Heyday
P.O. Box 9145, Berkeley, California 94709
(510) 549-3564
heydaybooks.com

Printed in East Peoria, Illinois, by Versa Press, Inc.

10 9 8 7 6 5 4 3 2 1

This book is dedicated to the Native peoples of California, to Ohlone past and very much present, and to activists who demand that Berkeley live up to its global reputation as a public university committed to social justice.

Fiat Justicia

This college, where we are now sitting, what lies beneath?
—*Virginia Woolf, 1928*

What is denied the Dead is denied the living ten times again.
—*Beth Piatote, 2019*

The antonym of forgetting is not remembering, but justice.
—*Josef Hayim Yerushalmi, 1996*

CONTENTS

IV. MISEDUCATION

EIGHT: MISANTHROPOLOGY

NINE: SORROW SONGS

TEN: MAKING HISTORY

EPILOGUE: RECKONING

A NOTE TO READERS

This book contains disturbing and painful imagery of Native people depicted as less than human in anthropological records. You would never know from university archives and popular histories that California's tribes lived full, vibrant lives for thousands of years prior to Spanish conquest and American genocide; that in the heart of what is now the Berkeley campus, the Ohlone built longstanding settlements, hunted in the hills, and fished in the creek; that the "East Bay remains a place that Indigenous people and their relations reoccupy."[1]

Connections

Stand too close to horror, and you get fixation,
paralysis, engulfment; stand too far, and you
get voyeurism or forgetting. Distance matters.

—EVA HOFFMAN, 2004[1]

I HAVE SPENT most of my eighty-year life in Berkeley as a student, faculty member, ex-faculty member, researcher, parent, activist, and resident. And yet it has taken me until now, in the words of T. S. Eliot, to "arrive where we started / and know the place for the first time."

Berkeley-the-university—formally known as the University of California, Berkeley, or colloquially and presumptuously to locals as "Cal," and around the world as "Berkeley," easily confused with the company town where it is situated[2]—was founded in the 1860s, and for its first fifty years was the only full-scale campus of the University of California that today includes ten sites.

Along with nearby Stanford University, it was the intellectual powerhouse of a new American state that, following the extraction of gold, appropriation of land, mechanization of agriculture, and access to national and global markets via shipping and rail, became one of the fastest-developing regions of the capitalist world economy. During its formative decades, the university delivered most of California's brain trust.

I've made several disconnected efforts in the past to know the place, starting with my experience as a student and faculty member in the 1960s and 1970s.

As a neophyte grad student fresh off the plane from medieval Oxford in 1963, I felt liberated in cutting-edge Cal Berkeley, where the foundations of the old white boys' club that had forever run elite universities began to shake. I quickly felt at home on a campus where students linked the struggle for civil rights in the South with the right of students to exercise free speech. In the School of Criminology, where I did my doctorate, I was fortunate to be part of a group that tried to break criminology's incestuous ties with government and criminal justice agencies.

It was here that I learned my first lesson about how quickly benign Berkeley could turn ruthlessly punitive.

After completing a doctorate, I did my postdoc in Chicago from 1966 to 1968, where I witnessed rampant police violence and was jolted into action by the antiracism movement. My return to Cal Berkeley as an assistant professor in 1968, the year of worldwide popular revolts, coincided with new ideas and practices storming through academia. My first academic job was in a lively, pluralistic criminology program that included old-school police officials and criminalists, liberal policy advocates inspired by the War on Poverty, and a small radical wing that advocated what is known today as abolitionism and defunding the police. While I joined anti-war activists on the streets, the school gladly took $140,000 (about $900,000 in today's value) from President Nixon's right-wing Justice Department to train police in how to control urban disorders. My leftist colleagues included a survivor of Manzanar "relocation camp," a Marxist activist, and a Freedom Rider veteran of the voting rights campaign in Mississippi.[3]

I joined organizations that advocated community-based governance of police, massive decarceration of prisons and jails, making crimes of violence against women a public matter, and holding corporations and government officials responsible for crimes against humanity. For an extraordinary few years, I was, in the words of Alice Walker, "called to life" by the movement. I experienced a seamless connection between ideas and practice, a sense of purposeful commitment in the classroom and in the community, teaching what I believed and believing what I taught. We were far too hopeful, as it turned out, but we did not know or care.[4]

Years later, benefiting from information available through the Freedom of Information Act, I would discover that informants in my classes were taking highly selective and sometimes hilarious notes for the FBI and CIA, and recommending my deportation. "Platt has continually and consistently displayed anti-American ideas," reported an FBI agent in 1969–1970. "He has expressed anti-police opinions in the past and has led discussions which had an anti–law enforcement tone. He was one of the first individuals to wear extremely long hair. . . . He is a dangerous individual."

Berkeley figured prominently in the paranoid imagination of the federal executive branch. Richard Nixon's national security adviser was "shell-shocked" by the anti-war movement, and Admiral Thomas Moorer, chairman of the Joint Chiefs of Staff, claimed in 1970 that a radical "command post" in Berkeley was plotting a military attack on the White House.[5]

Not surprisingly, I was not a criminology professor much longer. Berkeley Chancellor Albert Bowker regarded my first book, *The Child Savers* (still in print more than fifty years later), as "sharply biased" and evocative of "Orthodox Marxism of the 1930s." In a confidential memo, he berated my "agitating" against the police. "I do believe some of his colleagues would be somewhat relieved if he weren't around."[6]

By the mid-1970s, social movements were in retreat and radical ideas marginalized in academia. Despite campus protests, including a rally attended by thousands to hear Black Panther Party leader Bobby Seale defend the School of Criminology, in 1976 the university administration and Governor Reagan–led Board of Regents closed down the oldest such program in the United States and placed vetted senior faculty under the ideological guardianship of the law school.

This experience at Berkeley taught me a great deal about how academia functions not just as a servant of power but also as a powerful institution in its own right. But as was the case with many fellow activists in the 1970s, I didn't understand if the university's hard-nosed exercise of power against its own was extraordinary or precedented.

While working at Berkeley, I had another opportunity to make connections that I failed to take.

Berkeley's role in creating the Manhattan Project's first atom bomb during the Second World War was well known in 1972 when I cotaught a class that included an unedited, unembellished video made by the air force, but suppressed until 1967, on the impact and aftermath of the bombing of Hiroshima and Nagasaki. My co-professors and I asked the stunned students: Was this a war crime?[7]

My generation of New Left activists was steeped in the significance of Hiroshima-Nagasaki, but I didn't understand the details and context of how and why Berkeley got involved in the bomb-making business. Was this an aberration, an exception, or business as usual? I didn't know, for example, that the university governed the Los Alamos lab's day-to-day operations; or that it was deeply involved in the application of scientific knowledge, such as planning in which Japanese cities "the blast wave would create effective damage";[8] or that it administered the Bradbury Science Museum as a public relations department of the American military.

In 2010, I traveled around New Mexico for the first time, my eyes opened wide by colors, clouds, and light—a spectacular experience until I went through the security check into the Los Alamos compound, where some ten thousand employees worked on "The World's Greatest Science Protecting America." I also spent time in local museums, hoping—and failing—to learn how such an extraordinarily sensual terrain became home to the world record for mass killing in seventy-two hours.

Even after my visit to New Mexico, I was oblivious that the university and federal government unilaterally appropriated land for Los Alamos that included Pueblo burial grounds, exploited the labor of local tribes, and enabled the families of lab employees to treat Indigenous cultures as a source of entertainment and collectibles.

About the same time as my visit to Los Alamos, I published a book about the traffic in the human remains and ceremonial artifacts of Indigenous peoples. The University of California, especially its Berkeley campus, figured prominently in this trade—as excavators, authorities, dealers, and collectors—and amassed one of the largest collections in the world. *Grave Matters* documented with compelling evidence how the university had pillaged hundreds of Native

•

burial sites through either their own expeditions or local surrogates, and had subjected ancestors' remains to eugenic postmortems in the anthropological laboratory.[9]

But I didn't make any connections between the university's acquisition of Indigenous homelands in New Mexico and in California; or between Berkeley's military history and the Manhattan Project; or between the university's plundering of Native grave sites and Los Alamos residents' fascination with collecting Native artifacts. *Los Alamos* does not appear in the index of *Grave Matters*.

There is no excuse for my ignorance, but it's not surprising. The Berkeley campus's commemorative landmarks honor the victors in the Indian Wars, not those who died and resisted. Also, there are no visual reminders or solemn events on the Berkeley campus to trouble our consciences about one of the most consequential events in university and world history. Unlike the US ambassador to Japan, the University of California does not formally participate in ceremonies of remembrance to commemorate Hiroshima Day on August 6.[10]

Minimally, I hoped that *Grave Matters* would reinforce the efforts of tribes to repatriate their ancestors' remains and cultural and ceremonial artifacts, as demanded by the federal Native American Graves Protection and Repatriation Act (NAGPRA) of 1990 and the 2007 United Nations Declaration on the Rights of Indigenous People. But the university treated my research the same way that it treated Native claimants: ignoring, evading, and delaying through "glacially slow" procedures and "interminable consultation," as a gathering of California tribes concluded in 2017.[11]

In 2020, I took another opportunity to make connections that, in retrospect, were hiding in plain view. With a small group of faculty and staff I cofounded Berkeley's Truth and Justice Project. Our purpose was to investigate the history of the university's accumulation of Native ancestral remains and artifacts. What could we learn from the past that might explain the university's reluctance to comply not only with its legal obligations under NAGPRA and ethical guidelines suggested by the UN Declaration, but also with its reputation as the country's "top public university" and an incubator of social justice committed to "improving the world"?[12]

This book emerged from my praxis with the Truth and Justice Project. It took me a long time to make connections between Los Alamos and Berkeley, to understand how they both share a callous disregard for the human cost of knowledge. Now, I can't stop these associations from scurrying around my brain, as intricate and interconnected as a spider's web.[13] *The Scandal of Cal* is not *the* or even *a* definitive history of Berkeley-the-University. It's not a celebration of Nobel laureates, Pulitzer prize winners, MacArthur Fellows, scientific breakthroughs in genomics, or entrepreneurial innovators. It's a story less often told that encourages us to think in new ways about what we too often take for granted, to consider history not as an indisputable set of facts, but as "an argument about the past, as well as the record of it, and its terms are forever changing."[14]

To know the place I call home requires recuperating multiple erased histories and unpeeling institutional memories that tenaciously stick to History. The book's first section, **Origins Stories**, contrasts vibrant Ohlone communities, which preceded the founding of the University of California for thousands of years, with archaeological records and public histories that are embedded in the state's foundational stories and continue to reduce peoples to specimens, as well as minimize the horrors of conquest and genocide. Sometimes, as Saidiya Hartman warned us, "to read the archive is to enter a mortuary."[15]

To know the past requires recognition of how Cal Berkeley—where I was schooled in anti-war activism in the 1960s and 1970s—flourished in war and celebrated colonial violence as a harbinger of Civilization. The book's second section, **Conquest**, argues that California's "Golden Age" was birthed in unspeakable bloodshed, and that colonialism, imperialism, and militarism shaped the university's governance and academic priorities from the Indian Wars to Hiroshima, and beyond.

To know how Berkeley achieved such a rapid rise to prominence requires understanding the importance of its anthropological collecting practices. The longtime slogan *fiat lux* distilled the university's aspiration to bring light to a make-believe wilderness. The book's third section, **Accumulation**, investigates how Berkeley in the late nineteenth century followed the example of European colonial powers in pillaging Indigenous grave sites from Egypt to California, and hoarding a glut of artifacts and human remains. It was only through persistent tribal resistance and organizing that universities, museums, and other institutions finally and reluctantly in the late twentieth century put a halt to excavating and displaying the spoils of their plunder.

To know how the state validated conquest and genocide as the price of Progress requires an investigation into the role of academia in the production of knowledge or, in W. E. B. Du Bois's blunt phrase, "lies agreed upon."[16] The book's fourth section, **Miseducation**, examines Berkeley's contributions to popular narratives about California's fanciful history and to eugenic explanations of inequality; and explores how the university's "beautiful white buildings embowered in greenery" and its memorial landscape express a cultural self-identity as an outpost of European civilization.[17]

The book's epilogue, **Reckoning**, calls upon Berkeley to live up to its progressive reputation and grapple with how the past bleeds into the here and now. Such a challenge should not be delegated to subcommittees and task forces. It demands a system-wide investigation with tribal and Native community leaders occupying principal seats at the table. Their land, blood, ancestors, cultural heritage, and traditional knowledge are inseparably tied to the university's origins.

It will require the kind of paradigm shift that occurs when long-standing truisms—so rooted in everyday common sense that they are regarded as indisputable facts—are upended, when consensus becomes dissonance, when orientation is disoriented. From its origins story to its wishful historical narrative, the institution's persona needs a makeover. Facing the weight of the past means tackling hard issues—such as reparations—and a willingness to tarnish the university's well-polished brand as a catalyst of social justice.

It's time, in the words of Michael Yellow Bird, for "truth-telling and the revision of settler history."[18]

I

ORIGINS STORIES

ONE

Ghosts *of* Forgotten Histories

The ghosts of forgotten histories haunt
America's heartland, begging to be
remembered and exorcised.

—PHILIP DELORIA, 2020[1]

ARCHIVE OF DEATH

DURING TWO YEARS of the pandemic (2020–22), while more than 5.3 million people died from Covid-19—including 800 thousand in the United States—I spent a great deal of time quarantined in my office at home doing research, with occasional sanitized outings to Berkeley's Bancroft Library, immersing myself in an archive of death.

Heading up a research team that included law students and undergraduates, I followed choreographer Twyla Tharp's advice about the creative process: In addition to a good plan, we need to be open to unexpected detours. "It's only after you let go of your plans that you can breathe life into your efforts."[2] As I took off into uncharted territory, I stumbled into fissures that run deep beneath the ground.

Reading hundreds of archaeological field notes and published findings of expeditions in Indian Country has been a suffocating and numbing experience. It's a close encounter with ethnographies of excavators and grave diggers, stark photographs and skillful sketches of bleached corpses, records of the measurements of the dead, pieces of bones packed into crates, body parts sorted into discreet containers, specimens catalogued in an Archaeological Burial Record, skulls tagged and probed by lab assistants working their craniometers, and fun times camping on a dig. "I drove to Marysville for some shopping, dinner, and a mediocre evening at the movies," wrote a member of an archaeological team in 1935 after a day "working out the skeletons" from a burial pit.[3]

Prior to 2016, when Benjamin Madley's definitive *An American Genocide* was published and most historians stopped arguing about whether or not California's extermination policy constituted genocide, California's catastrophe was either ignored and minimized, or treated as a sad but inevitable stage in the evolution of Civilization. In 2012 I attended the Third Global Conference on Genocide, held in San Francisco. The gathering explored genocides, past and present, in many parts of the world, just about everywhere. Except here. In three days of panels and presentations, my talk was the only one that included California as a site of genocide. It wasn't until 2021 that the first Native-centered history of California was published.[4]

To mine the archive is to learn a great deal about cultural and academic perceptions of The Indian as trapped in prehistory, as a precursor to modernity, as a scientific specimen, as less than fully human. It is rare to find a twentieth-century archaeologist who imagined the dead as children, sisters, brothers, parents, spouses, or grandparents. A member of a Berkeley-led team that excavated a site in Contra Costa County in 1937 was more animated about digging up the remains of a bear than unearthing fifty-seven skeletons of adults and children. It was "the chef d'oeuvre of the day," wrote one of the crew.[5]

Occasionally, very occasionally, I came across an archaeologist who recognized the dead as kindred spirits, who acknowledged that excavators and excavated share a common humanity, who restored my regular breathing.

Llewellyn Loud (1879–1946), a self-described socialist who learned archaeology on the job in Berkeley's Department of Anthropology, did his share of digging up human remains and treating them as collectible objects, but now and again his leftist politics and sense of morality punctured his training in scientific neutrality. In 1912, while excavating a site in Monterey, he took time to matter-of-factly point out that "the Indians did not have much of a metropolis on Half Moon Bay. Their metropolis was doubtless where our metropolis will be, at Richmond, while they come down here for summer vacation, the same as we Whites do, and also to get abalone shells. 'History repeats itself.'"[6] At another site, Loud's compassion is glimpsed in his notes that include information about how "friends of the deceased" prepared the body for burial.[7]

The following year, Alfred Kroeber (1876-1960), Berkeley's most celebrated anthropologist who led the department from 1909 to 1946, dispatched Loud to excavate graves on Gunther Island (now known as Tuluwat Island) in Humboldt Bay, an important location for the Wiyot, who abandoned it after a bloody massacre in 1860. It took a struggle lasting almost 160 years for the Wiyot to reclaim what their tribal chair describes as "the center of our world."[8] Kroeber was actively involved in planning Loud's 1913 expedition, instructing him by mail in exacting detail to the point of thoroughly irritating his outspoken apprentice. "In general, I will say that you appear to be misunderstanding the situation very thoroughly and to be doing work which I have not authorized you to do," Kroeber lectured Loud, reminding him that he needed to devote all his time to exclusively archaeological matters, digging up corpses and arti-facts for Berkeley's collection. "I know of no reason," wrote Kroeber "why you should be planning to work up a historical paper."[9]

But the rebellious Loud insisted on including in his final report a detailed, six-page account of the 1860 massacre:

> A climactic act of barbarity and inhumanity on the part of a half dozen vicious whites. It seems almost beyond belief that men could do such a deed as was perpetrated by them. Indeed, there are no men who could commit such crimes unless they had long been trained to deeds of violence. . . . Mercilessly the hatchet descended on all alike, old and young, women, chil-dren, and infants. Their skulls were cleft, their spines severed, their bodies thrust with bowie knives.[10]

Robert Heizer (1915–79), a colleague of Loud who spent most of his academic career in Berkeley's Department of Anthropology (1946–79), was involved by his own count in one hundred excavations of Native grave sites. It wasn't until a few years before his death, his humanity stimulated by tribal protests and movements for social justice in the 1960s, that he had second thoughts about the unethical assumptions of his lifelong archaeological practice. He had learned his craft in the 1930s from his mentor Jeremiah Lillard at Sacramento Junior College. "On Saturdays we would go dig for Indian relics," he recalled. "Always we dug where we hoped to find some poor old buried Indian whose grave would produce some interesting thing."[11] Soon, he had a bachelor's degree from Berkeley and was participating in professional excavations, digging up burial sites before appreciative audiences. By the time he had his doctorate and joined Berkeley's faculty, he was supervising expeditions that routinely exhumed hundreds of Native ancestors.[12]

In 1964, unlike most of his academic colleagues, Heizer welcomed the "exciting days of the Free Speech Movement" that mobilized thousands of supporters to end Berkeley's longtime ban on political speech. As his "more intellectually alive" students gave him "hope for the future," he began to see historical connections that he had previously failed to recognize between, for example, the invasion of Vietnam and the Indian Wars. In both wars, the aggressors treated the enemy as "non-persons" and "abrogate[d] their humanity."[13] Heizer was among the earliest academics to use the g-word when describing the state's efforts to exterminate Native peoples in the nineteenth century. "No one troubled to name what was happening in California a hundred years ago genocide," he wrote with Theodora Kroeber in 1968. "It was only with the Second World War, after a Lidice, a Coventry, the almost successful attempt to wipe out a whole culture and religion in places like Auschwitz and Buchenwald, that the true meaning of the word, of the act, and of its inhumanity bore in upon the collective conscience."[14]

Many years before Congress put a stop to the desecration of Native graves in the name of science and cultural preservation, Heizer argued that "it would be difficult for any museum to insist, in the face of a demand by living descendants, that its human bone collection was the museum's legal property, and that Indians were simply being emotional about the whole thing."[15] Heizer did not come to this realization on his own nor was it the result of a sudden conversion. He had personally experienced fierce Native resistance to his excavations several times, beginning in 1949 when he ran into a group of Yurok women, including the formidable Alice Spott, Minnie Shaffer, and Olive Frank, who made his life miserable at a digging site in Tsurai (Trinidad, California).[16] In 1974, some twenty-five years later, the now fifty-nine-year-old Heizer decided to take a lonely stand and issue a public mea culpa, subtitled quite presciently "One Archaeologist's View." "I believe that we must consider this a human ethical question rather than one of professional ethics and that when we do, we will decide that this should no longer be done."[17] His colleagues ignored his advice. In 1987, eight years after Heizer's death, Berkeley's anthropology museum was still gratefully accepting "human osteological material."[18]

I go on at some length about Loud and Heizer because these voices of contemplation and accountability, albeit half-hearted and belated, are conspicuously rare in the archaeological archive. Maybe others pondered their actions or held solemn rituals before excavating graves or sorting corpses but neglected to put their experiences in writing. But it's not likely.

An institution that demands respect for the dead does not hire an amateur archaeologist who proudly shows off his spoils of crania like a big-game hunter, as Philip Jones did in 1901 when he dug up graves on Santa Rosa Island.[19]

An institution that encourages compassion for the descendants of the dead does not encourage *Life* magazine in 1948 to take a full-page photograph of its anthropology staff working dispassionately on dozens of "ancient Indian" crania and "boxes of tibiae and fibulae." Berkeley "has everything," says the magazine, "from books and bugs to skulls and sandbags." The text that accompanies another staged image of bathing belles lounging around the pool in the Hearst gym does not mention that the building's basement at that time contained at least 7,680 items of "human skeletal material."[20]

Above the Campus Mortuary, Hearst Gym, 1948
Photograph by Ralph Crane, The LIFE Picture Collection, Shutterstock (1346050oa)

In the aftermath of millions killed during World War II and revelations about the Holocaust, it didn't occur to anybody in the university's public relations department that *Life*'s coverage might evoke a genocide closer to home, even though one of the university's own faculty experts, Sherburne Cook, had recently published a study, albeit tainted by eugenic assumptions, that documented how Gold Rush settlers carried out a "social homicide" against California's tribes and "brought with them an implacable hatred of the red race. . . . All Indians were vermin, to be treated as such."[21]

ERASURE

The state's public history emulates the academic record of erasure. The region's tribes were so backward, concluded an "amazing story" of California's history in 1949, that they were incapable of resistance. Apparently, they went obediently to their doom during the genocide and had no objections when their ancestors' graves were plundered. "It is doubtful if the Indians realized they were being conquered."[22]

While California can hold its own with other regions of the world regarding human-made tragedies—extermination campaigns, land grabs, pogroms, ethnic cleansing, racial segregation, and eugenics—it doesn't have any monumental, officially endorsed, civic memorials to victims of mass injustice, such as the Memorial to the Murdered Jews of Europe in Berlin, the Shoah Memorial in Paris, Memory Park in Buenos Aires, or the African Burial Ground National Monument in New York. On a smaller scale, we have nothing comparable to the federal memorial on Bainbridge Island, Washington, that commemorates the region's removal of all citizens of Japanese origin under Roosevelt's 1942 order; or Reconciliation Park in Tacoma, a private-public initiative that remembers a horrific day in 1885 when a group of white men sought to ethnically cleanse Tacoma of Chinese residents, violently forcing hundreds of Chinese out of town.

Due to lack of funding, California has a weak public arts presence in memorial culture. It's rare to find the kind of government-funded artistic projects so commonplace in Berlin's daily life that you literally bump into reminders of Nazism at the top of subway exits, or walk past them on the way to work, or see them next to ads in neighborhoods, or stumble over them on the way into a café, or come across a kiosk in a park that seductively invites you to look through a peephole at a video of two men or two women kissing and to imagine their fate during the Hitler regime.

Prior to the last decade, there were so few public acknowledgements of California's record of atrocities against Native peoples that they could be counted on one hand. They include a historical

marker on Highway 20 in recognition of a massacre by soldiers of
Pomo women and children on Bloody Island in 1850; the Eureka
City Council's return in 2006 of sixty acres of Tuluwat to the Wiyot
Tribe as a gesture of reparations; and Bishop Francis A. Quinn's
personal apology during a mass for the "past mistakes and serious
misdeeds" of the Catholic Church during the Mission period. "The
Church apologizes for trying to take Indian out of the Indian. Let
the Miwok be Miwok."[23] It would take another fifteen years before
the Church began to take institutional responsibility.

For Native peoples in California who lost homelands, thousands of their ancestors' bodies, and an untold number of cultural
artifacts, there is not yet any official investigation into the case
for reparations, comparable to Clinton's Presidential Advisory
Commission on Holocaust Assets in the United States.[24] Nor
do we have any educational and cultural institutions devoted to
learning about the motivation, psychology, and organization of
perpetrators, such as Germany's Topography of Terror in Berlin,
the Documentation Center at the former Nazi Party Rally Grounds
in Nuremberg, and the House of Wannsee Conference Memorial
and Educational Site. Cal Berkeley does not have a Department of
California Genocide Studies.

ARCHIVE OF LIFE

In the university's early decades, anthropology was central to its
role and self-image as accumulator of objects of prestige (including corpses), as ideologue of conquest, and as creator of origins
stories. Thus, its archive of archaeological documents reveals a
great deal about how Berkeley imagined itself as "the Great Light
of the Pacific—a great public university, one that would serve
equally the children of immigrants and settlers, landowners and
industrial barons."[25]

At the same time, the archive contains a massive lacuna.
Where are the people not served by the great public university?

What about the facts not noted? Where are the unassembled databases? What about the narratives unrecognized by academia? What eras of historical significance are not acknowledged within the canon?[26] Doesn't the thousands of years of survival, adaptation, and creativity by Indigenous peoples in the region now known as California deserve at least one entry in *Fifteen Decisive Events of California History*?[27] Did the history of the state really begin in 1542, as affirmed by one of the first comprehensive high school history textbooks, "when the first white man set forth on the on the shores of California"? Or was it in 1769 "with the ringing of Father Serra's mission bells"?[28]

How can we "resurrect lives from the ruins?" asks Saidiya Hartman. "How does one revisit the scene of subjection without replicating the grammar of violence?"[29] In the case of Indigenous lives that are reified and deracinated in the archive, the answer, says William Bauer Jr., is to be found in "Indigenous ways of knowing" and stories "deployed as weapons against attempted oppression"; in "creation narratives [as] living understandings of what happened in the past"; and in paying attention to place rather than time in Native epistemology.[30]

This requires appreciating the long history of Native resistance, from guerilla warfare in the nineteenth century to struggles over land and repatriation in the twentieth and twenty-first centuries. Though California's tribes were in retreat after the genocide and daily life was drenched in hardships, defense of graves remained a priority, in part out of normal respect for elders, and in part because the land in which they were buried had shaped enduring identities.[31] Settlers, militias, and archaeologists constantly met Native-led opposition, ranging from deferential petitions to confrontational militancy, from polite letters to impolite, rambunctious in-your-face protests. Long before Congress passed the Native American Graves Protection and Repatriation Act (NAGPRA) in 1990, California's intertribal Northwest Indian Cemetery Protective Association (NICPA), founded in 1970, confronted archaeologists and put a stop to unauthorized excavations in the region, setting a precedent for national legislation some twenty years later.

Berkeley's slogan *fiat lux* (let there be light), still in regular use, implies that the people who lived here for countless generations prior to conquest existed in backward obscurity, waiting to be enlightened by their conquerors. To challenge how Berkeley brands itself requires starting the region's long history before there was a university.

Sometimes, if you are patient and lucky, you can use a grain of knowledge in the archive for "contrary purposes."[32] In September 2020, while plodding through boxes of archaeological records in the Bancroft Library, a brief handwritten note on a draft of a 1950 archaeological report caught my eye: "Perhaps there should be mention of remains. . . ." By remains, the writer was referring to Indigenous human remains found on campus some fifty years earlier. He included in his note the exact place where crania and body parts had been excavated. That nobody took up his suggestion to publish the evidence sparked my curiosity. What else, I wondered, has been covered over like the scrubbed surfaces of a palimpsest?

Rub away the top layer in "this place that is both nowhere and everywhere at once" and you'll uncover the previous imprints of history that are present in their absence: in the land's topography, in crates stored in temperature-controlled basements, and in ghosts trapped in a desecrated laboratory. "We see you in your tomb," says the chorus in Beth Piatote's play set in Berkeley, "suspended / Between the living and the dead."[33] Practice your exorcism skills and you'll quickly resurrect what is concealed. Like a glacier, a university is a repository of vast amounts of information beneath its glossy surface.[34]

The unexpected discovery of the scribbled query alerted me to Twyla Tharp's advice and started me on a meandering journey that would link the history of the university with gold mining in Sioux lands, extracting the dead in Egypt, silver mining in Peru, bomb making on Pueblo lands in New Mexico, the unsettling of California, and the plentiful lives of the Ohlone prior to conquest.

TWO

Present Absences

Every song, every story is a living moment that
we can access again many years later. We are
not sad, dying Indians.

—CUTCHA RISLING BALDY, 2018[1]

LIVING MOMENTS

ON OCTOBER 23, 2021, a deluge flooded Berkeley's parched greenery. Walking on campus the next day gave me a sense of how a fierce surge of water channeling through Strawberry Canyon influenced the decision by the Ohlone to make this place a homeland. And why the regents of the University of California decided in the late 1860s to relocate its campus from Oakland to Berkeley. When landscape architect Frederick Law Olmsted was hired to map out a residential neighborhood, he described the canyon as "a most valuable appendage" to the university.[2] "Its gentle slopes, spectacular views, rushing streams and venerable oaks," observed the university's historian, "were always described with reverence. Its very possession was an achievement of respectable order."[3]

The disreputable disorder of nature is a frequent motif in iconography of the land prior to the university's occupation. An early publication contrasted the "untamed beauty and waywardness" and "tangled disorder" of Strawberry Canyon with the "cultivated gardens" that the Botanical Garden tried to impose in the 1920s.[4]

At the first commencement ceremony at the new campus on August 16, 1873, regent and property lawyer John B. Felton described an unpeopled landscape ready for its ambitious occupants: "Sheltered by the mountains from the winds of the ocean,

Strawberry Canyon's "Copious Streams"
Photograph by Tony Platt, October 24, 2021

the student will drink in health and strength from a climate more beautiful and an air more pure than that which attracts to Italy the death-shunning invalid. Copious streams that shall hereafter be classic, descend from ravines in the mountains, and long lines of majestic trees stand like sentinels on the banks."[5]

Felton's hyperbole evokes an emptiness belonging to nobody *(terra nullius)*, eliding the fact that Strawberry Creek, which now mostly trickles through the campus, was once an important, flowing body of water that ran from east to west and sustained life for countless generations. Felton thought of the land as subject to the laws of ownership, forgetting that "deeds of property need to be read like poems," as Peter Bacon Hales reminds us. "Beneath their dry words lie the histories and myths of lands, men, and women."[6]

Before the university polluted Strawberry Canyon with sewage, chemicals, run-off from development, and sediment, it was a generous source of the basic requirements of everyday life: water, food, and shelter. According to a 2004 environmental report, it wasn't "like other streams." The creek's spring-fed flow from the hills to the bay, its link to the Sacramento River, and its proximity to high ground and a deep-water estuary below made it ideal for long-term habitation. Even during the drought of 1864, the creek was generating about one hundred thousand gallons a day.[7] As late as the mid-1880s, according to Berkeley anthropologist Thomas Waterman, "Strawberry Creek ran year round and abounded in trout."[8]

Ohlone Homeland, Strawberry Canyon, 1870
Photographer unknown, courtesy of UC Berkeley Office of Environment, Health, and Safety

Many different Ohlone communities flourished throughout the East Bay for a few thousand years.[9] They were well established here long before people like me traveled thousands of miles to attend a world-famous university; long before San Francisco became a base of military operations in the Pacific; long before fortune hunters passed by on their way to the gold mines; long before the Bay Area profited from the extraction and marketing of ancient redwoods for everything from construction materials to decorative doodads; and long before a Spanish expeditionary force stopped in 1772 on what is now the Berkeley campus, planted its flag, and claimed all that they could see in the name of Charles III and their Catholic god.

A plaque on campus by Strawberry Creek identifies the spot where supposedly the Don Pedro Fages expedition briefly made camp, thus linking Berkeley's origins story to the Spanish Empire. There are no plaques to connect us with our Ohlone roots.

"California Indians understood themselves as a people of a place," writes William Bauer Jr.[10] What kind of a place was the East Bay and the land that is now Berkeley? "For thousands of years, the Bay Area was one of the most densely populated regions on the West Coast. The People who lived there were the children of Coyote, who lived at Reed's Peak, and Eagle, who lived on Mount Diablo," write historians Damon Akins and William Bauer Jr. The fifty or so small bands that comprised more than fifty thousand people lived in the region that stretched from the Carmel River to San Francisco and San Pablo Bay.[11] The Ohlone bands were both autonomous and interrelated, speaking eight different languages, not dialects, "as different from one another as Spanish is from French."[12]

The Ohlone who lived in present-day Berkeley had a fabulous view of the bay, similar to the one we enjoy today from the eastern tip of the University. Living with water everywhere, the Ohlone built their villages over marshland, constructing huge shellmounds from the detritus of fish, earth, and ashes.[13] "The picture we get" from the earliest European adventurers, writes Malcolm Margolin, "is of a moist, even swampy land."[14]

When a French military expedition arrived in Northern California in the late eighteenth century, its commander was astounded to find a land that was "inexpressibly fertile. Our European cultivators," Jean François de la Pérouse recorded in his journal, "can form no conception of so abundant a fertility. . . . No country is more abundant in fish and game of every description."[15]

In the early twentieth century, architects of popular, widely read stories about "The West" would transform this history into mythology: that it took the ingenuity of American pioneers to make the soil productive, the deserts bloom, and the ocean release its bounty. Even Malcolm Margolin, whose foundational book on the Ohlone paints a complex portrait of a people who lived under conditions that were "plentiful beyond modern conception," confesses that he once believed that that the Ohlone were a "Stone-age people with a simple, crude culture."[16]

The second myth embedded in the narrative of American civilization enlightening a wilderness was that by the early twentieth century, the Bay Area Ohlone had declined into nonexistence.[17]

Alfred Kroeber's definitive *Handbook of the Indians of California*, first published in 1925, pronounced that "the Costanoan group [i.e., Ohlone] is extinct as far as all practical purposes are concerned." As for survivors, the testimony of visitors to San Francisco and Monterey in the early nineteenth century convinced Kroeber that there was nothing of cultural value worth preserving in a people who "were dark, dirty, squalid, and apathetic." Decades later he awkwardly tried to backtrack. By "extinct" Kroeber had meant to say that "knowledge of the aboriginal language and culture has become extinct among the survivors. The survivors are there," he conceded in 1955. "They may even be full-bloods; racially or biologically the stock is not extinct; but they can no longer help the anthropologist acquire the knowledge about the group that he would like to preserve."[18]

By then, it was too late to undo what had become popular opinion, reinforced in anthropological textbooks that "parroted Kroeber's extinction sentence."[19] Kroeber of course was not solely responsible for the spread of this disinformation, but his authority as California's leading anthropologist and expert on everything Indian carried enormous weight.

While the cumulative impact of Spain's mission system of forced labor and American genocide had enormously reduced the Ohlone population through disease and state terrorism, there were many survivors—about the same percentage as European Jews who survived the Holocaust. Unlike the Ohlone, however, the European Jews who escaped death did not have to assert their existence or their authenticity as Jews if they did not speak Yiddish, or had non-Jewish family members, or had converted to Christianity, as was the case with many German Jews.

Contemporary Native activists and writers push back against the narrative of erasure by emphasizing the productivity and creativity of their ancestors, and the persistence and ingenuity of survivors.[20] "We are good at adapting to unnatural circumstances," writes Shaunna Oteka McCovey (Yurok/Karuk).[21] We never were and are not now "passive victims," say Cutcha Risling Baldy (Hupa/Yurok/Karuk) and Kayla Begay (Hupa). "We center our histories of ongoing resistance, activism, political interventions, and continued fights for our land, water, fish, and cultures."[22] Today, two generations of Native youth "know no different than a life with ceremonies and cultural protocol."[23] Yurok elder Walt Lara Sr. is thrilled that "my children's generation is getting closer to capturing the true essence of Indigenous knowledge."[24]

A recent study, involving an unprecedented collaboration between genetic scientists and members of the Muwekma Ohlone Tribe, found that "the present-day Muwekma Ohlone share continuity with peoples who have inhabited the San Francisco Bay Area for at least two millennia." For the tribe, whose federally recognized status was revoked in the 1920s, this begins to repair the long-term harm done by anthropological and popular misconceptions. "Validation, finally," says Monica Arellano, vice-chairwoman of the tribe and a coauthor of the study.[25]

Given the relentless sense of Native anonymity and lifelessness that pervades so much of how California history has been and continues to be written—a double negation of past and present—it takes a fierce imagination to humanize the people who civilized the land for us.[26] Berkeley professor Beth Piatote (Nez Perce) would give up a chance to see planet Earth from outer space or celebrate New Year's Eve at the Eiffel Tower in exchange for an opportunity "to see what our ancestors saw, to dream their vivid dreams, to come over a mountain with my mother and sisters and suddenly see, in the wide open, an enormous blue meadow of blooming camas, an endless, unbroken field of periwinkle, lake, and lapis that you could barely imagine, a land breathing and rolling with blue."[27]

AN ARCHAEOLOGICALLY
SENSITIVE AREA

Today, Berkeley's narrative about its origins gives the impression that California's history—or History that matters—begins with the university's occupation of the land. Yet, administrators and faculty knew in the 1870s that they were the latest of a long line of residents. The Ohlone presence in Berkeley was not a secret, as the university's own evidence demonstrates.

Strawberry Canyon Occupied, 1875
Photograph by Carleton E. Watkins (no. 673), courtesy of California State Library (2005-0687)

Decades before the anthropology department was launched, the university's governing body publicized its interest in acquiring "Indian antiquities" from near and far.[28] The first generation of anthropologists documented how the university's site had been a homeland to the Ohlone. Some of Berkeley's leading academics—including Nels Nelson, Thomas Waterman, Leslie Spier, and Alfred Kroeber—are on record acknowledging a longtime Native presence on the land that became the university. These settlements were much more than temporary "camping grounds," as flippantly suggested in a comprehensive architectural guide to the university.[29]

In 1907, paleontologist John C. Merriam excavated shells of oysters, mussels, and clams that "extended for a known distance of nearly two hundred feet along the bank of Strawberry Creek." The thickness of the deposit, he concluded in his field notes, indicated "the occupation of this site as a dwelling place through a period amounting to many years. How long a time has elapsed since the site was occupied can only be conjectured, though some evidence is found in the fact that large tree roots passed through a skeleton."[30]

In his monograph on the *Shellmounds of the San Francisco Bay Region*, archaeologist and future president of the American Anthropological Association Nels C. Nelson referred to "several more or less obliterated camp and village sites of late and ancient date [that] are definitely known in the region, some of them even on the University Campus in Berkeley."[31]

Alfred Kroeber, who had recently assumed leadership of the Department of Anthropology, thought that the main village site on campus was a thousand years old, maybe older. Comparable shell-mounds have been dated to the seventeenth century.

> That this comfortable little hollow, with its growth of live oaks was inhabited pretty regularly is shown by the burial of several individuals. The aborigines would hardly have interred their dead at an overnight camp. The convenient combination of acorns, firewood and water on Strawberry Creek which in former times probably had some flow throughout the year, no doubt determined the selection of this site.[32]

About the same time, Kroeber's apprentice Thomas Waterman, whose mapping of *Yurok Geography* is still in print as a definitive guide to Yurok villages, told the *Oakland Tribune* that he believed "a great Indian village once lay along the present course of Strawberry Creek." He was convinced because "practically every time excavations are carried on in Strawberry Canyon, or the laying of pipes or sidewalks, or the foundations of new buildings, Indian relics are brought to light, the latest find being three skeletons. . . . The reasons for the selection of this site for a village were undoubtedly the presence of oaks, which supplied acorns and a sheltered spot for encampment, as well as drinking water, the trout in the streams, and the game in the hills."³³ Here, he added the following year, "the Indians also buried their dead."³⁴

In 1925, visiting professor Leslie Spier, another future president of the American Anthropology Association, excavated graves on campus and confirmed the presence of "an old Indian Burial Ground." ³⁵

On a regular basis the university's buildings and grounds department excavated human remains of Ohlone ancestors and turned them over to archaeologists who measured and recorded their findings according to the dictates of eugenic anthropometry that was in vogue in the new Department of Anthropology. An exhumation was also a newsworthy event for local press, as in the *Oakland Tribune*'s reporting on how workers digging a trench for a water pipe unearthed a "prehistoric Indian skeleton . . . possibly a thousand years old."³⁶

Internal museum records, now confidential and shared only on a need-to-know basis, document exhumations in 1901–2, 1906–7, 1914, 1925, and 1949.³⁷ "One incomplete skeleton of one young adult, won't hold together with glue," reads a typical accession record.

Today, California's Office of Historic Preservation lists the university and city of Berkeley as a "burial and habitation site."³⁸ Cal Berkeley has not officially acknowledged the specifics of this history. There are no markers or plaques on campus to commemorate what was widely recognized in the university's early decades.

Most of Berkeley's ethnology collection, according to an in-house history of the Phoebe A. Hearst Museum of Anthropology, came from California, including from the campus itself.³⁹ The first documentation of an artifact "found on the University grounds at Berkeley" in 1877 recorded "an Indian relic, a finely carved shuttle in soapstone."⁴⁰ Word about Berkeley as an archaeological site must have spread because by 1884 the Smithsonian had made casts of a "stone pestle made of serpentine" and six sinkers found on "University grounds, Berkeley."⁴¹ A few years later, Berkeley paleontologist John Merriam presented the National Museum with another cast of a "ceremonial stone," collected for the Smithsonian by William Holmes, its head curator of anthropology.⁴²

Between the mid-1870s and 1950s, finding and excavating Native artifacts on campus, including ceremonial and funerary items taken from graves, was a regular occurrence. Here are some examples that were sufficiently important to be noted in regents' reports and accession records:

> Arrow-head of yellow jasper, found near Zeta Psi Hall, Berkeley [1878]. . . . A rare Indian relic from the Berkeley Mound [1879]. . . . A small obsidian arrowhead, from the field south of the Campus, Berkeley [and] a lance or spearhead in obsidian, found on University grounds, Berkeley [1880]. . . . An Indian mortar found near the north line of the University grounds [and a] stone pestle made of serpentine [1884]. . . . Mortars and pestles [1890]. . . . 3 stone relics (Indian) [and] 1 large and perfect spear-head, Berkeley Grounds [1892]. . . . Ceremonial stone [1899]. . . . Mortars and pestles [1890].[43]

Well into the twentieth century, the university documented acquisition of artifacts and skeletal remains on campus, clear evidence of an Ohlone village site. During construction of buildings on campus in the 1900s, "numerous relics were found—cooking utensils, mortars, arrowheads, ornaments, and, yes, skeletons."[44] The "broken end of charm stone" was collected at "Berkeley Mound, Strawberry Creek" in 1901; obsidian knives in 1903 and 1905; fifty objects and shell fragments taken from graves in 1907; a serpentine artifact "in or under skull" and "heavy oval mortar bottom-up over skull" in 1914; twenty-nine funerary objects in 1914; a "small deep stone mortar" in 1922; ceremonial shells in 1925; an obsidian projectile point "picked up in Faculty Club Glade" in 1938; a "basalt scraper" found "north to South Hall, UC Campus" in 1957.[45]

This list of acknowledged artifacts doesn't include innumerable items that amateur pot hunters and university staff privately pocketed, took home, displayed on mantlepieces, showed off at family gatherings, or sold to collectors. In 1973, Berkeley Chancellor Albert Bowker turned over to the museum "one Maidu, one Paviotso [Northern Paiute], one Hupa and one Egyptian basket" that he and his wife kept in the basement of their university residence.[46] In 2011, the relatives of an engineer who had worked on building the football stadium in 1923 returned to the university three mortars, three pestles, and a pounding stone that had not been previously reported.[47]

University-commissioned archaeological and environmental investigations provide the final piece of compelling evidence that confirms what we know from Ohlone histories, anthropological reports, and museum records.

In 1982, archaeologist William Roop surveyed a site designated for construction of the Biological Sciences building. He noted that "three prehistoric sites . . . appear to be associated with Strawberry Creek."[48] Four years later, in a separate survey, Roop reported that the Lawrence Berkeley National Laboratory was sitting on land that "might have been suitable for prehistoric occupation. . . . The Cyclotron itself occupies what is probably the most likely area to have contained evidence of prehistoric human occupation or use."[49]

In a 1987 management plan for Strawberry Creek, environmental scientist Robert Charbonneau explained why the Ohlone must have found the area so welcoming:

> Native Indians of the Huchiun-Ohlone group lived in clustered settlements along streams such as Strawberry Creek. They once maintained a summer camp near the present site of the stadium. The Indians were hunter-gatherers who managed their land by controlled burning of the underbrush to facilitate acorn gathering and the growth of seed-bearing annuals. The landscape appeared as an open oak woodland and grassland filled with perennial bunch grasses and herbaceous flowering plants. Much of the tree cover was limited to the stream channels, and strips of riparian vegetation closely followed the stream corridors from the crests of the hills down to the alluvial flatlands. Deer, elk, bear, and mountain lions were abundant in the hills. Salmon and trout spawned in the upper reaches of the creek.[50]

In another archaeological report on land use at the Lawrence Berkeley National Laboratory, Carol Kielusiak alerted the university that "if any ground-disturbing activities are planned along Strawberry Creek and Chicken Creek, construction personnel should be alerted to the potential for the presence of subsurface archaeological materials. If such materials are encountered, work should be halted in the immediate vicinity, and an archaeologist contacted immediately to evaluate the find."[51]

In 2007–8, the university commissioned William Self Associates to evaluate the archeological significance of the football stadium, built over Strawberry Creek in 1923, in preparation for a major retrofit and renovation. The Buckley report concluded that "the entire project site should be considered an archaeologically sensitive area based on its proximity to Strawberry Creek and the fact that prehistoric archaeological deposits and features have been found along the creek within the vicinity of the project area. Consequently, archaeological monitoring is recommended during all construction and related excavations."[52]

The university went ahead with the remodel and issued a press release that omitted information about Strawberry Creek as an "archaeologically sensitive area."[53]

From the 1870s through the 1950s, university officials were quick to boast in their official reports about the acquisition of Indigenous human remains acquired in Egypt, Peru, and the United States, especially California—with the exception of the Berkeley campus. Faculty circulated and published reports about their work digging up Native graves throughout the Bay Area, including shellmounds that benefited from Strawberry Canyon's waterway, but did not do any serious investigations of sites in their own backyard. Max Uhle's 1907 report on his excavation of the Emeryville shellmound includes a map of shellmounds "in the vicinity of Berkeley" that ignores the shellmound near his own workplace.[54] Nels Nelson surveyed in great detail every shellmound he could find in the East Bay, with the exception of the campus shellmound, which disappeared into his field notes. When a Berkeley anthropologist suggested in the late 1950s that a forthcoming report should include information about human remains that had been excavated on the Berkeley campus in the early twentieth century, his advice was not taken.[55]

Why the apparently uniform embargo on this information? Why the disappearance of this history from university publications? Perhaps officials were worried about negative publicity, especially after the Yokayo Rancheria in Ukiah in 1906 threatened Berkeley anthropologists with felony charges for digging up their ancestors without permission. Press coverage was not favorable to the university: "Reds Want Bones of Forefathers," "Grave Robbers May Have to Answer for Crime," and "May Arrest the Professor" were the headlines in the *San Francisco Call* and Ukiah's *Dispatch-Democrat*.[56]

Another possible explanation is that the university didn't want anything to interfere with or slow down its building and expansion plans. Still, it's something of a mystery why I could not find any mention of exhumation of graves on campus in Berkeley's formal administrative records, not even in the records of the buildings and grounds department that quite regularly dug up corpses. All that remains are scraps of evidence in the briefest of anthropological accession records. Maybe my research wasn't sufficiently thorough. Maybe the regents decided that this kind of information should be kept off the books.

By 1968, when Verne Stadtman wrote the first definitive history of Berkeley's first hundred years, Ohlone legacies had been erased from institutional memory.[57] While university officials and anthropologists kept the details of what they knew to themselves, the topic remained of interest to writers, amateur historians, and purveyors of folksy lore, becoming a matter of historical curiosity rather than historical knowledge.

In a book about the loyalty oath controversy of 1949–1950—when the regents of the University of California required faculty members to take an oath affirming that they were not members of the Communist Party—George Stewart oddly compared Berkeley academics to a tribe who once lived on land occupied by the university and "vanished long ago." Just as early nineteenth-century Ohlone

had been divided over whether or not to resist "the sudden encroach-
ment of Spaniards, all powerful with horses, arrow-stopping armor,
and fire," so too Berkeley's twentieth-century faculty were like "a
primitive tribe," divided against themselves, unable to stand up to
the omnipotence of the regents.[58]

The areas around Strawberry Creek, noted a 1999 faculty memoir, "have for centuries been the gathering-place and eating-place
of local inhabitants."[59]

Even an online map of university landmarks, still in use in 2023,
suggests that the campus "may have once been the site of an Ohlone
Native American settlement that harvested fresh water and fish
from adjoining Strawberry Creek."[60]

But what the map does not tell us—nor does any official university publication—is how Native peoples' homelands financed
Berkeley's development.

LAND GRAB

In 1877, Regent John Franklin Swift used the opportunity of
his commencement speech to promote private property as the
hallmark of capitalist progress and to dismiss socialist ideas popularized in Henry George's proposal to make land into a matter
of ownership in common.[61] "We have here a land fair enough to
be the home of angels," Swift told the graduating students. Make
sure, he continued, to avoid any policy that smacks of "state ownership" because it is "no ownership at all, in the sense the term is
used in civilized countries, and to adopt it would be to take a distinct step backwards in the direction of nomadism and barbarism.

> Our Indian tribes have "State ownership" of land (or tribal
> ownership, which is the same thing), and were in the fullest
> enjoyment of its blessings, whatever they may be, long before
> the coming hither of Columbus. . . . Private property in this
> land has been carried, certainly in theory, to a higher and more

complete point in this country than in any other. . . . [T]he result has placed a greater number of families securely under a roof that belongs to them than can be found elsewhere.[62]

Ironically, it was state ownership of land that made it possible for the university to rise to national prominence.

Jonathan Turner, an early advocate of agricultural and industrial education throughout the United States, argued in 1852 that there was sufficient momentum to pass "an appropriation of public lands adequate to create and endow . . . a general system of population Industrial Education." He added, "There is wisdom enough in the State, and in the Union, to plan and conduct it—there are students enough to patronize it—there is useless land and wealth enough to endow it."[63]

Vermont Congressman Justin Smith Morrill endorsed Turner's policy and introduced legislation in Congress that would "enable industrial classes of the country to obtain a cheap, solid and substantial education." Another supporter, Representative Thaddeus Stevens, also endorsed the bill, hoping it would "establish a national system of education, bestowing national property for that purpose."[64]

The Morrill Land Grant Act, signed by President Abraham Lincoln on July 2, 1862, provided states with land from "unpeopled public domain" to fund new universities.[65] "It was the early days of the Civil War," explained University of California President Mark Yudof in 2012 at an event celebrating the act's 150th anniversary.

> The law granted federal land to states to fund colleges teaching agriculture and "the mechanic arts." At the time, our country was being split apart, yet Lincoln had the foresight to envision a future of peace and prosperity in a nation united and populated by an educated citizenry. . . . You can debate the politics that influenced the creation of these laws and some of the unintended consequences, but there is no question they collectively transformed our country.[66]

To Yudof, the Morrill Act "moved us from a divided, underdeveloped nation into one that is vigorously diverse, competitive, and advanced. And—we don't talk about this much—it made mass education, which is the bedrock of the country, the norm and not the exception."[67]

In his speech, Yudof didn't talk at all about the intended consequences of appropriating Native lands in order to finance the university or the downward mobility and desperate poverty of tribes recovering from a genocide. He could have quoted Congressman Morrill who, in 1857, stated that land for colleges was "acquired by the displacement of the red man."[68]

The federal legislation redistributed close to eleven million acres of land from twenty-four western states to fifty-two institutions across the country. In today's value, the grants were worth about half a billion dollars.[69] Each recipient could use interest from the sale or rent of the land "to promote the liberal and practical education of the industrial classes in the several pursuits and professions in life."[70] California's share was 150,000 acres, ratified by the California legislature in 1864. Income from investments subsidized what became the University of California in 1868.[71] Over the next thirty years, the university raised more than $700,000 ($19.2 million in today's value) from Morrill Act lands.[72]

The standard interpretation of the Morrill Act, as articulated by University of California President Clark Kerr (1958–67), is that the land grant movement was responsive "to a growing democratic, even egalitarian and populist trend in the nation." It opened the gates of opportunity to "qualified people from all walks of life" and initiated the "creation of a relatively classless society."[73]

In reality, according to Robert Lee and Tristan Ahtone's innovative research, the rise of "democracy's colleges" involved "a massive wealth transfer masquerading as a donation." Approximately 10.7 million acres of Morrill land were taken from some 250 tribes, bands, and communities through "violence-backed cessions." In California, land seized from the Chumash, Yokuts, Kitanemuk, Miwok, Tongva, Maidu, and Pomo tribes became the property of the University of California. In the late nineteenth century, about one-third of the university's operating expenses can be traced to the Morrill Act. To capitalize on its windfall, Cal Berkeley "ran a real estate operation that sold plots on installment plans, generating a lucrative combination of principal and interest payments."[74]

California's 1878–9 Constitutional Convention established the University of California as a public trust with extraordinary autonomous control over its lands and investments that would enable Berkeley to use "public power to become a private developer."[75] A 1918 amendment to the state constitution additionally gave the regents the right to acquire land through eminent domain, a right reinforced in 1957 when the legislature affirmed the university's practice of expanding its economic sphere of interest by forcing local property owners to sell. "Landowners in Berkeley and across the state who were unwilling to sell their property to the university," concludes LaDale Winling, "were powerless to stop the institution's expansion plans."[76]

No doubt, the Morrill Act benefited a new, rising middle class, but at the expense of tribes' enforced decline. There are many examples in American history of the unevenness of progressive victories, when some groups make gains towards equality, while others lose ground. For example, African Americans made remarkable, albeit short-lived political achievements during Reconstruction, while during the same time Native peoples experienced military defeat and carceral reservations, and their children were subjected to forced assimilation in boarding schools. As white women fought for and eventually won the right to vote, Puerto Ricans lost their right to citizenship. After World War II, when previously despised Jews moved into the middle-class mainstream, Japanese Americans were still recovering from the economic and psychological shock of their wartime imprisonment for crimes they did not commit. Divisions between antiracist and feminist organizations in the 1970s weakened the effectiveness of the Civil Rights Movement.

SACRED INDIAN LAND

Some eighty years after the Morrill Act, the University of California was party to another land grab far from the West Coast, and again the university benefited from the deprivation of tribes. From 1942 to 1946, the federal government created the clandestine Manhattan Engineer District—better known as the Manhattan Project—that perfected the atomic bomb. The land for the project in New Mexico was acquired through eminent domain by the US Department of War, which contracted with the University of California to administer the military site at Los Alamos. The federal government took over fifty-four thousand acres of remote but accessible land—once home to a private school, a game refuge, archaeological landmarks, and important Pueblo burial grounds—that they transformed into a fortified laboratory, led by Berkeley scientists who then designed and produced the bombs that were dropped on Hiroshima and Nagasaki in 1945.

The lands surrounding the lab, according to the lead article in the first issue of *The Atom*—published by the University of California in 1964 and issued by the Los Alamos Scientific Laboratory Office of Public Relations (now known as the Bradbury Science Museum)—included a "sprinkling of Indian ruins" that had "been forgotten."

> The region might be valuable if it was accessible and worth anything. It could also offer some interesting possibilities in law enforcement or tax collecting. Bandits hiding out there could dodge the sheriff by ducking over the nearest county line in a few jumps. Just think: it would take a three-county posse to stage a round-up, with the Indians cutting them off at the pass! . . . All of this is sacred Indian land, held in trust by the U.S. Department of the Interior for the San Ildefonso pueblo because of the many small ruins in the area. It can probably never be used for anything, which is the main reason nobody has worried about it all these years.[77]

During the war, Los Alamos was off limits to outsiders. After the war, like the Morrill Act, Los Alamos "offered the illusion of free land," its longtime, previous inhabitants disappeared into History, their homeland glorified as testimony to American scientific ingenuity.[78]

In California, as historian Philip Deloria reminds us, the "violent plunder of Native land and its conversion into vast American wealth" was one of "two foundational sins" (the other of course being slavery).[79] For the University of California, whose initial funding relied, in the words of a campus committee, on "capital derived from appropriation and genocide" and whose location in Berkeley and New Mexico was built on land that had been sustained since time immemorial by Native settlements, this officially unacknowledged history is constitutive.[80]

CHOICES NOT MADE

As Berkeley was becoming a university of national distinction in the early twentieth century, it faced choices: how to write its own history, who to remember, who to forget, and how to symbolize its aspirations.

Berkeley could have constructed an origins story that honored the peoples who preceded the university, who had lived with the land "since time immemorial" and had by all accounts thrived until the shock and awe of Spanish colonization and American genocide. It could have acknowledged that there was much to learn from and build upon the experiences of the Ohlone who made the land "inexpressibly fertile."

But it didn't.

Or Berkeley could have recognized, in the words of Lee and Ahtone, that "land-grant universities were built not just on Indigenous land, but with Indigenous land."[81] It could have crafted an origins story that acknowledged its economic debt to Native peoples whose land was unjustly expropriated and brokered by the federal government. Instead of a pro forma generic land acknowledgment,

the university could have crafted a historically specific land acknowledgment that raises the possibility of reparations.

But it didn't.

Instead, Berkeley created and sustained an origins story that
paid tribute to "conquerors in a new land."[82]

By the 1910s, Berkeley had repurposed the canyon that had
nourished thousands of Native lives into a rifle range for student
cadets.[83]

II

CONQUEST

THREE

The Sound *of* History

when the strongest winds blow, the skulls
will rattle wildly, bone against metal,
a crack and chatter of bone against metal,
the true sound of history, this metal striking bone.

—JIM HARRISON, 2019[1]

BLOODY LEGACIES

NOWHERE IS CHARLES TILLEY'S aphorism "war made the state and the state made war" more apt than in California, where the new university came to life in an era of ferocious nationalism, conquest, fratricidal war, and a genocide of malevolence and negligence that caused the premature deaths of a majority of the Indigenous population.[2] The Golden State exemplified violent nation making that occurred worldwide in the nineteenth century: the sound of metal striking bone.[3] The university's history is deeply entwined with militarism. "From its beginnings at the University," noted the chair of the military science department in 1968, "instruction in military science has spanned advancements in military tactics from musketry and horse-mounted cavalry to nuclear weapons and counter-insurgency."[4]

When the University of California greeted its first students in Berkeley in 1873, there was no avoiding the state's bloody origins or the pervasiveness of war. Militarism was central to the university's founding mission and identity well into the twentieth century, from students' rote drilling on campus and the cultivation of an officer corps, to ushering in the era of atomic warfare. "Now I am become Death, the destroyer of worlds," said Berkeley physicist Robert

Oppenheimer after witnessing the first detonation of a nuclear weapon (code-named "Trinity") in a New Mexico desert on July 16, 1945—a trial run for Hiroshima.

The university's birth and development and the region's ubiquitous violence were interdependent.

In 1867, while the California legislature was wrangling how to finance and define the University of California's educational objectives, General George Crook led US Army soldiers and state militia at Goose Lake, near the Oregon border, to kill, not capture Paiutes, Achumawi, and Modocs. "I never wanted dynamite so bad," Crook recollected. Earlier in his military career, then Lieutenant Crook, a West Point graduate, had led a campaign "with murderous effect" against the Achumawi in Siskiyou County. The *Shasta Republican* heralded Crook as "one of the best Indian fighters attached to the service in the State."[5]

During 1868, when the California legislature authorized creation of the University of California and construction began in Berkeley, soldiers and vigilantes carried out one of the last official expeditions of state-authorized violence against Owens Valley Indians in Yolo County, Northern Paiutes in Surprise Valley, and Nongatl fighters near the Van Duzen River.[6]

In 1871, while the University of California welcomed students to its temporary buildings in Oakland, vigilantes murdered nineteen Chinese men in Los Angeles—seventeen by lynching, two knifed to death. "The Los Angeles massacre," notes a definitive history of anti-Chinese terrorism in the second half of the nineteenth century, "was probably the largest single mass lynching in California."[7]

In 1873, as the University of California moved to its new campus in Berkeley, race-specific laws targeted Chinese immigrants for living in a tenement with insufficient space, carrying baskets on sidewalks, and operating laundries in wooden buildings. The police were authorized to cut off men's queues. In other words, being Chinese was criminalized. By 1881, Chinese men comprised almost one-fifth of California's prisoners. The demonization of opium users and proliferation of images of "yellow peril" triggered legal and vigilante actions against the Chinese.[8]

In October 1873, while Berkeley's Museum of Ethnology was displaying its acquisition of "remarkable stone implements and skulls from the Pacific Coast,"[9] the US Army hanged four leaders of the Modoc rebellion—Black Jim, Boston Charley, John Schonchin, and Kintpuash (Captain Jack)—at Fort Klamath and shipped their heads to the Army Medical Museum in Washington, DC.[10]

In 1876, a year after the university announced that it was in the market for "Indian antiquities," General George Armstrong Custer and 263 soldiers of the Seventh Cavalry were killed in a battle with Plains Indian warriors at Little Big Horn, Montana.

In 1877, as African Americans in the South experienced the brutal and long-lasting defeat of Reconstruction, the university recruited Confederate refugees to its governing board and faculty, and elevated John LeConte to president (1875–81). A regent promised John and his brother, geology professor Joseph LeConte, that their support for the Confederacy, during and after the war, would not count against them at Berkeley. And it didn't.[11]

In 1878, after former state Supreme Court Chief Justice and ranch owner Serranus Hastings donated $10,000 to the University of California, the regents named its first law school—Hastings College of Law in San Francisco—after "a man who helped to lead the assembly, financing, and state-sponsored . . . genocidal Eel River Rangers militia expedition in 1859." According to historian Benjamin Madley, then Justice Hastings was the "wealthy mastermind" who orchestrated a military campaign that hunted and indiscriminately killed hundreds of Yuki men, women, and children.[12]

WAR OF EXTERMINATION

Native peoples in California did not experience the respite that Reconstruction (1865–77) provided African Americans in the South, only what historian John Caughey in 1940 recognized as "the heartless liquidation of the California Indian."[13] By the mid-1860s, observed Byron Nelson Jr., the Hupa experienced "a kind of violence the area had never known." Gold Rush settlers "came to consider themselves the owners of the valleys and rivers and mountains filled with grass, minerals, fish, timber, and fertile soil."[14] Native women in particular—their bodies, their sexuality, their reproductive capacity, their children, their ceremonies—were targeted in "this genocidal landscape."[15]

It is now well established that what was done to the tribes of California in the era from statehood to at least 1873—when South Hall, the University's oldest surviving building was built—meets United Nations legal standards of genocide: "acts committed with intent to destroy, in whole or in part, a national, ethnic, racial or religious group."[16]

According to Madley's definitive study, the decades of violence that followed California's statehood were "more lethal and sustained than anywhere else in the United States or its colonial antecedents."[17] You need a strong stomach to get through his *An American Genocide*, as it relentlessly excavates atrocities and cruelties from the historical record, piling high the corpses until they are made visible even to those who prefer to forget or sanitize what happened.[18]

Until quite recently, academics and writers generally blamed the excesses of the Gold Rush on a marginalized riffraff of young hoodlums unmoored from the restraints of civilization, a view popularized by Hubert Howe Bancroft's view of California as a "paradise for wild men."[19] Berkeley anthropologist Llewellyn Loud argued that desperation and ruthless competition on the frontier, reinforced by racism, promoted anarchy among "an ignoble, mean, shiftless, ignorant, vicious, and treacherous element of brutes, who boasted that they were white men and went armed to the teeth with rifle, pistol, and bowie-knife ready to back up their assertions."[20]

More recently, historians have begun to attribute responsibility not only to the "ignorant and benighted," but also to political elites—"the humane, knowledgeable, and perceptive"—who gave the orders for reckless slaughter.[21] As Claudia Koonz has observed about Nazism, genocide paradoxically necessitates an appeal to "communal ideals of civic improvement," even as it mobilizes an extraordinary campaign of repression.[22] To be effective, agents of genocide must convince a broad swath of active participants, accomplices, and collaborators about the righteousness of their crusade. Carrying out the killing, dispossession, removal, neglect, enslavement, rape, and daily humiliations of tens of thousands of Native people required the support, tacit and active, of state agencies, and the involvement of many good Californians—especially the honored and educated whose work as bureaucratic functionaries was critical to the tasks of articulating, planning, and organizing death on a grand scale.[23]

California's genocide was broadly supported. The state's political system authorized twenty-four state militias to operate as a "killing machine." When militias ended their involvement in the slaughter, the US Army became a "major killing force."[24] With the exception of the Civil War and its aftermath, throughout the nineteenth century the army was primarily deployed to subdue Native peoples in the West.[25]

Peter Hardeman Burnett, the appropriately named first governor of California (1849–51), presided over the early days of a cataclysmic moment of shock and awe that tribes experienced as a time when the stars fell. Burnett had grown up in a slave-owning family in Tennessee, where his murder of an enslaved man he suspected of theft was ruled a justifiable homicide. Moving first to Oregon, he advocated the exclusion of African Americans from his new homeland. "Peter Burnett's lash law," as the legislation he authored in 1844 was known, called for the punishment of between twenty and thirty-nine stripes upon the bare back of any "free negro or mulatto [who] shall fail to quit the country as required by this act." The object of the law, he informed the *Jefferson City Inquirer*, was "to keep clear of that most troublesome class of population."[26]

As governor of California, Burnett recognized that the state's tribes had "some ideas of existence as a separate and independent people, and some conception of their right to the country, acquired by long, uninterrupted, and exclusive possession," but nevertheless argued that conquest trumped ancient communal rights. "The two races are kept asunder by so many causes and having no ties of marriage or consanguinity to unite them, they must remain at enmity." Therefore, it is "with painful regret," he declared in his annual message to the legislature in 1851, that "a war of extermination will continue to be waged between the races until the Indian race becomes extinct."[27]

Burnett's prediction came close to being fulfilled. The "grisly statistics" tell the story: California's Indigenous population fell hard from between 300,000 and 700,000 in 1769, to 200,000 in 1821 under Spanish occupation (1769–1834), to 30,000 in the 1850s under American rule, to a nadir of about 15,000 in the 1900s.[28] It was a decline of well over 90 percent, comparable to that of Tutsis under the Hutu regime in Rwanda, albeit over a much longer period of time—a relentless campaign that ranged from killing sprees to deaths from illnesses triggered by malign neglect.

There is a tendency to divide what happened in the West into two master narratives: One emphasizes the unfortunate, unintentional result of diseases that shredded Native immune systems throughout the Americas from the late eighteenth to mid-nineteenth centuries—what Thomas Bender refers to as "the greatest human demographic disaster in the historical record."[29] "The Indian population was drastically reduced, especially through disease," I learned in 2012 from a wall text in San Francisco's Mission Dolores about the high death rate of the Ohlone during the Spanish occupation. But apparently it was nobody's fault. "Whether Spanish, English, Russian, or even if no settlers had preceded the Americans, the result would have been the same."[30]

The Spanish missionaries gave the neophytes a short course in Christianity before trying to convert them en masse. But when they died en masse, they received burials fit for non-humans: they are stacked anonymously ten or more deep in pits underneath mission grounds and buildings of one of California's oldest and leading tourist attractions. "We don't know the exact location of their burial," a guide at Mission Dolores told me, referring to thousands of mostly Ohlone corpses. I am reminded of a witness to the genocide of Armenians in Turkey in 1916 who reported that the dead were "past counting."[31]

The second narrative emphasizes the role of human agency in population reduction in the second half of the nineteenth century, variously attributed to state policies of extermination, killings by settlers involved in the extraction of lucrative natural resources, and destruction of social systems of interdependence. Despite guerilla-style resistance, particularly in the rugged northwest, Native fighters were no match for the sudden influx of hundreds of thousands of miners and settlers, backed up by greed, a sense of entitlement, and armed militias.

Many Indigenous people—perhaps as many as 50 percent—died during California's genocide from malnutrition, disease, and despair. Between 1850 and 1950, Yurok life expectancy halved.[32]

Native deaths resulting from disease and malice are interrelated, just as the estimated 20 percent of Jews who died in concentration camps from malnutrition and exhaustion were victims of genocide.[33] No doubt Spanish and American colonialisms forged their own particular regimes of domination, but they shared an assumption that the benefits of Progress had to be backed up by relentless force. "Civilization did not simply spread of its own accord," David Graeber and David Wengrow caustically note. That is why colonial powers were "obliged to spend the last 500 years or so aiming guns at people's heads in order to force them to adopt to it."[34]

The loss of life under Spanish colonialism was driven by contagious diseases facilitated by a mission system that was authoritarian and brutal, marked by "the sight of men and women in irons, the sound of the whip, the misery of the Indians."[35] The susceptibility to life-threatening illnesses was facilitated by policies that removed people from their lands, banished their cultural traditions, disrupted familial relations, and tried to replace long-standing epistemologies with Catholic dogma under Spain's missions and, later, Protestant dogma in American boarding schools. "Colonizers bear responsibility," note Tai Edwards and Paul Kelton, "for creating conditions that made Natives vulnerable to infection, increased mortality, and hindered population recovery."[36]

What happened to the Indigenous peoples of California was similar to the forced assimilation and genocidal destruction experienced by many other self-sufficient, precapitalist agrarian communities—such as Indigenous peoples throughout Latin America and the Ainu in Japan.[37] "Their story," observed historian Albert Hurtado, "clearly shows the human costs of bringing California into the ambit of the modern world economic system."[38]

While the state-organized military campaign ended in the early 1870s, its assumptions had a much longer life. Officially, the genocide ended, but the war on Native peoples continued.

The exploitation of the survivors of genocide reminded a local newspaper of "cottondom." From the beginning of American occupation, California Indians were "required to obtain employment and not permitted to wander about in an idle and dissolute manner," as a military commander ordered in 1846. "If found doing so, they will be liable to arrest and punishment by labor on the public works."[39] The legislature reduced California Indians to rightless subjects, made the prosecution of anti-Native crimes almost impossible, and colluded with landowners and ranchers to sell thousands of survivors into what Madley calls "state-sponsored servitude."[40]

Legislation passed in 1850 and 1860, paternalistically titled "An Act for the Government and Protection of Indians," enabled the state to arrest and lease out to private employers perhaps as many as ten thousand Indigenous people found guilty of vagrancy, "strolling about," or "leading an immoral or profligate course of life." Children were bound out to white families, young women to household service and rape, and men to hard labor. The new state received revenue, while employers had access to a labor force that was cheap, without rights, and recovering from extermination campaigns. Because Native people could not testify in court against Anglos, the law in effect encouraged entrepreneurs to kidnap and sell them as unpaid apprentices to farmers, ranchers, and miners. According to an estimate made in 1862, children fetched a market price of $30 to $200. The laws of so-called protection facilitated crimes against humanity because, like the post-Reconstruction Black Codes in the South, they were enforced by terror. "Have I not with my own eyes seen Americans steal Indian women and girls for slaves?" asked a visitor from Switzerland as he traveled through California in 1851.[41] As was the case with Armenian parents during the 1915–1916 Turkish genocide, many Native families faced the anguished choice of contracting out their children or risking their death from impoverished misery.[42]

Beginning in the mid-1870s, California emulated the practice of settler colonial governments in Canada, Australia, and New Zealand that forcibly separated Indigenous children from their families and tribes in an effort to uproot cultural and collective traditions and indoctrinate a new generation into values of individualism and economic subordination.[43]

Meanwhile, the new University of California recruited a governing board, administrators, and faculty who legitimated settler colonialism as an inevitable stage in human evolution and articulated the nation's imperialist ambitions in the Pacific Rim, setting the stage for military interventions in Cuba (1895–8, 1917), the Philippines (1900s), Haiti (1915–34), the Dominican Republic (1916–24), and Mexico (1914–16).

BLOOD BROTHERHOOD

Militarism figured prominently in the university's founding iconography. Many of the first generation of regents—the university's governing body that included state officials and university presidents—had intimate experiences with war.[44]

Several regents had been educated at military academies or served in the military, from Romualdo Pacheco (Board of Regents, 1871–5) in the US Navy in 1846, to Buron R. Fitts (1926–8) in the US Army 1917–18.[45]

California's statehood in 1850 profited from the US's military invasion of Mexico (*Intervención estadounidense en México*, 1846–9) that annexed one-half of Mexico's territory—some one million square miles—including large chunks of what is now California. Mexicans became strangers in their homeland, lynched at a per capita rate equivalent to that of African Americans in the South.[46] Regent John Bidwell (Board of Regents, 1880) had been a second lieutenant in the

California Battalion during the war against Mexico in 1846. Richard P. Hammond (1868–73) rose to captain in Mexico in 1847 as aide-de-camp to Brigadier General Shields, who later was promoted to general during the Civil War. Jesse D. Carr (1885–6) used his experience in the army to make money as a sutler during the Mexican War, selling provisions to the military. Samuel La Fort Collins (1947–53) was with the US Army on the Mexico border in 1916.

Within the first few years of the university's move to its new home in Berkeley, the US government had abandoned the promise of the Emancipation Proclamation and Reconstruction (1865–77) by allowing the Confederacy to devastate the first Civil Rights Movement and institute a regime of terror in the South. While the university welcomed all veterans of the Civil War—no questions asked—it only welcomed victors in the Indian Wars. Berkeley students who marched in the university battalion in San Francisco's Golden Jubilee celebration in 1898 were led by Commander J. J. O'Connell who had previously been posted to the Pine Ridge Indian Reservation.[47]

Regent William H. L. Barnes (Board of Regents, 1899–1902) was on the staff of Union General Fitz-John Porter; Ernst A. Denicke (1896–1900) was a colonel in the Union Army; Charles N. Ellinwood (1901–8) had experience trying to repair devastated bodies as a surgeon with the Seventy-Fourth Illinois Voluntary Infantry; John Mansfield (1880–83) was a colonel in US Army and fought at Gettysburg; Henry H. Markham (1891–1905), was severely wounded at the battle of Whippy Swamp in 1865; William S. Rosencrans (1884–5) became a brigadier general, fought at the Battle of Rich Mountain in 1861, defeated the Confederacy in Virginia in 1861, and was himself defeated at Chickamauga in 1863; Regents Chester Rowell (1891–1912), Irwin C. Stump (1892), and James A. Waymire all fought for the Union Army.

Henry S. Foote (Board of Regents, 1892–1900) had been a member of the Confederate House of Representatives and his son fought in the Confederate Army; John LeConte (1875–81), was a Confederate officer in the Civil War, as was William T. Welcker (1883–7), who had trained at West Point and was in the US Army from 1851 to 1861. John LeConte's brother, geologist Joseph LeConte, was a munitions manufacturer for the Confederacy.[48]

Phoebe Hearst (Board of Regents, 1897–1919) was the most influential regent and its only woman during Berkeley's early decades. Her massive funding and hands-on involvement in the university's design, administration, and curriculum propelled the campus from a provincial agricultural college into an academic powerhouse. She inherited her wealth from her husband, George Hearst (1820–91), who grew up in a slave-owning family in Missouri and remained a resolute white supremacist until his death.

Prior to leading the Cavalry Bureau and fighting alongside General Sherman in Georgia, George Stoneman (Board of Regents, 1883–7) moved up through the ranks to major general fighting in the Indian Wars. Under the leadership of Captain Nathaniel Lyon in California, he was involved in a brutal campaign against the Pomo in 1850 that was "among the most lethal of all Native American massacres." Stoneman was elected governor of California in 1882.[49]

Nathan G. Curtis (Board of Regents, 1880–90) was a major general in the National Guard in 1860. John Galley (1932–8) was a surgeon in the National Guard 1896–7. David P. Barrows (1919–23) served as a US Army major in the occupation of the Philippines and returned to California as a major general in the guard fighting the American labor movement. In 1934, he led troops against the maritime strike in San Francisco.[50]

Some regents advocated war-like measures against perceived domestic enemies. John Franklin Swift, who served as regent from 1872–88, aided the US attorney general in obtaining a decision before the US Supreme Court upholding the constitutionality of the Chinese Exclusion Act of 1888.[51] James Duval Phelan (1898–9) was active in anti-Asian movements. "Keep California White" was one of his slogans in a successful campaign for the US Senate.

CITIZEN SOLDIERS

Berkeley has had a well-known reputation for anti-war activism since the 1960s, but for most of its history pro-war activism ruled. It wasn't until 1962, after decades of student organizing going back to the 1930s, that mandatory military training was ended.[52]

A visitor to the Berkeley campus between the 1870s and 1920s would have been impressed not by a stately seat of higher learning in a bucolic retreat, but rather by a military camp preparing for war.

Students Training for War, 1912
"Battalion Crossing Shattuck Avenue at Center Street," photographer unknown, courtesy of the Bancroft Library, University of California, Berkeley (UARC PIC 4:124b)

Three years before the University of California moved to Berkeley, it established in compliance with the Morrill Act a Bureau of Military Instruction that required all male students to take classes and participate in campus drills. State law also required that "students be organized for military instruction and discipline." The military science curriculum included field fortifications, principles of strategy, and theories of artillery fire.[53] The new university prided itself on going beyond the requirements of the federal legislation. In 1872, the regents expressed concern that "citizen soldiers" were ill-equipped with Springfield rifles and urged acquisition of "the newest patterns of breechloaders, and still better, of repeating rifles." In addition to teaching infantry tactics, the chief military instructor gave a series of lectures on:

> The composition and organization of armies, both ancient and modern, showing the nature, use, proportions, and respective advantages of the different kinds of troops. The supply of armies, showing the methods of arming, equipping, clothing, and feeding troops in the United States and the leading military powers of Europe. The moving of armies, treating of the marching and transportation of troops, both in time of peace and war, in a friendly country and in the vicinity of an enemy; passage of rivers by all the usual methods, including the construction and service of pontoon bridges; field fortification; theory of fire and target practice; the main principles of strategy; the history of small arms.[54]

For two hours every week on the new campus, students were trained in "tactics, dismounted drill, marksmanship, camp duty, military engineering, and fortifications." An armory was built in North Hall and an armorer, John Mitchell, hired to maintain weapons and ammunition. The first two hundred students formed a battalion of four companies.[55] Students who wanted to be exempt from drill had to get a note from a doctor at a cost of $2.50. Most, like Elmer Drew, were eager to "get rifles from the Armory and practice at the target, having only to pay the government price for cartridges, one cent each. I went out last Wednesday for the first time," he wrote a friend, "and on the first round made 11 out of 25, with one clean miss. Next time I made a miss also but scored 15 on the rest. 5 shots to the round, 200 yds." He was excited to witness a fellow cadet experiment "with an explosive bullet" that involved inserting a .22 cartridge into a .45 cartridge. "It worked very well on a redwood fence-post." Drew, according to a profile in the Bancroft Library, was inspired by "an army officer who was fresh from chasing Apaches."[56]

"The military feature of the University is important and beneficial in many respects," said President Daniel Gilman at his commencement speech in 1873. "It promotes good order and decorum in the daily routine about the University buildings . . . and contributes largely towards the cultivation of a proper *esprit de corps*. It may, besides, when the University is established at Berkeley, afford a ready and efficient means for the general protection of the public buildings and grounds."[57]

By the turn of the century, some one thousand cadets were drilling on campus, organized as a regiment with a marching band. When World War I offered an opportunity to establish the Reserve Officers Training Corps (ROTC), the university shifted its military program to training commissioned and noncommissioned officers.[58]

In February 1917, the Faculty Club convened a meeting to vote on support for "preparedness, including universal citizen training for army, navy, aviation, engineering, or contributory public service in the present emergency." The three hundred faculty present voted in favor of the motion without any dissent.[59] Around the country, many faculty were fired for opposing US support for the war or came under suspicion of treason. "In many ways what happened to academic freedom during the First World War," observes historian Ellen Schrecker, "was similar to what would happen to it after the Second. Both times, the entire nation was aroused against an external enemy whose alleged agents seemed both particularly menacing and readily identifiable. Both times the academic community sought to purge itself of such dangerous souls."[60]

German Americans lost more than their jobs during the First World War: some 6,300 were imprisoned in camps as "suspect aliens"; many were jailed for dual loyalties; some were lynched. Once thriving arts institutions were driven underground. "Americanizers," concludes historian Cecilia O'Leary, "effectively eradicated German American culture, forcing the disappearance of German Americans as a publicly identifiable group."[61]

At Berkeley, the regents approved President Benjamin Ide Wheeler's request "to offer the War Department such use of the grounds, buildings, and equipment . . . as may accord with the plans

Mobilizing for War, 1918
"Students' Army Training Corps," photographer unknown, courtesy of the Bancroft Library,
University of California, Berkeley (UARC PIC 4:70b)

and needs of the department in the training of troops." In the wake of political and physical attacks on German Americans throughout the country, anti-German prejudices prevailed. The regents ordered the university to fire any "disloyal faculty member," an edict with which it enthusiastically complied. At least three faculty members were "dismissed" for actions "inimical to the United States," and students in the German department were required to sign a loyalty oath. The regents also imposed a pro-war Advisory Committee of Deans on President Wheeler who a few years earlier had advocated US neutrality, saying "It seems terrible to go to war with a nation which does not want to go to war with us."

Berkeley quickly mobilized for war. In 1917–1918, some 1,000 students joined the army; 113 faculty members served as consultants or commissioned officers; and the School of Military Aeronautics contracted with the US Army to train 3,000 cadet pilots.[62]

MANLY WICKEDNESS

The human cost of war is evident everywhere on campus—from a concrete bench with small bears (the university's mascot) that marks "the heroism of the sons of this University who died in the Great War," to wooden benches asking us to "Remember 9.11.01."[63] There are no soulful monuments that ask us to at least consider the horrors and human waste of war, such as you find in most small villages throughout France where the slaughtered, unheroic youth of World War I are remembered not by triumphal arches or resolute combatants, but by the figure of a melancholic woman or man, shoulders sloped, glazed eyes looking off into the unknown.

War changes the meaning of a place. As Berkeley created its landscape and buildings in the 1870s, a national conversation was taking place about how to remember the Civil War. Frederick Douglass's warning in 1871—we must never "forget the difference between the parties to that terrible, protracted and bloody conflict"—was quickly forgotten. By the end of the nineteenth century, a chauvinist patriotism prevailed. Former military antagonists reunited as a "blood brotherhood" of officers, first in wars against tribes and then in the Spanish-American war and occupation of the Philippines.[64] Berkeley's recruitment of supporters of the Confederacy as regents, administrators, and faculty was a clear rejection of Douglass's warning.

The Indian Wars were a matter of national debate at the celebration of the US centennial in Philadelphia on July 4, 1876, nine days after the Battle of Little Big Horn, where General George Armstrong Custer's regiment was routed. Custer's humiliating defeat was transformed into a necessary sacrifice for the nation, a narrative that echoed during the university's formative decades.

Custer's "Last Stand" refers to his role in his final battle. A military man all his short life (1839–1876), he graduated from West Point and fought in the Civil War and Indian Wars. He died at war. Given how well his name is known (though inevitably paired with "Last Stand"), you might think that he was an unblemished military leader who had a bit of bad luck at Little Big Horn, or that he was a warrior of extraordinary courage—the last one standing in the battle. Historical evidence suggests neither is true.

In 1867, during the Kansas-Colorado campaign, Custer ordered deserters shot without trial and left his post without permission, for which he was sentenced to a one-year suspension from the military without pay. In 1868 he returned from exile to defeat the Southern Cheyenne at the Washita and was rumored to have encouraged his soldiers to rape women captives.[65] He regarded Indians as a once "noble race" who had degenerated and were doomed to extinction: "The Indian cannot be himself and be civilized: he fades away and dies."[66]

If, as the Sioux chief Sitting Bull put it, "the love of possessions is a disease among them," Custer was somebody who enthusiastically spread the virus. In violation of the 1868 Fort Laramie Treaty, signed by the Sioux and US government, Custer led a military expedition looking for gold into the Black Hills of Dakota in 1874. The US Army's subsequent "pacification campaign" in sacred terrain made it possible, three years later, for George Hearst, Phoebe's husband, to make his first great fortune from what would become the largest gold mine in the United States. The Homestake Mine in South Dakota generated 2.7 million tons of gold and caused long-standing environmental damage to Indigenous lands, rivers, and the watershed. "I will hurt a good many people," Hearst confided in his business partner.[67]

In 1876, as a sort of poetic justice, Custer blundered into the largest gathering of Plains Indian fighters ever assembled in central Montana. With the story of the "Last Stand," he became the celebrity in death that he never fully achieved while alive.[68] We know from military and Native histories that "Last Stand" is not an accurate description of what took place at Little Big Horn. The battle was chaotic and overwhelming, with Custer and his men quickly swept away. The actual fighting took about "as long as it takes a hungry man to eat a meal," according to one account. There was no heroic Last Stand at the Battle of the Greasy Grass, the much less romantic name that Native fighters used. Like war in general, it was nasty and brutal, with the defeated fleeing in panic. According to an oral history with Wooden Leg, a Northern Cheyenne fighter, the battle "looked like thousands of dogs might look if all of them were mixed together in a fight." A day or so later, Custer and his men were found strewn about in the stifling heat, naked and torn apart, their bodies covered in flies and swollen with gas.[69]

So how did a leader associated with one of the nation's worst military defeats become a national hero? According to historian Richard Slotkin, the celebration of the United States centennial on July 4, 1876, nine days after the battle of Little Big Horn, provided an opportunity to remake Custer's humiliating death into a "redemptive sacrifice" on behalf of the nation's quest to "bring light, law, liberty, Christianity, and commerce to the savage places of the earth." The myth of "Custer's Last Stand" was popularized in the print media as a call to defend the nation against rebellions from below, whether tribes fighting back, or a labor movement demanding workers' rights, or "barbarian" immigrants threatening capitalist civilization.[70]

The making of the myth of the Last Stand was a massive literary and artistic production, as well as a makeover of Custer's body image.

Custer, 1869, Before Makeover
"Gen. George A. Custer, U.S.A.," December 1869, courtesy of Brady-Handy Photograph Collection, Library of Congress, Prints and Photographs Division (LC-DIG-cwpbh-04951)

In "A Death Sonnet for Custer," written a few days after his death and published in the *New York Daily Tribune*, Walt Whitman represented Custer as a Christ-like figure, "the loftiest of life upheld by death. . . .

Thou of the sunny, flowing hair, in battle,
I erewhile saw, with erect head, pressing ever in front,
bearing a bright sword in thy hand,
Now ending well the splendid fever of thy deeds,
(I bring no dirge for it or thee—I bring a glad, triumphal sonnet;)
There in the far northwest, in struggle, charge, and saber-smite,
Desperate and glorious—aye, in defeat most desperate, most glorious,
After thy many battles, in which, never yielding up a gun or a color,
Leaving behind thee a memory sweet to soldiers,
Thou yieldest up thyself.[71]

This theme of the gloriousness of death in battle and of the purging qualities of violence resonated at Berkeley, especially in the ideas of Josiah Royce (1855–1916), who was born in the mining town of Grass Valley, graduated with Berkeley's first class of undergraduates in 1875, received a Ph.D. from Johns Hopkins three years later, and taught in the English department at Berkeley from 1878 to 1882 before settling into a distinguished career in philosophy at Harvard.[72]

In his influential 1886 book on *California*, subtitled *A Study of American Character*, Royce lamented the carnage inflicted by settlers who practiced "blindness to our social duties and an indifference to the rights of foreigners, whereof we cannot be proud." But conquest also nourished "our best national traits," Royce continued. "Our pioneer community in California was persistently cheerful, energetic, courageous, and teachable." Echoing Whitman's search for salvation in Custer's death, Royce told his readers not to obsess about the "horror of the crimes," for "one's horror is itself a weakness. . . . [California's] manly wickedness is full of the strength that, on occasion, freely converts itself into an admirable moral heroism." What is remarkable about the state's early history, he concluded, is that the pioneering generation evolved "to purify itself within so short a time, not by revolution, but by a simple progress from social foolishness to social steadfastness. Even thus a great river, for an hour defiled by some corrupting disturbance, purifies itself, merely through its own flow, over its sandy bed, beneath the wide and sunny heavens." To Royce, hope for the future resided in the "the better families of the community [who] were superior to the average of Mexicans, having generally a purer Castilian blood, since in many cases the colonists had come almost directly from Spain."[73]

A couple of decades after Royce left for Harvard, another faculty member, biologist Jacques Loeb, took on the "false biological assumption" advocated by "war enthusiasts" who think that war is good for preserving the "virile virtues" of a nation. But Loeb—an atheist, pacifist, socialist, Jewish immigrant— didn't last long at Berkeley.[74]

CHOICES MADE

In 1876, at the height of the genocide, while settlers purified themselves with unrelenting violence, Yurok writer Lucy Thompson witnessed some "three thousand Indians at a White Deerskin Dance." Cutcha Risling Baldy reminds us that a place saturated in blood and terror is also a "place of world renewal," of dancing to "the stomp of our feet and the warmth of our fires."[75]

Berkeley could have chosen an origins story that soulfully reflects on what it means to build a university in "the valley of the shadow of death."[76]

But it didn't.

Berkeley could have chosen an origins story that reflects on the victims, survivors, and resisters as well as victors of war and conquest.

But it didn't.

Instead, the university chose and continues to choose to honor the leaders and beneficiaries of California's genocide and military ventures, to enshrine them as founding fathers and occasionally founding mothers, and to celebrate them for bringing Progress to the Golden State.

Arming the University, 1900

Photographer unknown, courtesy of Oliver Family Photograph Collections, the
Bancroft Library, University of California, Berkeley (BANC PIC 1960.010 ser. 2:0936)

In 1905, Berkeley erected a monument in the Esplanade, the campus's most revered space, to the university armorer, a military veteran whose claim to fame was being part of a military expedition that drove the Comanche, Kiowa, Southern Cheyenne, and Arapaho tribes from the Southern Plains.

FOUR

A Matter *of* Life *and* Death

History keeps me awake at night.

—DAVID WOJNAROWICZ, 2018[1]

I HEAR AN ARMY

IN 1937, ON "one of those radiant days that October brings to Berkeley after the fog and even cold of the summer," poet-to-be Robert Duncan was sprawled out on the grass with two undergraduate friends. He felt the same kind of ambivalence about being at Berkeley that another budding writer, Jack London, had felt in 1895 when he was briefly an undergraduate, a year after being convicted of "having no fixed abode" and sentenced to a month in the Erie County Penitentiary in Buffalo where he experienced "things unbelievable and monstrous . . . [in] the awful abysses of human degradation."[2] A working-class socialist from Oakland, London lasted only a year at Berkeley. Channeling his experiences through a character in his semiautobiographical novel, he felt alienated from his fellow students who

> had been studying about life from the books while he had been busy living life. His brain was just as full of knowledge as theirs, though it was a different kind of knowledge. How many of them could tie a lanyard knot, or take a wheel or a lookout? His life spread out before him in a series of pictures of danger and daring, hardship and toil. He remembered his failures and scrapes in the process of learning. He was that much to the good, anyway. Later on, they would have to begin living life and going through the mill as he had gone.[3]

There would be many more Jack Londons and Robert Duncans, torn between "scorn and longing," between the lure of entitlement and a deep sense of alienation.[4] In the 1960s, Free Speech Movement activist Mario Savio hoped that Berkeley would be a "place where people begin seriously to question the conditions of their existence" but instead discovered that "students are permitted to talk all they want so long as their speech has no consequences."[5]

For Robert Duncan, it was militarism, not unfree speech, that drove him away. One sunny day in October 1937, Robert and his friends Lilli and Athalie were reading aloud and discussing a poem by James Joyce—"I hear an army charging upon the land, / And the thunder of horses plunging, foam about their knees"[6]—when the campanile bells sounded, calling students to military drill. "It was a condition of our being educated at all at a state university that we be prepared, that we march. Keep time," thought Duncan as he got up to leave. "You don't have to go," said Lilli. "Stay with Joyce." Athalie added, "Rejoice with Joyce." Torn between the command to "keep time in ordered ranks" and "obedience to the beauty of a thing," Duncan chose "the authority of the poem." As the student cadets assembled, he joined his friends' "conspiracy against the army," deciding there and then to boycott classes that he "found a sham" and to enlist in "a poetic order more commanding than my fear of military authorities."[7]

Duncan's resistance to Berkeley's pride in militarism wasn't new. "There is and always has been an undercurrent of hostility to the military department on the part of both faculty and students," said Berkeley's Commandant Colonel George C. Edwards in 1884.[8] In 1904, students pelted Captain John Nance, head of the Cadet Corps, with clods of earth when he required them to march into his class on military tactics.[9] Even Robert McNamara, who as President Kennedy's and Johnson's Secretary of Defense (1961–68) enthusiastically orchestrated the war against Vietnam, admitted in his memoir that he had cautiously rebelled against compulsory military service at Berkeley in the

1930s. "My classmates and I saw it as a pointless ritual, irrelevant to our world. On the day of our final parade, when we had to march before the president of the university, we threw down our rifles as soon as we were done—the hell with it!"[10]

McNamara no doubt recalled a lively and well organized anti-war campaign at Berkeley in the 1930s that called for abolition of compulsory military service, contested the ban on political organizing on campus, and as late as 1940 held "The Yanks Are Not Coming" rallies.[11] Robert Nisbet remembers leftists "trapping their professors into class arguments," reminiscent of how as a neophyte academic I experienced debates between Marxists and national liberationists in the 1970s.[12] In 1938, the student government's Peace Committee reported that opposition to required military classes and training was widespread, as evidenced by students who gave an ironic fascist salute and hummed fascist anthems when marching past the university president.[13] A majority of students and faculty, however, eagerly or silently complied.

From the founding of the university through the US occupation of the Philippines and involvement in World War I, it was common to see students "in their army uniforms marching, hup-hupping all the way to their classes. . . . One could summon up images of West Point just by looking out on the Berkeley campus." With a global war looming on the horizon in the late 1930s, Nisbet no longer had to worry about being trapped into classroom debates by argumentative leftists.[14]

By the time that the United States entered the war in late 1941, the anti-war movement had dissipated, and the university turned over its "arsenal of knowledge" to the government.[15] Berkeley provided research, technical support, and officer training, and transferred a dormitory to army personnel and International House to a naval program. By 1944, about a quarter of all male students were working with the navy. The military, according to a public relations press release, "beefed up its presence on campus to churn out recruits from the officer training corps."[16]

More significantly, the university formally and secretly committed its scientific programs to national offense. Prior to the bombing of Pearl Harbor in December 1941, Berkeley physicist Ernest Lawrence advocated the development of a new kind of weapon system. Shortly after the Japanese attack, the federal government funded Lawrence's work at Berkeley's Radiation Laboratory in the hills above the Greek Theatre and football stadium. At its peak, the lab employed 1,250 staff at a cost of about half a million dollars per month. In the summer of 1942, a group of scientists, led by physicist J. Robert Oppenheimer, met regularly in LeConte Hall (named after the brothers who had sided with the Confederacy and remained lifelong white supremacists) where they prepared the first blueprint for the atomic bomb and discussed the possibility of creating a thermonuclear bomb. "If such weapons had to be created," concludes a history of the University of California, "it was in the interests of the free world that the United States make them first."[17]

After the war, no detectable vestiges of the anti-war movement remained, and militarism continued to figure prominently in the university's memorial culture, creating a seamless link between past and present until the Vietnam War (or what is called the American War in Vietnam) once again disturbed the appearance of consensus.

DEMOCRATIC IDEALS

Arriving on the Berkeley campus through its main entrance, I'm greeted by a lovely grove of cherry trees, installed in 2013 by the Japanese American Alumni Association, that "stands as a legacy to the graduates of Japanese ancestry in recognition of their contribution to our society and as a tribute to the educational excellence of the University of California."[18] The plaque at the grove does not mention the five hundred Japanese American students expelled by the University of California during World War II in compliance with President Franklin Roosevelt's Executive Order 9066 in 1942.[19]

Japanese Americans Exiled from Berkeley, 1942

Photographer unknown, courtesy of the Bancroft Library, University of California, Berkeley (BANC PIC 1983.097)

Stadtman's authoritative account of the "one of the world's great academic institutions," completed in 1970, chose to erase memory of this shame from "the first complete narrative history of the University to be published since 1930."[20] This kind of selective remembering is also evident in a recent exhibition in the Bancroft Library on "the incarceration of Japanese Americans." It emphasizes that "notable Berkeleyans joined efforts against the federal injustices being inflicted against their fellow citizens," but does not explore the university's silent complicity in federal government policies that forced families to abandon their homes and jobs and be imprisoned without trials for crimes they did not commit. The exhibit is also silent on Berkeley's direct involvement in the bombing of Hiroshima and Nagasaki.[21]

Yoshiko Uchida, a Berkeley student, remembers being given notice by Western Defense Command to "clear out in ten days a house we've lived in for fifteen years." Together with her mother and sister, they "packed frantically and sold recklessly." Another Nisei student wrote to the *Daily Californian*: "In the hard days ahead, we shall try to re-create the spirit which has made us so reluctant to leave now, and our wish to those who remain is that they maintain here the democratic ideals that have operated in the past. We hope to come back and find them here."[22]

Walking unaware through the campus you would never learn that the University of California has administered three national laboratories involved in nuclear weapons production since their creation, or that it played a significant role in the development of weapons of mass destruction that contributed to the mass murder of civilians in Japan in 1945.[23] Berkeley's lead physicist in Los Alamos, Robert Oppenheimer, is the subject of several books, two plays (*In The Matter of J. Robert Oppenheimer* and *Oppenheimer*), an opera (*Doctor Atomic*), and a film (*Oppenheimer*), but is invisible in Berkeley's public spaces.

I'm reminded of my 2010 visit to New Mexico, when I visited the Los Alamos National Laboratory's Bradbury Science Museum. The museum, which caters to students, families with children, and tourists, receives about ten thousand visitors a year. "Don't miss the first nuclear bombs, Little Boy and Fat Man," invited the Bradbury's brochure. Surprised to find out that the museum is operated by the University of California (on behalf of the U.S. Department of Energy), I expected something more than jingoistic propaganda on behalf of American militarism. I naively thought that university sponsorship means visitors will be exposed to debates, conflicting opinions, and moral engagement. I recorded the experience in my field notes.

Inside the small museum, free to visitors, there is extensive information about the history of Los Alamos, as well as the scientists and staff who were part of the hush-hush operation known as the Manhattan Project. We are informed how the Lab was built in 1942–3 and about the scientific details that went into testing the world's first nuclear device at the Trinity site on July 16, 1945, in the desert. The buildup to dropping bombs on Hiroshima on August 6 and Nagasaki on August 9 is described in detail. If you look carefully, you can even learn that the bombs killed an estimated three hundred thousand people in Japan.

Visitors get facts, presented clinically and dispassionately as if science is value-free. We are sheltered from seeing the human cost of nuclear war. There are replicas of the first bombs, photographs of the devastated cities, and, of course, mushroom clouds. But no images of vaporized people, agonizing deaths, or the long-term suffering produced by radiation sickness. Nothing to make us recognize the common humanity of us and them. The Japanese are absent, faceless, abstract.

Reading my notes now, I'm reminded of how Berkeley's archaeologists transformed ancestors into specimens.

> The museum exhibits don't include political debate or ethical dilemmas about the decision to kill, without warning, one-third of the population of Hiroshima and eighty thousand civilians in Nagasaki in order to end the war and "save American lives." And there is nothing about the Cold War and spiraling arms race initiated by the United States. A sixteen-minute film, *The Town That Never Was*, shows off a nuclear fireball, but no people burning to death or staggering through the splintered streets. In a small space at the back of the museum, behind all the exhibits, out of the way, there's a hard-to-find book in which you can write comments that express "an alternative perspective to the official views presented by the museum."
>
> In the museum's bookstore, I buy a booklet written by the Los Alamos Historical Society that tells us everything we might want to know about The Bomb except what it did to its victims. It concludes with an empathetic account of the "crashing letdown" felt by the Lab's staff at the end of the war but is silent on the feelings of the Japanese victims who died instantly or were unlucky to survive.[24]
>
> After the Bradbury, I visited the New Mexico History Museum in Santa Fe, expecting less propaganda. But it's more of the same. A gleaming white room is decorated on every wall and the ceiling with graffiti-like quotations from people who worked on "the most daring scientific project ever attempted." The impact is disorienting and hip, but anti-intellectual. The

only hint that the Lab's staff was working on a weapon of mass destruction is a small case displaying an oscillograph that recorded data from the Trinity blast.

Beyond the white room, we briefly learn that "the atomic bomb project changed New Mexico"—its labs, bases, defense contracts, and high-tech industries becoming a "crucial part of the state's economy." But unlike a visit to any Holocaust museum, we are not asked to ponder the enormity of human loss or express a moment of solidarity with innocent victims. Nor are we expected to grapple with the fact that the state's economic development was fueled by industries of death. Oblivion continues in the gift store, where I buy a packet of fifteen "Historic Postcards" of the White Sands Missile Range, with celebratory before and after photographs of the Trinity test and snapshots of missiles from the V-2 to the Patriot.

Even an obligatory visit to Georgia O'Keeffe's gorgeous adobe home in nearby Abiquiú leaves me with a bit of a sour taste. From her studio we look out at the cottonwood trees, jimson weeds, Chama River valley, and white hills that she captured so vividly in her paintings. But her fully stocked, state-of-the-art bomb shelter—built in the late 1950s at the height of the Cold War when many people thought that an underground room could protect them from radiation and fireballs—is off limits to tourists.

MANKIND WILL CURSE

The small team that met on campus in LeConte Hall to brainstorm an atomic bomb needed more space, more personnel, and more security to implement its vision. In 1942, the University of California and the US Department of Energy selected a site in New Mexico to locate the Los Alamos National Laboratory where the Manhattan Project designed and developed the two bombs, "Little Boy" and "Fat Man," that were dropped on Hiroshima and Nagasaki on August 6 and 9, 1945. The University of California, primarily

Berkeley, managed the project and provided key scientific leadership and personnel.[25]

In addition to administering the Bradbury Science Museum when it opened to the public in 1954, the university also published the lab's public relations magazine, *The Atom*, first issued in 1964. In both cases, the University of California provided an imprimatur of academic legitimacy while delegating all curatorial and editorial decisions to the lab's public relations office. "I've never heard of UC faculty being involved in any Bradbury exhibit development," the current director of the museum told me.[26]

For its operations, labs, three thousand personnel, and families, the university and federal government carved out fifty-four thousand acres from the Pajarito Plateau that Indigenous communities had occupied since 900 CE, and that by the 1800s were centers of bustling activity. A century later, cattle ranchers, timber companies, and homesteaders competed for control of natural resources.[27] According to the Atomic Heritage Foundation that is "dedicated to the preservation and interpretation of the Manhattan Project," Los Alamos "prohibited many Native Americans from enjoying their ancestral lands and sacred ancestral sites."[28] Peter Bacon Hales notes that by the 1940s the federal government owned most of the region, making it easy for the Manhattan Project to "turn scientific discovery into a tool for the control of nature, and the control of nature into a tool for war."[29]

"Official histories of the Manhattan Project," writes Hales, "tend to begin with scientific discovery and military necessity," reminding me of how in official histories of Berkeley "the land and its people, their histories together, rarely appear, except perhaps as necessary sacrifices."[30] The university-run operation in New Mexico denied Native communities access to longstanding burial grounds and ignored the plateau's ecological and human histories in much the same way that the university treated its land in Berkeley as uninhabited, virgin territory, disconnected from its multiple pasts.[31]

"This section of New Mexico was mostly uninhabited except for a few isolated homesteads and the Los Alamos Ranch School for Boys," explained a University of California brochure announcing the opening of the Los Alamos Scientific Laboratory Science Museum in 1954. The museum's first exhibition included "a display of artifacts ranging from arrow heads to pottery that have been found here"—disconnected from the people who used these items every day for generations.[32] As observed by historian Hal Rothman, Los Alamos was a product of the Cold War, an "economic colony and federally funded protectorate . . . dropped into a world to which it bore no relation."[33]

Unlike Berkeley, where the university treated local tribes as if they were invisible or disappeared, in New Mexico they were visible, close, and an invaluable part of the Manhattan Project's labor force, as well as objects of curiosity and cultural exploitation. The local Pueblo communities provided workers who cleaned homes, cooked, looked after children, maintained gardens, poured concrete, and stoked furnaces. The lab cultivated relationships with Pueblo leaders, such as the governor of the Tesuque Pueblo, who believed "the people must be taught that in order to make a good living, they must learn how the white man thinks."[34] Pueblo women who worked as maids were nearly always called "girls," no matter their age or status. To Phyllis Fisher, wife of physicist Leon Fisher, her "household help looks as though she couldn't lift a feather. But whether or not she can clean the house is immaterial. I'm sure she'll be worth her wages in entertainment value alone. She is sweet and picturesque, and I love to watch her."[35]

Scientific staff and their families assumed they had a right to walk through tribal lands and visit the homes of their employees unannounced. "I never dreamed that an Indian Pueblo could be so attractive," Phyllis Fisher wrote her parents about attending a ceremony. Her son was "quite carried away by it all and finally joined lustily in the war whoops."[36] *The Atom* magazine encouraged the lab community to explore "a thousand years of human history [that] lie at your feet." Members of the Cochiti Pueblo were hired to make the area "more accessible to hikers" and to amateur archaeologists interested in visiting "the large and mysterious circle of stones called a shrine for lack of a better name" or collecting "pottery shards and chips of obsidian sprinkled profusely around some of the stone circles."[37]

As in Berkeley, though on a much smaller scale, the residents of Los Alamos were overcome by "collector's mania" and were passionate about "Indian art objects." Luke-warm warnings about cultural sensitivity issued by the Manhattan Project did not stop plundering of archaeological sites nor holding public events that promised participation by local Indians "in full war paint." As the Pueblos became more economically dependent on the military for jobs and to meet the insatiable demand for artifacts, Pueblo culture experienced profound changes in work patterns, gender roles, and creativity. Pottery production in San Ildefonso, according to a longtime local resident, shifted from "bowls made as gifts of love" to mass production for tourism.[38]

Meanwhile, Los Alamos's primary production was a new kind of weapon of mass destruction. At a meeting on May 31, 1945, Berkeley physicist Oppenheimer predicted that an atomic bomb— with the explosive yield of about 15,000 tons of TNT—would kill "some 20,000 people" if exploded over a city.[39] Oppenheimer helped to select Hiroshima for the first bombing. In 1954, at a confidential hearing held by the US Atomic Energy Commission, he was asked about his prediction:

Q: You knew, did you not, that the dropping of that atomic bomb on the target you had selected will kill or injure thousands of civilians, is that correct?

A: Not as many as turned out.

Q: How many were killed or injured?

A: 70,000.

Q: You supported the dropping of the atom bomb on Japan, didn't you?

A: I did my job which was the job I was supposed to do.[40]

Oppenheimer's second estimate also undercounted the number of victims by at least 30 percent. We will never know the actual number of dead in Hiroshima and Nagasaki, but recent studies range from 110,000 to 210,000. What is undisputed is that the overwhelming majority of dead and injured were civilians, including many schoolchildren and some 30,000 conscripted Korean laborers.[41] If the United States had been defeated in the war, the men responsible for intentionally killing thousands of civilians could have been charged with war crimes.

"Effective Damage," Hiroshima, August 6, 1945

Photographer unknown, National Archives, Harry S. Truman Library and Museum (98-2459)

In 1954, Oppenheimer was closely questioned by members of the Atomic Energy Commission who suspected his loyalty to the United States. They wanted to know if he had any second thoughts about using atomic weapons against Japan or had his doubts about using nuclear bombs against Cold War enemies. At first, Oppenheimer parried his interrogators. Had he ever opposed the development of the hydrogen bomb? he was asked. "I would think that I could very well have said this is a dreadful weapon, or something like that," he replied. "I have always thought it was a dreadful weapon. Even from a technical point of view—it was a sweet and lovely and beautiful job—I have still thought it was a dreadful weapon." Asked if he had "a moral revulsion against production of such a dreadful weapon," he answered, "That is too strong. . . . I had a grave concern and anxiety."

Q: You had moral qualms about it?

A: Let us leave the word "moral" out of it.

Later in the interrogation, Oppenheimer stops playing word games and is more forthright.

Q: Any moral scruples or qualms about the development of [thermonuclear weapon]?

A: Of course. . . . It is not an academic thing whether you can make a hydrogen bomb. It is a matter of life and death.

Q: Did you have moral scruples about [dropping the bomb in Japan]?

A: Terrible ones.

Q: Would you have opposed the dropping of a thermonuclear weapon on Japan because of moral scruples?

A: I believe I would, sir.[42]

It also nagged Oppenheimer that the need for state secrecy conflicted with scientific norms, that "the very absence of criticism and discussion tended to corrode the decision-making process."[43] The failure of Oppenheimer, his colleagues, and the University of California to reveal harm to staff caused by radiation accidents at Los Alamos violated the free flow of information associated with academic research. It took a long time before we learned, in the ever-so-euphemistic language of the Department of Energy, about "the larger than desirable" radiation exposures that, as far as we know, killed and injured Los Alamos staff in 1945, 1946, and 1958.[44] Clarence Kelley died in excruciating pain from radiation poisoning, his family's misery compounded by an unauthorized autopsy that removed eight pounds of organs and tissue from his body.[45]

"Normal accident" theory, developed by sociologist Charles Perrow in the 1980s, predicts the inevitability of a nuclear accident as a result of human error. There have been many near misses. "As with the Manhattan Project," notes Alex de Waal, director of the World Peace Foundation at Tufts University, "demand for ever more powerful munitions justifies risk-taking of a kind that the scientists involved don't really fully comprehend."[46] According to Hal Rothman, a "series of leaks, spills, and emissions [went] unreported for more than forty years" at Los Alamos. When they were revealed, "the faith that was at the core of the science and the system at Los Alamos was forever shaken. Los Alamos finally caught up with the rest of the nation."[47]

In a speech given at his retirement as director of Los Alamos in October 1945, attended by a shocked UC President Sproul, Oppenheimer warned that "if atomic bombs are to be added as new weapons to the arsenals of a warring world, or to the arsenals of nations preparing for war, then the time will come when mankind will curse the names of Los Alamos and Hiroshima. . . . The peoples of the world must unite or they will perish." A few days later, Oppenheimer met with President Truman, who wanted to congratulate him on his scientific discovery that ended the war. Instead, Oppenheimer wanted to discuss the urgent need to create international regulation of atomic technology: "Mr. President, I feel I have blood on my hands." Truman quickly ended the meeting with the "cry-baby scientist."[48]

If you had joined the fourteen thousand visitors to the Los Alamos Scientific Laboratory Museum in 1954, when it opened to the public, you would not have learned anything about Oppenheimer's troubled conscience or debates about the use of the atom bomb against civilian populations. Nothing had changed when I visited the Bradbury Science Museum in 2010.

Berkeley had another opportunity to create a national discussion about targeting Japan with atomic weapons when Michael Heyman, a former Berkeley law professor (1959–74) and chancellor (1980–90) was appointed the chief executive (secretary) of the Smithsonian National Museum. The Smithsonian was planning an exhibition at the National Air and Space Museum on the controversies surrounding the decision to bomb Hiroshima. The fuselage of the Enola Gay would be a centerpiece. The Smithsonian's role was not "solely to affirm 'good news' and traditional patriotic values," said Heyman in a speech to the Commonwealth Club in San Francisco in 1994. "We must explore and present the complexities of our subjects."[49]

One of the exhibition's lead curators, Tim Crouch, wanted to tell a balanced story. Instead of it being a "purely celebratory exhibit," he reflected in 1996, "it dared to offer alternatives to the actions that were taken." In addition to the Enola Gay, he wanted to include "a lunch box containing carbonized rice and peas, all that parents could find left of their daughter."[50]

Eighty-one days after Heyman's speech in San Francisco, in the wake of protests from a military lobbying group and right-wing political leaders, Heyman cancelled the exhibition and replaced it with a celebration of the plane that dropped the bomb. He took the advice of Preble Stolz, another retired Berkeley law professor, who told him that "it is probably asking too much of people who have thought for fifty years that they owed their life to President Truman's decision to drop the bomb to reflect objectively about whether his decision was morally justified."[51] At the national convention of the American Legion in Indianapolis in September 1995, Senate Majority leader Robert Dole chastised "educators and professors" for trying to "disparage America."[52] Heyman, writes Richard Kohn, "chose to surrender the Smithsonian's independence in order to save it."[53]

The Smithsonian's decision to succumb to political pressure sent a chill throughout American museums, making it clear that putting education above ideology was a risky proposition. "The real danger," said Lonnie Bunch in 1996 in his capacity as head curator of the National Museum of American History, "is that the Smithsonian has abdicated its leadership in the museum field. *Enola Gay* is going to have a continuous ripple effect." Tim Crouch felt the consequences personally. His family received abusive phone calls and letters calling him a communist and anti-American.[54]

The Berkeley-Smithsonian model of amnesia and silence became the national model for the next two decades until it was finally broken in 2016 by the National Museum of African American History and Culture, a museum that dared to face the inglorious past and pose hard questions about the persistence of structural racism. It took its founding director, Lonnie Bunch, twenty-two years to repair the damage done by the *Enola Gay* exhibition.

Meanwhile, the University of California emerged from the Second World War as a significant beneficiary of the "military-industrial complex," with lucrative contracts from the Atomic Energy Commission and other federal agencies, a relationship that endures to the present at the Lawrence Livermore National Laboratory, where the university co-manages the country's preeminent nuclear weapons research facility.[55]

Berkeley became "the classic Cold War multiversity," writes LaDale Winling, "the proving ground for mass education and Cold War planning." Regent Edward Heller promised to "yield to no one in my detestation of communism and communists. There is no question that they have no place in the University, and I will enthusiastically vote to remove any found on our faculty."[56] Berkeley's loyalty oath implemented Heller's vision,[57] while silence about crimes against humanity in Japan ensured that there was nothing to keep us awake at night. Meanwhile, reverence for Berkeley's secular saints of capital remained undisturbed. The campus is dotted with *Hearst*s in recognition of a dynasty whose fortune was made from the spoils of war, and whose patriarch (George), widow (Phoebe), and son (William Randolph) established a reciprocal relationship between private wealth and public education.

FIVE

Berkeley, Inc.

All naming must be consistent with the
University's role as a public trust.

—UNIVERSITY OF CALIFORNIA, BERKELEY,
DIVISION OF ACADEMIC PLANNING[1]

BY THEIR MUNIFICENCE

"WE MUST LOOK to men of wealth," President Daniel Coit
Gilman said in his 1872 inaugural address, "to provide the richer and
more complete endowments which will place our University by the
side of her older sisters at the East. The rich Californians, who have
made this wilderness rejoice and blossom like a rose, who have built
these banks and warehouses, these railroads and steamships—the
men who by their enterprise have made a University desirable and
possible, and who now need it for their children—must make it actual
by their munificence."[2]

Men of wealth and a handful of women of extraordinary wealth
obliged. The land on which the Berkeley campus was built benefited
from the holdings of its predecessor, the private College of California;
Phoebe Hearst's donation of $200,000 financed the university's
architectural plan that garnered attention in Europe; Regent Edward
Tomkins donated land to be sold to endow a professorship of Oriental
languages in honor of Harvard biologist Louis Agassiz; James Lick
funded the installation of what was then the world's most powerful
telescope; Hugh Toland bankrolled the university's school of medicine; banker Michael Reese endowed library acquisitions; and Jane
Sather financed the landmark Sather Gate and Campanile in honor of
her husband, banker Pedro Sather.[3] And so a precedent was set.

The influential role of philanthropic capital in the shaping of *private* universities was, of course, widespread and routine by the time that the University of California was founded, but the new university claimed to be predominantly *public*. It would be more accurate, however, to describe Berkeley from the beginning as a *public-private* partnership or as a *private-public* partnership. By 1940, more than half of the university's land and buildings had been funded by non-government sources. "A tradition of generous private support," observed an official university publication in 1967, "has made possible the steady climb to eminence."[4]

The regents of the University of California, Berkeley's governing body, originally consisted of eight members appointed by the governor, six members representing state political leadership, and another eight members appointed by the regents. It was a cozy, inbred group. Following the 1879 Constitutional Convention, the regents now enjoyed "the privileges of virtually an independent arm of state government."[5]

During the university's first thirty years, beginning in 1868, not only did the regents have extensive military experiences, they also represented the state's dominant agricultural, ranching, mining, and financial interests.[6] Regents Charles Reed (California Quicksilver Mining Company), Samuel Butterworth (New Almaden Quicksilver Mining Company), Pierre Barlow Cornwall (Black Diamond Coal Mining Company), and Robert Waterman (Stonewall Jackson Mine) owned and ran mines. New Almaden produced more than $70 million worth of mercury that was an essential ingredient in gold mining, making it one of the world's most profitable mines.[7]

Regents Frederick Ferdinand Low, Isaac Friedlander, and Joseph Mora Moss made their fortunes in shipping and global trade. Isaias Hellman was president of Wells Fargo, Leland Stanford president of Central Pacific Railroad, and Samuel Merritt owned the California State Telegraph Company. Frederick Billings was a major investor in the Northern Pacific Railroad.

Some regents benefitted personally from the university's lands dealings, investments, and educational priorities. Isaac Friedlander, known as the "Grain King," accumulated 196,000 acres of Morrill

Act land before he joined the Board of Regents in 1868. Benjamin Redding, the former mayor of Sacramento and California Secretary of State, was a land agent for the Central Pacific Railroad when he purchased 160 acres from the regents in 1877. Three years later, he was appointed to the Board of Regents.

In 1885, Phoebe Hearst donated $3,500 to create a machine shop in the department of mining, the first of many investments in the university.[8] She financed the design and construction of the Hearst Mining Building, completed in 1907, at a time that the family business was significantly involved in global mining operations. She also subsidized Donald McLaughlin's education at Berkeley that launched his career as chief geologist at the Cerro de Pasco Corporation in Peru, a company cofounded by George Hearst, Phoebe's husband.[9] In 1916, the Hercules Powder Company donated one thousand pounds of dynamite to the university to be used in an underground laboratory on campus to train students in "drilling, drifting, blasting, timbering, and mine surveying."[10]

More importantly, as a body the regents promoted and guarded the collective interests of the state's extractive, agricultural, and financial development. Many were politically active capitalists, moving fluidly between their economic and political roles—real estate and city hall, mining and the state legislature, banking and the US Senate, finance and global diplomacy. John Franklin Swift, who later was appointed minister plenipotentiary to Japan, worked with the US attorney general to defend the Chinese Exclusion Act of 1888. Phoebe Hearst's husband represented the family's mining interests in state and national politics.

BUILDERS OF BERKELEY

This pattern of private investment in a public university continued throughout the twentieth century. Looking back on his time at Berkeley as a student and faculty member, Robert Nisbet concluded that the university is "a public campus with a difference, a stunning reflection of private taste and design" and one of the "most heavily endowed—by private money—of any of the state universities in America." He didn't think there was "all that much difference between private Stanford and public Berkeley."[11]

Ninety-one years after President Gilman's speech, in which he implored the private sector to make Berkeley competitive with the Harvards of the world, Clark Kerr reported that "the modern American university," such as Berkeley, is "a new type of institution, it is not really private and it is not really public." As Berkeley's first chancellor (1952–57), president of the now-multicampus University of California (1958–67), and a well-known advocate of the "multiversity," Kerr appreciated that postwar Berkeley had "demonstrated how adaptive it can be to new opportunities for creativity; how responsive to money."[12]

Today, the campus is filled with buildings and programs named after successors to the first generations of investors—a who's who of brand-name donors from industries, tech companies, investment firms, and financial institutions throughout the Pacific Rim: Amadeo Peter Giannini (Giannini Hall), Isadore and Jennie Zellerbach (Zellerbach Hall), Stephen D. Bechtel (Bechtel Engineering Center), Richard Blum (Blum Hall), Kevin and Connie Chou (Chou Hall), Richard and Rhoda Goldman (Goldman Hall), Walter Haas Sr. (Haas Business School), Walter Haas Jr. (Haas Pavilion), Li Ka-shing (Li Ka Shing Center), Sehat and Pantas Sutardja and Weili Dai (Sutardja Dai Hall), Tan Kah Kee (Tan Kah Kee Hall), Jack C. C. Tang (Tang Center), Y. Charles and Helen C. Soda (Soda Hall), to name a few.[13]

In the engineering building's majestic vestibule, dedicated to George Hearst, $5 million-plus corporate donors get a special mention. Walls that greet you on your way into Doe Library are etched with the names of $1 million-plus donors. An empty wall waits for the names of Berkeley graduates who have taken a pledge to "incorporate philanthropy into [their] growth mindset" and join "UC Berkeley's entrepreneur ecosystem."[14]

The university's long-time dependency on and aggrandizement of wealthy benefactors is problematic in two important ways.

First, by making wealthy donors synonymous with the "builders of Berkeley" and giving them pride of place in the university's topography, other kinds of builders are marginalized or disappeared: the tribes and Native settlements whose lands financed Berkeley's rapid rise to prominence; the workforce who literally built and maintain the campus; and the activists who eventually forced the university's white, old boys' club to begin to diversify the curriculum, student body, and faculty.

Secondly, in return for accepting large sums of money, the university agrees in effect to serve as a public relations firm that promotes one-dimensional, relentlessly positive images of donors, not looking for or acknowledging anything that might tarnish reputational value, even when everybody knows better. Maybe it's understandable how the university in 1907 enshrined George Hearst in a plaque that described him as "a plain honest man and good miner. . . . Taking his wealth from the hills he filched from no man's store and lessened no man's opportunity." But there is no justification for continuing to display this monument to greed and racism by whitewashing a man who made his fortune by *inter alia* filching tons of gold in the Black Hills and occupying Sioux homelands.

A PLAIN HONEST MAN

It's impossible to walk through the campus without being reminded that the Hearst family fortune financed Berkeley's development. *Hearst* is ubiquitous, from the magnificent to the mundane: the William Randolph Hearst Greek Theatre, Phoebe A. Hearst Museum of Anthropology, Hearst Memorial Mining building, Hearst Memorial Gymnasium, Hearst Avenue, Hearst Parking Structures, Hearst Food Court, and Hearst Tennis Courts. George Hearst-the-patriarch (1820–1891) looms large on campus as he does in historical lore and popular culture.[15]

Hearst's $14 million estate (worth more than $436 million today) enabled his widow Phoebe Hearst, inspired by a visit to the World's Columbian Exposition in 1893, to imagine Berkeley as a "City of Learning."[16] She benefited from the profits George had accumulated through shrewd financial deals and investments in extractive industries, including gold, silver, and copper mines in the Black Hills, Utah, Nevada, and Peru. He also invested in land in Mexico and owned a cattle ranch in New Mexico.[17]

George grew up on a wheat farm in Missouri where his father William G. Hearst owned more land than most farmers in the county and nineteen of the forty-one enslaved Africans in Maramec Township.[18] He had fond memories of his childhood "in a wilderness. The Indians were around in every direction, and every summer visited us," as did wolves on the hunt for chickens, geese, and sheep.[19]

George Hearst remained a resolute pro-South Democrat and opponent of Reconstruction and African American voting rights throughout his political career. As noted by one of his many and mostly admiring biographers, Hearst never abandoned the antebellum, ruling worldview of Franklin County, Missouri: white supremacy, nativism, and patriarchy.[20]

While Phoebe promoted admission of women to universities during her husband's lifetime and quickly joined the cautiously conservative wing of the suffrage movement after his death, her husband toed the Democratic Party's line against women's suffrage.[21]

Like his cousin Joe Clark, George sided with the South in the Civil War. Some of his relatives fought for the Confederacy, including his cousin William Hearst who was captured and imprisoned in Alton, Illinois. There was even a rumor, proved untrue, that George had become an officer in the Confederate Army. In 1861, while in St. Louis, he was arrested for uttering "alleged seditious language" in support of the Confederacy, a charge that he somehow got dropped. He described his situation in a letter to the *Nevada City Morning Transcript* that published his account on September 12, 1861. "Mr. Hearst represented Missouri as an intolerable place for a neutral man to live in. Indeed, such a thing as neutrality was out of the question."[22]

While an appearance of neutrality served him well in some of his business operations, he didn't disguise his views on race in his public political positions. In December 1865, the California legislature approved by a two-thirds vote the Thirteenth Amendment to the US Constitution that abolished slavery and involuntary servitude. Forty-five-year-old Hearst, then representing the Assembly's Eighth District (San Francisco), voted against Joint Resolution Number 1.[23]

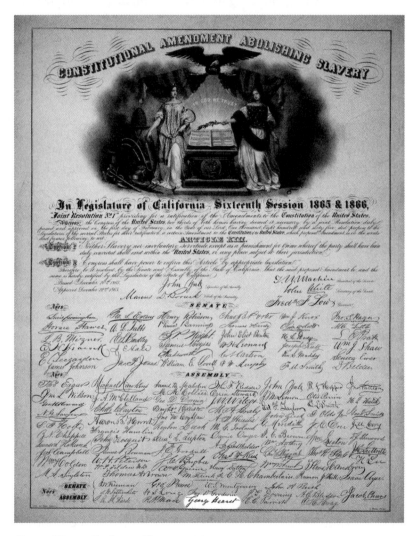

George Hearst Endorses Slavery, 1865

"13th Amendment to the U.S. Constitution abolishing slavery, in Legislature of California sixteenth session, 1865 & 1866," courtesy of California State Library Archives (990013690020205115)

More than two decades later, now in the US Senate (1886–91), his last political act was to help fellow Democrats filibuster to death the Federal Elections Bill (1890). When Massachusetts senator Henry Cabot Lodge introduced the bill that was designed to protect African Americans' voting rights in the South, he called for federal oversight of Congressional elections:

> The United States must extend to every citizen equal rights. It is a duty which they cannot avoid. If they do not perform it now, they will perform it later, and the longer it is postponed the worse the consequences will be.
>
> Moreover, this cry about the danger of negro [sic] rule, this bitter appeal to race supremacy, which is always ringing in our ears, is made a convenient stalking horse to defraud white men as well as black men of their rights. It is an evil which must be dealt with, and if we fail to deal with it, we shall suffer for our failure. If all is fair and honest and free in Southern elections this law will interfere with no one but will demonstrate the fact to the people of the United States.[24]

Southern Democrats fiercely and successfully opposed the Federal Elections Bill that they shrewdly nicknamed the "Force Bill," a portent of twentieth- and twenty-first-century efforts to restrict voting rights in the name of states' rights.[25] An obituary for Hearst noted that he celebrated the bill's defeat on his deathbed.[26]

Hearst also supported the Chinese Exclusion Act (1882) and six years later defended an amendment that restricted Chinese Americans abroad from coming home.[27] His position on the Chinese Question was opportunistically motivated by his political campaign for the US Senate. "The great objection I have to the Chinese," he said in a posture of support for American workers, "is they work so cheap." Meanwhile, he advocated substituting child labor for Chinese labor. "If there were no Chinamen in California, a great deal of the fruit . . . would necessarily have to be gathered by children, and this would make them industrious."[28]

For the most part, George Hearst's racism and economic ventures were interdependent, and he didn't have to pretend that he cared about workers' well-being.

Hearst personally benefited from the US Army's expedition, led by Brevet General George Armstrong Custer in 1874, into South Dakota's Black Hills, backed up by ten cavalry companies, Gatling guns, a cannon, and a military band. Facing military defeat, the Sioux were forced to sell their lands for a pitiful amount and "the stage was set for George Hearst's coming involvement in the Black Hills."[29] Hearst and his partners invested in the Homestake Mine, knowing the dangers involved once Custer withdrew. In the same 1878 letter in which Hearst confided to his partner J. B. Haggin, "I will hurt a good many people," he continued, "And it is quite possible that I may get killed. . . . All I ask of you is to see that my wife and child gets [*sic*] all that is due them from all sources and that I am not buried in this place."[30] It was worth the risk, he told a reporter, because the Black Hills mine "beats anything in the way of gold quartz you ever saw. . . . Take the Homestake alone, and there is profit of a million a year in sight, and it will last for 25 years at that rate of profit." The mine generated 2.7 million tons of gold and caused longstanding environmental damage to Indigenous lands, rivers, and the watershed.[31]

As a member of the US Senate's Indian Affairs Committee in 1886, Hearst personally benefited from insider information that Goyahkla (Geronimo), the Chiricahua Apache leader, had been captured by the Army in Mexico. He quickly bought up thirty-three thousand acres at twenty to forty cents an acre in Chihuahua, increasing his holdings to a million acres of property that rapidly increased in value.[32]

As a member of the Senate's Mines and Mining Subcommittee with mining investments in Utah, Hearst introduced a bill in January 1888 to legalize mining on Ute Tribe land on the Uintah Reservation, to force the tribe to sell their lands, and to retroactively legitimize squatting "as if the lands had been public at the attempted time."[33]

Though he did not live to realize his grandiose vision of extracting copper in Peru, his estate personally benefited from the Cerro de Pasco mine and Phoebe Hearst is acknowledged as a "founder," according to a mining think tank.[34] Along with his business partners James Ben Ali Haggin and Lloyd Tevis, George Hearst invested in mining operations for some forty years, including the Ontario silver mine in Utah that he bought in 1872. The company that became the premier mining investment firm in the United States began to investigate the possibility of owning mines in Peru in 1887, four years before Hearst's death.[35] The attraction was not only one of the largest deposits in the world, but also an abundance of cheap labor, mostly Indigenous miners from the Andes, who worked under a system of indentured servitude (*"enganche"*), backed up ruthless punishments.[36]

Cerro de Pasco's industrial system of modernization, introduced in the early 1900s, made the most of this practice of debt peonage. According to an investigation carried out in 1913 by a pro-indígena organization, Cerro de Pasco preached the moral and civilizational superiority of its north American owners while practicing a "frightful waste of human life." A miner's working life lasted an average of five years. The survivors were bequeathed a landscape saturated with toxic tailings that infected generations of children with lead poisoning. "The Indian," concluded the report, "is torn away, by cheat and fraud, from his rustic home, subjected to laws which only help to enslave him, and persecuted by soldiers when he tries to escape from his masters."[37]

When anthropologist Max Uhle returned from an archaeological expedition to Peru in 1902, he brought back to Berkeley thousands of ceremonial artifacts and human remains, and seventy photographs of Cerro de Pasco for his financial sponsor, Phoebe Hearst.[38]

WITH THE EXCAVATORS

Berkeley's remembrance of Phoebe Apperson Hearst (1842–1919) offers a case study in the double standards of institutional memory. In the university's first two decades, she was the most prominent funder of wide-ranging projects. Today, she is honored in memorials, at public events, and on websites as Berkeley's founding mother, "great educator," and "matriarch of access and excellence."[39] While Berkeley emphasizes how she was a pioneer in advocating admission of women as undergraduates, it ignores her exclusion of women of color and her participation in all-white professional associations. The university lauds how she battled her way into the male domain of archaeology but ignores her involvement in the pillaging of Indigenous graves from Peru to California.

Anthropology was at the heart of Hearst's philanthropy. She gave it her special attention and hands-on involvement. When Berkeley established its anthropology program in 1901, it had to play catch-up if it wanted to be competitive with the rivals it aspired to emulate—the Smithsonian, Harvard's Peabody Museum, the American Museum of Natural History, Chicago's Field Museum, and European museums stocked with artifacts collected by naval expeditions and purchased from international traders. To be successful at this level, the university needed the funds of a patron of culture, somebody with big pockets and an outsize ego, somebody like George Heye, who accumulated eight hundred thousand Native artifacts, enough to fill his own museum in New York, somebody who imagined himself to be making and not just collecting history.[40] For wealthy collectors and middle-class hobbyists, archaeology was a man's game.[41]

In Phoebe Hearst, Berkeley found its woman. Without her patronage, there would have been no anthropology museum, no archaeological collection of national significance, maybe no anthropology department, certainly no University of California as we know it.[42]

In the early 1890s, Phoebe Hearst focused her philanthropic projects on the University of Pennsylvania, in part because her personal physician was the university provost. When William Pepper died suddenly in 1898, she transferred her loyalty, collections, and philanthropy to the University of California.[43]

Four years before the university created a Department of Anthropology, it appointed Phoebe Hearst the first female regent in acknowledgement of her funding of Berkeley's architectural design and infrastructure. In 1900, President Benjamin Ide Wheeler elevated her to act as president in his temporary absence.

To Hearst, anthropology was much more than a vanity project or philanthropic niche. She had, by her own account, "no technical knowledge of archaeology, having only the enthusiasm acquired through general reading and visits to the world's greatest museums," but she was sufficiently informed and engaged that the American Archaeological Association made her honorary president in 1899.[44]

Phoebe Hearst created the material foundations of the anthropology department before there was faculty, staff, and students. She understood that Berkeley needed to be competitive with Europe's colonial powerhouses in the business of stockpiling Indigenous "specimens." Determined to make Berkeley a player on the global as well as national stage, she hired George Reisner at $10,000 per year for five years between 1899 and 1913 to direct an archaeological expedition in Egypt; and paid Max Uhle $3,500 annually to head up excavations in Peru and Mexico from 1899 to 1902. With seemingly unlimited funds from Hearst, Philip Jones, a doctor and amateur archaeologist, went on a buying spree in California, piling up crates of artifacts and ancestors' remains for the university's anthropology department, scheduled to open the following year.[45]

These far-flung expeditions put important museums and anthropology departments around the world on notice that Berkeley was to be reckoned with as a center of collecting as well as extracting Native ancestors, artifacts, and knowledge; and that the university considered California to be its exclusive sphere of anthropological influence. "I should very much like to keep you out of the state altogether," Alfred Kroeber wrote Franz Boas, his former mentor, in 1905.[46]

Archaeologist George Reisner was educated at Harvard, where he received his Ph.D. in 1893, studied in Berlin, and became a leading expert on Egypt's history. For most of his career he taught at Harvard and was director of Boston's Museum of Fine Arts. Before his appointment at Harvard and despite his lack of formal training in archaeology, he convinced Phoebe Hearst to fund several expeditions to Egypt that involved hiring assistants and a large crew of workers on-site. During these expeditions, he acquired seventeen thousand "catalogued objects" and a valuable collection of papyri.[47] His patron, Phoebe Hearst, was there on one occasion to witness

Reisner opening a tomb. "You might have thought it right to class me with the excavators," she wrote a friend.[48]

"With the Excavators" in Egypt, c. 1905

"Phoebe A. Hearst (center), Giza, Egypt," photographer unknown, courtesy of the Phoebe A. Hearst Museum of Anthropology and the Regents of the University of California (15-18884)

There are more than 23,000 entries in the university's database for Reisner's collection, including 1,118 skeletons (of which 170 were mummies) taken from tombs and cemeteries. Occasionally, he bundled together and catalogued as one item several human remains—such as "mixed bones of 6 individuals"—but for the most part the self-trained Reisner kept accurate records and was thorough in his documentation.[49]

Born and educated in Germany, Phoebe Hearst's other beneficiary Max Uhle received his Ph.D. from the University of Leipzig in 1880, was director of the Ethnology Museum in Dresden, and worked at the Museum für Völkerkunde in Berlin from 1888 to 1892 before doing field work in Latin America and then getting hired by Hearst, first in Philadelphia, then in Berkeley.

During his three years collecting for Hearst in Peru, Uhle shipped back to the university thousands of funerary and ceremonial artifacts, and between one and two thousand human remains. Typical examples of his collecting include: "Cranium of child Peru grave" and a "mummified human head with straw hat, broad silver band, and colored feather."[50]

Uhle taught junior archaeologists how to excavate Indigenous cemeteries, stressing the importance of graves as a source of valuable artifacts and of crania as objects of scientific information:

> On no account should the archaeologist employ more men than he can watch and keep constantly busy; the laziness of some always has a contagious effect on the others.... I had excellent results digging the shallow graves of the Aborigines of Arica with one or two men.... The importance of graves for the study of civilizations is based on the general occurrence, among primitive nations, of the belief in continuation of life in the other world, and the care which in consequence is taken to accompany the dead with everything necessary for the life hereafter. For this reason, it is the utensils most necessary in this life that are found in the tombs as the furnishings for the journey to the other.... Any skull encountered in a grave should be secured.[51]

Uhle was a tireless but sloppy anthropologist who had a reputation for "obscure reasoning" and "skimming the cream off an archaeological site and then moving on, never to come back to it except for casual visits."[52] His documentation of the number of ancestors he excavated is untrustworthy because a single catalogue entry often bundled multiple remains: "Several jaws and fragments of skulls" ... "various bones" ... "five human bones."[53]

The university, however, appreciated Uhle's excavations in cemeteries and on his return from Peru in 1902 put him to work digging up the Emeryville shellmound a few miles from the university. Uhle noted that "Mrs. Phoebe A. Hearst generously made the undertaking possible by providing ample financial support for the exploration work."[54]

Hearst did much more than fund specific archaeological projects. Unlike most donors who made contributions to the regents with a request that they be used in a particular way, Hearst directly financed anthropology during its first decade. It was not so much a private-public partnership as a personal fiefdom.

Hearst approved and paid the annual budget for salaries, administration, and special requests, such as building a warehouse to store her collection.[55] In 1906, for example, she budgeted $21,255.36 for "research, publications, and instruction of the Department of Anthropology."[56] In the department's first director, Harvard anthropologist Frederic Ward Putnam (1839–1915), known then as "the Father of American Archaeology," she cultivated a fawning subordinate who would fulfill her vision. "I should have nothing to do with the establishment of a museum that did not meet with the approval of Mrs. Hearst," wrote Putnam, "for I should consider it disloyal to her when she has given the start to the whole matter." Hearst shared Putnam's view that anthropology should teach "how prehistoric man had lived his life [and] fought his way up from primal ignorance to civilizing knowledge."[57]

"Hearst assumed," according to her biographer, "that her official position, work, and major gifts to the University of California entitled her to have control over the department and museum." When Alfred Kroeber become de facto administrator of the department, she paid his salary and "set his budget."[58] At one point, she lobbied to get Kroeber fired when his plans to professionalize the department interfered with her goal of creating a grand museum that, in the words of Putnam, would display the story of Progress from "beginning in geological time, through savagery and barbarism to the periods of [Man's] civilization."[59]

Considering the collections Hearst donated to the university and her funding of the department's routine operations and infrastructure, it was conservatively estimated in 1908 that Phoebe Hearst's value to the university's anthropology program alone was worth $500,000 (about $17 million in today's value).[60]

By the second decade of the twentieth century, with Phoebe Hearst's vision of a grandiose museum on the Berkeley campus unfulfilled, she gave up the direct funding and administration of anthropology. By then, she had normalized a significant role for private investors in shaping the priorities of the university and had laid the basis for the university's archaeological acquisitiveness that resulted in four million items by the early 1990s.[61] Hearst's funding legacies include an emphasis on accumulation over knowledge, chronic undercounting of human remains, negligent scientific practices, and routine looting of ceremonial and funerary artifacts from inside and around Indigenous graves.

III

ACCUMULATION

SIX

The Love *of* Possessions

The love of possessions is a disease in them.
These people have made many rules that the
rich may break, but the poor may not! . . . They
claim this mother of ours, the earth, for their
own use, and fence their neighbor away. . . . If
America had been twice the size it is, there still
would not have been enough.

— SITTING BULL, 1877[1]

FETISHES OF CONQUEST

BY THE TIME that the University of California recruited Harvard's
Frederic Ward Putnam to launch its anthropology program in 1901
and hired a young Alfred Kroeber to build Berkeley's reputation
and collections, it had to make up a great deal of ground with its
competition. Organized expeditions, government agencies, self-
taught archaeologists, and entrepreneurs had already accumulated
and traded millions of Native American artifacts. Long before
Berkeley acquired its first collection of artifacts and skulls to display
in its Museum of Ethnology, before it received twenty-four skeletal
remains that an amateur archaeologist had excavated from Chumash
territory on San Nicolas Island between 1897 and 1902, there was an
extensive global market for everything Indian, from body parts and
sacred artifacts to functional utensils and popular tales.[2]

Hundreds of thousands of artifacts ended up in private collections and public display cases throughout Europe and North
America, from Moscow to San Francisco, as museums traded items

with each other like baseball cards in order to acquire "a kind of Noah's ark collection, two from each area, two of each type."[3] Curators and scientists were unable to keep up with an avalanche of materials that flooded shelves and basements, a precedent that Berkeley would follow.

Colonial military operations accelerated the harvesting of Indigenous artifacts around the world. Hearst-funded archaeological expeditions in Egypt, Peru, and Mexico followed in the footsteps of their European counterparts, all competing to stockpile and flaunt what Philip Deloria calls "fetishes of conquest."[4]

Captain George Vancouver's Pacific expedition (1790–95), which surveyed the Pacific coast on the ship *Discovery* on behalf of Britain's imperial ambitions, included several individuals who amassed personal collections of Native-made artifacts. Surgeon's mate George Hewett, like any serious hobbyist, recorded his haul of more than five hundred objects, item by item, in a small notebook.[5] "Mr. Hewett was evidently fond of natural history, and made note of anything that struck him as remarkable," observed archaeologist Charles Read in an 1891 talk.[6] Though Vancouver recognized that even "savage nations" take seriously their "funeral solemnities" and was under orders to be "a diplomat as well as an explorer," he could not stop his men from exploring burial sites in search of ceremonial and funerary items. When Vancouver's naval force sailed into Trinidad harbor in what is now Humboldt County, California, in May 1793, the flagship *Discovery* was "visited by two of the natives in a canoe; they approached us with confidence," wrote Vancouver, "and seemed to be friendly disposed." The Yurok, who "traded in a very honest and civil manner," were already used to doing business with Europeans. Vancouver was not at all impressed by the "trivial articles" his crew received in return for iron.[7]

No party to this exchange could have imagined that elk-antler spoons acquired during this stopover would be reverentially displayed in the British Museum more than two hundred years later as objets d'art—"very fine carving" with "finely incised decoration."[8] For North American archaeologists, wrote Berkeley anthropologist Arnold Pilling when he visited London in 1952, "the most important single body of material in the British Museum is the Vancouver Collection made by Hewett in the early 1790s."[9]

European museums and monied afficionados stocked up on huge numbers of Native artifacts from the Americas. "These Indians made objects that would deserve praise even in Europe," Vasily Golovnin, a Russian navigator, conceded about baskets and hats that he acquired in the San Francisco Bay Area in 1818. "In my collection of curiosities I have many items made by them. . . . They are not only well made but are very attractive."[10] Ferdinand Deppe, a former gardener for the Royal Court of Prussia, sold baskets he had collected in California to the Zoological Museum in Berlin in 1836. A few years later, the Royal Museum of Ethnology acquired a large collection from the Smithsonian and from German collectors.[11] In 1894–95, two visitors from England acquired several artifacts in San Luis Obispo that they added to Hewett's collection in the British Museum.[12]

The drive to accumulate Native material and physical collectibles in the late eighteenth and early nineteenth centuries was integral to a culture of conquest, extraction, and accumulation. Its institutional expression was the modern museum that combined elements of a privatized spectacle with a new kind of popular education. The nineteenth-century museum continued a longstanding tradition of acquiring and displaying natural, found, and made objects regarded as exotica or subjects for scientific investigation. It dramatized the "cabinets of curiosities" that had been reserved for men of wealth and status since the Renaissance. Instead of hundreds of items crammed into a room or display case to impress a small circle of friends, the new institution could now store and perform for huge public audiences the latest imports from the Americas.[13] "Collecting is a hereditary disease," confessed a British Museum curator in the late nineteenth century, "and I fear incurable."[14]

A survey of European museums in the 1980s reported the presence of tribal artifacts from California in museums in Prague, Vienna, Copenhagen, Helsinki, Nuremberg, Zurich, Auckland, and regional museums in England.[15] When I visited the Ethnologisches Museum of Berlin in October 2010, I found items Alfred Kroeber had sold, including a soup basket and an elk-antler spoon, displayed in a cabinet filled with "objects of value and prestige"—reminiscent of how the museum's competition across the Channel in London shows off its prized collection. The trade in collectibles was often led by patrons of the arts, such as Phoebe Hearst, who financed a frenzy of accumulation. As the market for Indigenous artifacts boomed, entrepreneurial traders, local museums, amateur archaeologists, hobbyists, and heritage historians joined the hunt.

In the nineteenth century, with the rise of anthropology and related academic disciplines in the metropole, colonial expeditions were encouraged to also return home with crania and skeletal remains to feed the demand for knowledge about the origins of the species and human differences, and to document the dogma of social development from primitive origins to advanced civilizations.

In the 1830s, British scientists brought back Tasmanian Aborigine corpses to London. Hundreds, possibly thousands of Aboriginal remains from Australia ended up in universities and collections in England and Scotland. Dutch colonists sent the head of an Ahanta king from Ghana back to the Netherlands in 1838, where it was kept at Leiden University's Medical Centre until repatriation in 2009. By the end of the nineteenth century, there were perhaps three hundred Māori preserved heads in collections around the world. Similarly, in the 1900s German archaeologists transported hundreds of Herero Namibian remains from southwest Africa to Berlin, where they were researched and displayed by museums, hospitals, scientific organizations, and private collections. It was estimated in 2018 that 120 ancestors remained in Germany, compared to at least 10,000 in Berkeley's basements and around 18,000 in the Museum of Mankind in Paris.[16]

The scope and volume of this practice in the United States, however, was unprecedented. Between the early 1780s, when Thomas Jefferson dug up perhaps a thousand skeletons from "repositories of the dead" near his home in Virginia, and the 1970s when the Red Power Movement put amateur and professional archaeologists on the defensive, the exhumation of Native graves was promoted as good sport, entrepreneurial initiative, sound science, and salvage anthropology. We do not know exactly how many Native ancestors were exhumed in the United States during these two centuries, but estimates range from the Native American Rights Fund's conservative figure of six hundred thousand to one million suggested by other experts.[17]

By the early nineteenth century, the country's leading museums and universities vied to become showplaces of American Progress through scientific study of the dead. The publication in 1839 of *Crania Americana* by Samuel Morton, a Philadelphia physician considered the "father of American physical anthropology," heralded the respectability of scientific racism. Morton boosted interest in studying the Native body in order to learn about the "secrets of human origins," to bolster claims about European superiority over Native degeneracy, and to find biological evidence for the *natural disappearance* of Indigenous people. Morton believed that cranial capacity was racially determined—the bigger the better—and that races could be ranked by the size of their brains. By the time of his death, he had amassed close to one thousand skulls.[18]

Morton's successor, Aleš Hrdlička (1869–1943), a Czech anthropologist on the staff of the National Museum, continued and outdid Morton's collection, amassing close to twenty thousand skulls and publishing in 1904 a how-to manual that instructed amateur archaeologists where to find Native grave sites and how to package and send crania to the Smithsonian. While recognizing that the harvesting of Native brains was a "delicate and difficult matter," he nevertheless provided detailed guidelines about how to remove, preserve, and transport a brain. "Open the tentorium as you come to it wholly, and, helping with one hand from within, receive the brain into the palm of the hand." Better still, advised Hrdlička, "whenever possible, all work connected with removing the brain may be obviated by sending the entire head. . . . The fresher the product, the better."[19]

Like Morton, Hrdlička thought the brain was the key to understanding the "different grades within the human species itself."[20] He described his work as investigating "the racial affinities and past family relations of peoples [that] throw light on the intraneous and extraneous blood relations of the California Indians." Physical

anthropology, he explained, illuminates "the racially more important characteristics, which are observed partly on the living, and
partly on the organs of the body, especially the skull and the skeleton."[21] In 1914, Hrdlička showed off some of his vast collection of
skeletons and crania at the Panama-California Exposition, all neatly
arranged into a tableau of racial hierarchy, from "thoroughbred"
white Americans to "full-blood American negro," and so on.[22] At
the same time, he was beginning to have doubts about the efficacy
of "the science of improving the human stock." During a conference
organized by Kroeber in San Francisco, he admitted that "in a great
majority of cases we know not as yet how to remove or compensate
for a given defect, or how to strengthen permanently and especially
create a desirable quality, or how to prevent or cause the transmis-
sion of tendencies or qualities."[23]

This did not stop anybody from plundering graves. The going
rate for a skull in the late nineteenth century was between $3 and
$5, depending on its condition. In 1903, a "mummified body," found
in a burial on Kern River, was sold to the Smithsonian for $50.[24]
Even antiracist anthropologists insisted on digging up Native
human remains because they wanted to prove the commonalities
of a single human race. "It is most unpleasant work to steal bones
from a grave, but what is the use, someone has to do it," Franz Boas
noted in his diary in 1888. "Yesterday I wrote to the Museum in
Washington asking whether they would consider buying skulls this
winter for $600, and if they will, I shall collect assiduously."[25]

In 1897, Boas provided housing at the American Museum
of Natural History for six Inuit whom the explorer Robert Perry
had imported like an exotic commodity from Greenland to New
York. When one of them, Qisuk, died from tuberculosis, Boas and
his young assistant Alfred Kroeber presided over a mock funeral,
orchestrated for the benefit of Qisuk's son, Minik.[26] Meanwhile, the
Museum surreptitiously kept Qisuk's skeleton and sent his brain
to Hrdlička. In 1916, Kroeber, now in charge of Berkeley's anthropology department, offered to send the brain of a Yahi man to the
National Museum. "I hardly need say," Hrdlička told Kroeber,
"that we shall be very glad to receive and take care of Ishi's brain."

He instructed Kroeber that the brain should be "packed in plenty of absorbent cotton saturated in liquid in which it is preserved." Kroeber complied.[27]

CATCHING UP

California's potential for unprecedented economic growth attracted the attention of federal agencies and scientific investigations. In the 1870s, the US Coast Survey dispatched a team to survey the Pacific coast and the Secretary of War authorized a massive geographical survey of the western United States. This included collecting data on the region's tribes, including their land and resources, and excavating Native cemeteries for skeletal remains and ceremonial artifacts. By this time, the Smithsonian was seriously collecting in California, where decimated Native communities, recovering from Spain's mission system of attempted cultural erasure and American genocide, were unable to protect their ancient village sites from professional expeditions, collectors, diggers, and looters. The harvesting of corpses in the name of science and education was especially prevalent in California. "No other state in the Union," observed Hrdlička in 1906, "is more interesting and important anthropologically than California."[28]

Educated as a civil engineer, with minimal training in archaeology and anthropology, Paul Schumacher worked on the Pacific coast for the US Coast Survey, but "found time," in his words, "to search for graves." Excavations of "ethnological material" in Chumash and Tongva burials in southern California, he reported, "were particularly rich and we collected about four thousand skeletons, which we brought into daylight." In 1874, he sent the Smithsonian eight boxes, weighing between seven and eight hundred pounds, that included funerary artifacts and several skulls, some of which he repaired with shellac.[29]

That same year, George M. Wheeler, a first lieutenant in the Army Corps of Engineers, hired Frederic Ward Putnam to supervise and edit the army's archaeological survey of the West.[30] Some twenty-seven years later, Berkeley would recruit Putnam to chair its first anthropology department.

The *Archaeology* survey begins with a brief overview of "the discovery of the Peninsula of California in 1534" and Cortés's encounter with "naked savages." The Franciscans who established missions throughout the region in the late eighteenth century are commended for their "disinterested motives and benevolent intentions," but chastised for the disastrous consequences of their good works. "Naturally indolent, unclean, licentious, and thoughtless of the morrow," wrote Putnam, "deluded Indians were reduced to slavery, confined in towns, subdued in spirit, and treated . . . like herds of animals. In consequence of this treatment, they became diseased, and the natural result soon followed. . . . From this time the doom of the race, settled at the first period of contact with the European became apparent, and of the thousands of free and indolent savages who formerly inhabited the beautiful garden-land of our Pacific coast, how few and how degraded are those now left in the vicinity of their old homes." As Putnam was particularly interested in "shellheaps and graves," he included in his final report an ethnological study of the Santa Barbara region.[31] H. C. Yarrow, the author of the study, left the interpretation of his findings to Putnam, "confident that, with the rich materials gathered as a basis, he will elucidate many hitherto mysterious problems connected with the custom of this extinct race, and bring to light much of their now hidden history."[32]

By the time that Yarrow, an acting assistant surgeon with the army, surveyed Native homelands in California, he already had considerable experience excavating Native grave sites and documenting human remains from Utah, New Mexico, Arizona, and Colorado. In the scientific tradition established by Morton, he carefully measured the length, breadth, capacity, and angles of crania.[33]

In southern California, Yarrow was "abundantly rewarded [by] careful excavations" of burial grounds. "Good finds" included "a few bones and arrowheads," "an entire skeleton *in situ*," "quantities of broken bones being met with at every stroke of the spade," "glass beads and human teeth," "a number of excellent crania," "the skull of an infant covered with an abalone shell," and hundreds of cere-monial and funerary artifacts. At another site, a local rancher gave Yarrow's team "a hearty welcome" and invited them "to dig any-where we might think proper." They accepted the offer and exca-vated ten to fifteen tons of "specimens"—including "no fewer than 30 skeletons" dug up from one of the trenches—that they shipped back to Washington, DC.[34]

In the second half of the nineteenth century, California was fair game for professional and amateur archaeologists. An expedition led by Horace Smith, a gun manufacturer and cofounder of Smith and Wesson, dug up "much material" at a ranch in Santa Barbara that he donated to the Smithsonian.[35] In the 1890s, anthropologist David Barrows, a future lecturer in the Department of Anthropology and president of the university (1919–23), did field research for his dissertation at the University of Chicago on "The Ethno-botany of the Coahuilla [*sic*] Indians of Southern California."[36] Crews building roads and railroad tracks, construction workers, and farm laborers regularly displaced grave sites that generated body parts and artifacts that ended up in private collections, museums, and the University of California.[37]

By the 1890s, Stanford's faculty and students were regularly exhuming Native grave sites. During the early days of the univer-sity, reported the *Palo Alto Times*, "you really hadn't lived until you had gone down to Castro and dug yourself up a skeleton or two."[38] Mary Barnes, a historian with no training in archaeology and the first woman faculty member to be hired by Stanford, took her students to excavate a mound at the Robles Rancheria. "The boys of the vicinity assured us that there were plenty of skeletons in it," she observed in an article for *Popular Science Monthly*.[39]

California was also an important site of Indigenous knowledge collection, from exotic tales of frontier life and *Indianology* to anthropological investigations. The popular fascination with the Native dead was typically linked with stories about "lost tribes" and ancient civilizations. "A collection of over three hundred human bodies, perfectly petrified," reported the *Daily Alta California* in the early 1850s, had been found in what became known as "the cave of the sepulchers" near the town of Vallecito in Calaveras County. The skulls indicated "a race distinct from Indians." About a hundred years later, a team of Berkeley anthropologists would return to the site and dig up "hundreds of human corpses" that were maybe more than three thousand years old and distinctly Indian.[40]

Between 1860 and 1863, Alexander Taylor, an amateur anthropologist described with backhanded praise by Alfred Kroeber as "indefatigable in his inquiries and a most industrious compiler," published 151 articles on Indian life and customs in the *California Farmer Journal of Useful Sciences*.[41] Writer Stephen Powers traveled on foot and horseback along the West Coast in the summers of 1871 and 1872, reporting on California's tribes for national magazines, often in sensational and racialized terms.[42] Doubling as a self-trained archaeologist, he also sent "four boxes of Indian collection" to the Smithsonian and seven skulls to the Army Museum.[43]

These early journalistic sketches—a mix of romantic nostalgia and racial defamation, dogged inquiries and pseudo-science, selective facts and historical fantasy—provided the bedrock of what in the twentieth century would become a cottage industry of publications about California, in which Berkeley's academics would play a significant role.

It was not only a one-way street from California to Europe, New York, and Washington, DC. In the late nineteenth century, the University of California's "Museum of Ethnology"—essentially a storage room, oversighted by an entomologist-cum-janitor promoted to curator—filled up with a mishmash of stuff, from important artifacts to mundane items and pieces of human remains from near and far, including Alaska, Polynesia, Canada, Mexico, Peru, and Egypt, as well as California.[44]

Decades before Berkeley's Department of Anthropology was created in 1901, the university had let sellers and donors know that it wanted their collections.[45] The call received immediate results, including a student who "presented the Ethnological Museum with a fine Indian skull from Santa Cruz."[46] In the late 1870s, Berkeley was already publicizing its prized possessions:

Spoils of Accumulation, 1893

"Ethnology Museum," South Hall, 1893, photograph by O. V. Lange, Phoebe A. Hearst
Museum of Anthropology and the Regents of the University of California (UARC PIC 500:15)

> The War Hatchet, Pipe, and Snow-shoes originally belonging
> to the celebrated chief of the Seneca Indians, Red Jacket. . . .
> Spoon belonging to Medicine-man of the Indian Tribes of
> British Columbia. . . . A perfect skull of a Kanaka warrior. . . .
> A compressed skull of one of the Clellam tribes of Flatheads,
> from New Dungeness. . . . A chief's girdle from Fiji Islands. . . .
> Skull of an Apache warrior, Globe district, Arizona. . . .[47]

In their annual reports, the university's governing body meticulously
documented every gift, casually interspersing human remains among
the artifacts:

> Arrow-head of yellow jasper [and] an Indian's skull, found on
> the sands of Humboldt Bay; [a sinker from Bear River and a]

Human Skull from Santa Cruz; two canoe paddles, a freshly
exhumed Indian skull [and] an Indian skull, having a tooth
abnormally situated; a small, well-shaped Indian mortar
[from Napa Valley], two Indian pestles [from Cloverdale], two
Indian skulls from a mound near Redding, [and] wampum
from Modoc graves.[48]

By 1890, the university had gone from receiving and excavating the occasional skeleton or skull to acquiring crates of human
remains, too many to specify: two boxes that included a "skeleton
of an Indian exhumed in 1876 at Shell Mound Park," located in what
is now known as Emeryville; seven boxes of material exhumed in
West Berkeley that included "fractured human skulls," "human jaw
bones," "human leg and arm bones," and "the principal bones of the
skeleton of an Indian killed in battle."[49]

Philip Jones, a doctor with no formal training in archaeology,
is honored on the Phoebe A. Hearst Museum of Anthropology's
website for his contributions "to the development of California
Archaeology as an academic discipline [that] still maintain a high
historical and research value today."[50] Between 1899 and 1901,
Phoebe Hearst bankrolled Jones's expedition to excavate burial
grounds in the Channel Islands, California's southern coast, and
the Central Valley. He documented his digs with photographs. In
one, taken on Santa Rosa Island, he poses like a big-game hunter
behind a table stacked with a pyramid of six skulls, framed by two
large bones. "In the course of the day," he records in his notes, "I
unearthed about 25 skeletons."

At another site in the San Joaquin Valley, with the permission
of ranch owners "who treated us with every courtesy and did everything in their power to further our work," Jones documented "many
skeletons dug up" in a chilling photograph of crania staged on top
of recently excavated graves. Except for a large shovel placed in the
foreground near a pit, the barren landscape stretches to the horizon
like no-man's territory in a war zone.[51]

During the founding year (1900–01) of Berkeley's anthropology
department, Phoebe Hearst sent Jones off on a buying spree:

Collection of Plains Indians material, valued at $3,000 . . . 2
sacks Indian Curios and Baskets from Chehalis Reservation
. . . two packages of material from Blackfoot Reservation,
including feathers, cost about $325 . . . Indian curios . . . largely
composed of feathers, value $500, from Round Valley Indian
Reservation . . . head dresses, Ukiah baskets . . . Indian curios
from Alexander Valley and Stewart Point, feather head dresses
. . . Klamath bow, quiver, and arrows; Sioux moccasins, Indian
games, Navajo blankets, baskets, mortars and pestles.[52]

Phoebe Hearst's archaeological expeditions to Egypt, Peru,
Mexico, and California returned to Berkeley with more than enough
mummies, skeletal remains, crania, funerary artifacts, and purchased
collections to equip an established anthropology program.[53]

A WELL-ESTABLISHED SCIENCE

It was a coup for the University of California to entice Frederic Ward
Putnam to become the anthropology department's first chairman
(1901–9). As director of Harvard's Peabody Museum of Archaeology
and Ethnology, a position he held from 1874 until 1909, Putnam was
the most influential anthropologist in the United States. The author
of an ethnological report published by the US Army in 1879 bowed
to his analytical expertise because he was "perhaps better fitted for
this most entertaining task than any other person in the country."[54]

As a result of his prominence as the lead curator for the World's
Columbian Exposition, held in Chicago in 1893, and president of the
American Anthropology Association in 1905, his endorsement of
Berkeley's program was clearly more valuable than his administrative
expertise. He kept his position at Harvard and was rarely present
in Berkeley, leaving the unglamorous, day-to-day tasks of fixing
broken plumbing, ordering coal, routine correspondence, and
bureaucratic report-writing to a young Alfred Kroeber, fresh from
his Ph.D. at Columbia University, who was hired as an instructor,

the lowest rung on the academic ladder. Acknowledging Phoebe Hearst's interests and philanthropy, University President Benjamin Ide Wheeler made anthropology a high priority at Berkeley and joined Regent Hearst, Putnam, and paleontologist John Merriam on the anthropology department's executive committee.[55]

Putnam was an excellent fit for a department bankrolled by Phoebe Hearst. His interests in archaeology and building Berkeley's collection conveniently matched her desire to showcase her acquisitions. "The constantly increasing patronage, by wealthy men and women, of archaeological research at home, as well as in foreign lands, is most encouraging," he told the American Association of Science in his farewell speech as president in 1899.[56] The metaphor of *fiat lux*, with its assumption about the inevitable benefits of modernization, also suited Putnam's worldview. He had been in charge of anthropological exhibits at the World's Columbian Exhibition of 1893 in Chicago which, according to historian Robert Rydell, "did not merely reflect American racial attitudes, it grounded them on ethnological bedrock."[57]

Putnam's expertise on the dead as repositories of scientific information can be traced to his twenties when he spoke to the Boston Society of Natural History about an "Indian grave" unearthed in Salem, Massachusetts.[58] His work for the army's geographical surveys in the 1870s deepened his knowledge of the rising profession of archaeology that he helped to shape. When he accepted an appointment to lead Berkeley's anthropology department, he created some space for Kroeber and other faculty to do research and write about the emerging fields of cultural anthropology. During the department's first decade, the University of California Press published several studies of Native languages, religions, and basketry.[59] At the same time, Putnam insisted on the prominence of physical anthropology, not only out of deference to Phoebe Hearst, but also because he believed that it would legitimate anthropology as "a well-established science."[60] The very junior Kroeber scrupulously followed orders: "Somatology has not been neglected," he informed his colleagues through an article in the *American Anthropologist*. "Measurements of living Indians has [sic] been undertaken."[61]

Even after Kroeber was promoted to assistant professor in 1906, he exercised caution, knowing that his focus on cultural issues and building an education program rather than a museum irritated Hearst. He asked Putnam if she "really wants to keep me or whether she would be relieved if I should go." Putnam advised Kroeber how to handle their patron. "Whenever you advise me what you wish us to do," Kroeber groveled to Phoebe Hearst, "I shall immediately proceed according to your instructions."[62]

Meanwhile, impressed by Hrdlička's research, Putnam made sure that "osteological work" was a departmental priority. He ordered from Germany "a measuring glass large enough to hold the contents of a skull" and investigated how he could acquire "one of Hrdlička's measuring machines" from the Smithsonian. "These two instruments," he wrote to Kroeber in 1906, "will give you full equipment for getting the capacity of skulls in conformity with measurements taken by Hrdlička and the Peabody Museum."[63] As Kroeber noted in an article for *American Anthropologist*, Hrdlička's research had "stimulated interest" in anthropometry and increased Berkeley's "somatological collections."[64]

In 1906, the fledgling University of California Press published a research report by Hrdlička, the country's leading authority on essentialist, biological, and racially determined differences between Native and European Americans. His study, based in part on twenty crania from Berkeley's "osteological collection," confirmed his assumption that "the data do not speak well for either the physical or mental development of the Californians [i.e., tribes]. [It is] . . . inferior to that in the average whites."[65]

The following year, Putnam reported to the Board of Regents that the "study of the physical character of the various groups of Indians combined with that of the skeletons found during the archaeological explorations, is being made in order to determine the physical relations of the tribes of California with the peoples of other regions."[66] He personally excavated a "prehistoric cemetery in ancient Chumash country," where he recovered "several perfect skulls and other important bones for study."[67]

Putnam's primary goal at Berkeley was the construction on

campus of an impressive museum "of great size" that would match the university's classical buildings, such as the Campanile, Doe Library, Hearst Mining Building, and Greek Theatre. It would illustrate "man's grouping into races . . . as exemplified by his osseous remains, his mental conceptions, and the work of his hands, from his primitive condition to his accomplishments in the highest intellectual and artistic realms."[68] The museum, he hoped, would provide an opportunity to put to good use some of the thousand or more human remains that were piling up in cabinets and basements. Putnam was enthusiastic about making human remains into an entertaining display.

As it was "no longer considered sacrilegious," he wrote in *Science* magazine in 1899, "to exhibit skulls, skeletons and mummies in connection with the work of the same peoples," he advocated replacing "heterogenous collections of ethnological and archaeological objects" with skeletons, objects, and texts that "should show the life and history of man . . . from his beginning in geological time, through savagery and barbarism to the periods of his civilization."[69]

The museum that Putnam and Hearst had in mind was not a monument to "past splendors" and the "extravagant glorification of the great people of previous times" in the style of European art museums.[70] Rather, they imagined a place that would combine elements of a shrine to holy relics—such as a piece of a scarf taken from the head of an Inca princess found in a tomb in Peru[71]—with educational exhibitions illustrating the Progress of Man, culminating in the final chapter of History with us in the here and now, the apogee of modern civilization. The massiveness of the anthropology museum's collection would itself testify to modern civilization's capacity for unlimited accumulation in contrast with premodern societies that were stuck in the past like amber—"slaves of custom," in the words of David Graeber and David Wengrow, "living in a kind of eternal present."[72] Moreover, it was not the inherent beauty or craftsmanship of the "specimens" that was to be highlighted; instead, "what they stand for . . . is the ultimate business and opportunity of the museum to show the world."[73]

What they stood for was a teleological narrative of Progress, in which Indigenous peoples represented the nadir of civilization—"a race living in a stage where all our ancestors have lived through," as one of Putnam's apprentices, Alice Cunningham Fletcher, explained in a campus lecture in 1901.[74] This paradigm, according to Indigenous critiques, characterizes our ancestors as a primitive or pre-civilization, fixed and immutable, incapable of significant change or the ability to consciously learn from past experiences.[75]

Putnam continued to lobby the administration for "a Museum of Art, Archaeology and Anthropology, $1,000,000, to hold the immense collections already accumulated by Mrs. Hearst at a cost of over $500,000." He reminded President Wheeler that when "the Department of Anthropology was established in 1901, its first purpose was to cooperate in the broad plans of Mrs. Phoebe A. Hearst, and [in order] to carry out her views it was made an integral part of the University."[76]

If Putnam had been on hand more often, or were a more effective fundraiser, or had not divided his loyalties between Harvard and Berkeley, maybe his vision of a museum "worthy of the rich materials it will contain" would have been realized.[77] Instead, he had to settle in 1902 for a "temporary" warehouse that was not dismantled until 1953; and a museum housed in "temporary quarters" in an old building in San Francisco from 1903 to 1931.[78]

It wasn't until 1959 that Berkeley constructed an anthropology museum on campus. Even then, Putnam would have been disappointed by its mundane architecture and limited space, which necessitated the storage of some 109 van loads of "specimens" in the basement of the women's gym.[79]

SHAPE-SHIFTER

By the time that Putnam left Berkeley in 1909 and receded from professional life, Alfred Kroeber had made himself indispensable. Promoted to associate professor in 1911, his prodigious scholarship, recruitment of talented faculty, and development of a solid curriculum enhanced the national reputation of Berkeley's program in anthropology. He also became a savvy bureaucrat, attentive to the university's expectations and a deft juggler of the faculty's disparate interests within the department. As a public intellectual, he was a shape-shifter, expressing contradictory positions that allowed him to successfully endure in academia until his retirement in 1946.

Kroeber had studied with Franz Boas and was the first recipient of a doctorate in anthropology from Columbia University. He was a member of a rambunctious cohort of aspiring academics who, in the words of Charles King, believed that the "only scientific way to study human societies was to treat them all as parts of one undivided humanity," and who did not assume that "all history leads inexorably to us."[80] Kroeber was twenty-six years old when he went to work as Putnam's gofer, thirty-four when he succeeded him. "Practically every specimen that is catalogued," he wrote Putnam in 1905, "has to be handled, placed, and named by me."[81]

Kroeber's reputation among tribes today is mixed. Many respect him for his advocacy, albeit belated, of Native land rights. "The solution of the California Indian problem," he told a Commonwealth Club audience in 1909, "lies above all in giving him [sic] land—property which he can call his own, and by which he can properly subsist and thereby be independent." The land, he continued, should be "good for something, not a quarter section on a granite hillside barely able to furnish pasture for a single cow."[82] Almost half a century later, close to the end of his life, he testified in a "masterful performance" for the plaintiffs in California Indian Land Claims Commission hearings, making a case that tribes had a material and spiritual right to lands that they had lost due to force, theft, and trickery.[83]

Kroeber's long-term relationships with Native informants made it possible for him to record stories, rituals, languages, and sacred sites that, in the words of a Yurok leader, "would not have been documented if it hadn't been for Kroeber."[84] His ethnographic field notes helped Yurok communities to preserve, revitalize, and celebrate young women's coming of age ceremonies. "We looked at any place we could find a reference to the [flower] dance," recalls

Lois Risling.[85] Without the assiduous work of that "good Doctor Kroeber," another Yurok elder once told Thomas Buckley, "we wouldn't know a thing today about who we really are."[86] Kroeber acknowledged that it had taken him a long time to "sense and value the qualities of a culture" into which he had not been born.[87] After his death, the Council of California Indians acknowledged how "in later life [he became] our greatest hope for long delayed justice."[88]

It would have pained Kroeber to know that recently his name has been unceremoniously removed from the anthropology department's building at Berkeley and that he is disparaged by a generation of Native activists who by the 1960s had succeeded his confidantes and who constitute today's elders.[89]

To most California tribes, especially those in the San Francisco Bay Area, Kroeber's legacy is more bitter than sweet. Why is this the case?

First, Kroeber failed in his responsibility to speak out publicly about the genocide that followed the Gold Rush. "What happened to the California Indians following 1849—their disruption, losses, sufferings, and adjustments—fall into the purview of the historian," he wrote in 1954, "rather than the anthropologist whose prime concern is the purely aboriginal, the uncontaminatedly native." He was of course well aware of the "shattering" of tribal communities and had heard many "tales of their deprivation and spoliation."[90] The transformation of everyday life after contact was traumatic, Kroeber conceded in a 1959 article, but, he added, "it is not gone into here." It wasn't that he hadn't known. He just hadn't gone into it. "I am not aware," anthropologist Karl Kroeber told me, "that my father wrote anything of the kind you are seeking on the topic of genocide."[91]

Kroeber's hands-off attitude towards the genocide influenced anthropological discourse in California for the first half of the twentieth century. One consequence of this moral cowardice and academic specialization was that until the 1960s a crude and racist imagery about California Indians dominated the state's public discourse, making it easier to frame their near extermination in the imagery of natural history, subject to inevitable processes of erosion and decline, rather than as the result of a planned human intervention. Many people hold Kroeber accountable because he had resources and authority to influence public opinion. Of course, one person, even Kroeber, did not wield such influence, but he became the personification of meticulous amnesia.

Secondly, Kroeber did not explore the extent to which his subjects' recollections of precontact life were mediated by their direct or indirect knowledge of the catastrophe that swept through their tribes in the second half of the nineteenth century. What Kroeber considered to be inherent in Native cultures from time immemorial—their melancholy "punctured by choler" and their tales suffused with an "almost elegiac emotion"—were no doubt survivors' depression and recall of dreadful times, as well as a reluctance to trust anthropologists.[92]

Thirdly, as Karuk scholar Julian Lang has noted, Kroeber was so preoccupied with precontact cultures that "he never introduced us to the living people."[93] This is not just a critique of Kroeber's specialized focus, but also of his failure to document how Native peoples survived against all odds and lived to fight another day. Activists looking for inspirational accounts of struggle, organization, and resistance find little solace in Kroeber's work, which tends to be nostalgic for the good old days rather than forward-looking. Again, it was not a matter of ignorance, for he had personally experienced the "dangerous mood" of the Yokayo Rancheria in 1906 when its lawyers had threatened Kroeber with criminal prosecution after his crew was caught digging up ancestors' graves in Ukiah, California.[94]

Kroeber was not particularly interested in Bay Area tribes, proclaiming in 1925 that they bequeathed nothing of important cultural value and that racially pure Ohlone were extinct.[95] This seemingly authoritative pronouncement, note today's representatives of the Muwekma Ohlone Tribe of the San Francisco Bay Area, "shaped the politics of powerlessness for the Ohlones for many decades [and] and reinforced the widely held notion that cultural transformations among native peoples erase their indigenous identity."[96]

Fourthly, Kroeber chaired a department that plundered Native grave sites and made eugenic anthropometry a respectable component of its curriculum and research.

Kroeber first met the teenage Edward Gifford (1887–1959) at the California Academy of Sciences where he was working as an assistant curator of ornithology and already a "passionate collector." Kroeber recruited him in 1912 to become his right-hand man at Berkeley's Museum of Anthropology, and later a researcher and professor at the university.[97] Gifford moved up the ranks without a college degree, trained by Kroeber to specialize in physical archaeology. Gifford's *California Anthropometry* (1926) followed in the eugenics tradition of Samuel Morton's *Crania America* (1839) and Ales Hrdlička's *Directions for Collecting Information and Specimens for Physical Anthropology* (1904). His quest for the biological basis of racial differences was consistent with the ideas and assumptions of the racist wing of the eugenics movement that had a considerable following in California between the world wars.[98]

Gifford's most far-reaching influence was in public education.[99] The responsibility for developing the museum's curriculum and offering hundreds of classes to thousands of schoolchildren was delegated by Kroeber to a faculty member who believed that Indigenous peoples had been stuck in premodernity. His research made the case that "during the long course of the Indian occupation of California," there had been "no change" in their "physical type" or "material culture." His science was constructed on essentialist gobbledygook: "Chins on the whole are less prominent than Caucasian chins," Gifford wrote in 1926. "The lips of the California Indians may be characterized as medium in thickness, occupying in this respect a position halfway between the lips of whites and of Negroes.... True foreheads are lacking."[100] Gifford's work resonates with Agassiz's observation some fifty-seven years earlier about "the square build of the trunk and shortness of limbs in the Indian."[101]

Gifford was promoted to director of the museum in 1925 and to anthropology professor in 1945. After his death in 1959, the anthropology department named a classroom in his honor. Last time I looked, the tribute was still on the door.[102]

SEVEN

Hoarding

Hoard (twentieth-century verb): the compulsion to continually accumulate and the reluctance to relinquish.

Let not your sorrow die, though I am dead.

—WILLIAM SHAKESPEARE, "AARON'S CURSE," *TITUS ANDRONICUS*

THE LARGEST COLLECTION

BERKELEY HAS A hoarding problem.

The university recorded its first acquisition of Native skulls in 1872 and some of its last "osteological material" in 1987. "There are now, indeed, few parts of the world," President Benjamin Ide Wheeler reported to the governor in 1912, that have as much information as California does about their "aboriginal inhabitants and prehistory."[1] By 1987, Berkeley could boast that it owned "the largest collection of California Indian material in the world."[2] Thirteen years later, a university administrator revealed more in sorrow than pride that Berkeley owned "one of the largest collections of human remains in the world."[3]

How and why did it achieve this claim to infamy?

Between the 1870s, when the first students were admitted, and passage of the Native American Graves Protection and Repatriation Act (NAGPRA) in 1990, the university accumulated, according to its own dubious numbers, 11,109 "skeletal remains" and 492,425 "Indian specimens" from North America.[4] As is typically the case

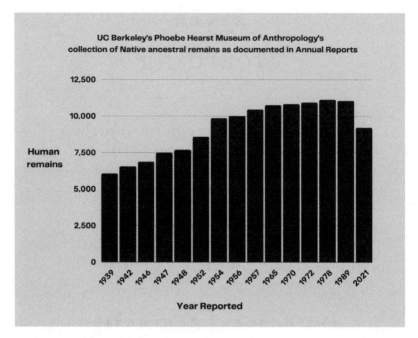

One of the Largest Collections of Human Remains in the World
"Infographic UCB Human Remains 2021," graphic by Danielle Elliott

with hoarders, the museum stashed items all over the campus, lost track of human remains and artifacts, and did not begin to account for what was in its collections until forced to do so by the federal government.

The habit might have started on Frederic Putnam's watch and under Phoebe Hearst's governance in the first decade of the twentieth century, but it took tenacious hold after their departure.

Prior to 1909, Kroeber did more than follow Putnam's orders and tolerate physical anthropology. As de facto executive officer of the department, he issued "an appeal for material and contributions for an exhaustive treatise on the myths, languages, and customs of the California Indians."[5] He also supervised excavations of burial sites along the Russian River and in the Bay Area, including the West Berkeley shellmound where, according to archaeologist Joseph Peterson, "there was an abundance of human remains."[6]

In 1907, he was in charge of an extensive survey of 439 Bay Area shellmounds, in which exhumations figured prominently.[7] "The somatological collections have been increased," he announced in *American Anthropologist* in 1906. "Systematic collection of photographs and measurements of living Indians has been undertaken," with plans to "cover the entire state."[8]

As Alfred Kroeber grew into his role as both chair of the anthropology department and a key player in the university's efforts to make its archaeological collections globally competitive, Phoebe Hearst's dominance ebbed. With Frederic Putnam's absence from Berkeley after 1909 and then death in 1915, she lost her main ally. She cancelled the bequest of $500,000 in her will that she intended for the construction of a museum. The standard explanation for her change of mind is that her wastrel son needed money to pay off debts.[9] But maybe she got wind of how the secretary to the Board of Regents had embezzled more than $52,000 from donations to the university, including $8,522.90 that she had earmarked for anthropology.[10] Or maybe she soured on the university when she finally realized she wouldn't be able to procure the kind of showplace that she was willing to finance. By the time of her death in 1919, most of her collections were in storage rather than on display.

Beginning in 1909, as chair of the department and director of the San Francisco–based museum, Kroeber oversighted excavations of Native burial sites almost every year, with the exception of during and immediately after World War I.[11] He helped to make a professional avocation into a popular hobby. Typically, an anthropology student dug up an "Indian burial ground" while on vacation on the Russian River in 1916.[12] As a founding member of the Society for American Archaeology, Kroeber retained a serious interest in archaeology. "In spite of the fact they informed only a part of his total scholarly work," observed a professional obituary, "Kroeber's contributions to archaeology are more substantial and important than those of most men who have devoted their entire career to the subject."[13]

He may not have been involved in the actual physical work of digging trenches and excavating the graves of Native ancestors, but Kroeber visited sites, participated in debates about what could be learned from burials, and encouraged amateur archaeologists all over the state to dig up and send crania to the university. "He did what he had to do," one of his biographers told me.[14] In 1911, for example, he contacted the president of the California State Dental Association for help in analyzing teeth and jaws in the museum's collection. In 1921, he authorized payment of ten dollars for "the skull of an Indian" dug up in Kern County. Moreover, Kroeber used extensive data derived from exhumations—dates of settlements, diet, causes of death, mortuary rituals, and so on—to reconstruct how "people in ancient and more recent times lived their lives."[15]

Kroeber hired Edward Gifford in 1912, guided his training, put him in charge of public education, mentored him in physical anthropology, and made him the university's point man for answering inquiries about crania and Native history, trading skeletons, and acquiring human remains. "It appears a typical Indian skull," Gifford wrote in 1925 in response to a high school student who had sent him a scale drawing. "If at any time it is decided that the school is not a safe place for the skull, the university would be very glad to receive it as an addition to its collection of California crania."[16] In his most important anthropometric treatise, Gifford thanked Kroeber for providing research data and "for his unflagging willingness to discuss the problems which these materials suggested."[17]

Kroeber was the key academic in a department and museum that rose to fame—literally and scientifically—on the bodies of the Native dead. When he retired in the late 1940s, the university proudly showed off to *Life* magazine its "bone collection [that] has filled two museums and overflows into the Campanile."[18]

Personally, Kroeber was more interested in the acquisition and trade in Native artifacts than in physical archaeology. "I do not want to collect in this state for any institution but our own," he told his former mentor Franz Boas in 1905—a pledge that he had not and would not observe. In 1902, philanthropist-tycoon Collis Huntington paid him to collect some 270 artifacts, including deerskin dance regalia and eagle feathers, for the American Museum of Natural History in New York. Even after Kroeber asked colleagues in Germany to "abandon the California field all together," he accepted a contract of $600 (the equivalent at that time of about four months' of his salary) from Berlin's ethnology museum in 1910 to collect "something from all cultural property of a tribe."[19] By then, though, Kroeber was becoming more proprietary about the university's collections. In response to a request from Stockholm's Royal Ethnographical Museum to borrow or buy artifacts, Kroeber told the regents that he did "not favor an exchange" and wanted to "control at least partially the outflow of ethnological material."[20]

Under Putnam and Kroeber's leadership, the Department of Anthropology acquired artifacts in two ways. First, by digging in, around, and through graves. Second, by forced sales.

"We bury our individuals with the trappings of their life," a Yurok tribal historic preservation officer told me, "in order to show their status in the afterlife. To separate the dead from their artifacts is to separate them from their identity."[21] Max Uhle applied in California what he had learned in Peru: the dead were typically buried with ceremonial items and everyday utensils that are valued in "the life hereafter" and therefore have commercial value in museums and collections.[22] Uhle understood that "many tribes of a low grade of civilization [*sic*] follow the custom of burying their dead underneath their feet in the ground upon which they live to protect the graves of their dead against being disturbed and also to enjoy the protection against their enemies of the spirits of the departed ones." This knowledge did not stop him from disturbing the dead, and extracting human remains and some six hundred "relics" from the Emeryville shellmound.[23]

While Kroeber was more focused on acquiring artifacts than skeletons, the practices of physical and cultural anthropology through the first half of the twentieth century made them practically inseparable. Until quite recently, all over the world people buried the dead where they lived out their daily routines—in part for reasons of security, in part out of respect for ancestors and a sense of the interdependence of life and death. This "promiscuity between the living and the dead," according to historian Philippe Ariès, was a common practice until the rise of modern funerary practices that swept ancestors out of sight and mind.[24]

Kroeber was well aware that tribes conceived of "life as established on a spot. Settlement there gives final repose and marks accomplishment of natural courses. This attitude is reflected in tale after tale; and in life by the custom of dying where one was reared."[25] He knew that digging up artifacts of the living and bones of the dead were interrelated. The physical and cultural branches of anthropology observed a division of labor and knowledge within the profession, but such a distinction was rare in the field or on expeditions where diggers and collectors accumulated both artifacts and body parts. "A large portion of the Emeryville mound consists of remains," Max Uhle observed in his field notes in 1902.[26] Moreover, in Berkeley's case, record keeping was so poor that it is very difficult to reconstruct with any certainty exact provenience or whether artifacts in the university's collection were ritualistic or practical or both.

The archaeological record is filled with accounts of the intermingling of human remains, ceremonial artifacts, and functional objects. In 1926, a visiting anthropology professor excavated skeletons and "strange animal figures" near Lodi.[27] In the 1930s, an amateur archaeologist, following the advice of Edward Gifford, "dug up several Indian skeletons [and] picked up quite a collection of artifacts" at Point Reyes; a University of Southern California excavation in Chumash sites unearthed skeletons and "burial mortars"; a crew led by Robert Heizer in Contra Costa dug up burials "rich in artifacts," including tubular pipes, pestles, and ornaments; another Heizer-led dig in San Jose created a chart of "burial artifact tabulation"; an expedition in Contra Costa removed olivella beads from a skull. In 1946, a professor of soil science donated to the anthropology museum a collection of "143 artifacts and 12 human skeletons collected in the course of an Indian-mound soil survey." In 1960, a report on excavations in Mendocino County documented "exceptionally fine, long pestles" extracted from burials.[28]

The second method of acquiring artifacts involved taking economic advantage of desperate people trying to survive—reminiscent of how the Nazi regime during the second world war and postwar speculators forced Jews to sell heirlooms and rare artwork for a pittance. With the destruction of traditional subsistence practices and forced displacement from homelands, many survivors of genocide faced starvation.[29] "I am here to tell you," Yurok leader Robert Spott informed a Commonwealth Club audience in 1926, "that we are almost at the end of the road." He had served as a "native son of these United States" in the trenches of France during World War I, only to return home to the Klamath to find sickness and desperate poverty.

> There are many Indian women that are almost blind, and they only have one meal a day because there is no one to look after them. Most of these people used to live on fish, which they cannot get, and on acorns, and they are starving. They hardly have any clothing to cover them. Many children along the Klamath River have passed away with disease. . . . It is 24 miles to Crescent City, where we have to go for doctors. It costs us $25.00. Where are the poor Indians to get this money from to get a doctor for their children? . . . I would like to know today if we will ever get our country back.[30]

The university's purchase of artifacts, either directly from Indigenous people by its agents or indirectly through purchase of private collections, was not an informed, consensual, equitable transaction because so many sellers were either the landless and impoverished survivors of genocide, dispossession, and criminalization, or their descendants.

What is clear from the archive is that thousands of Berkeley's acquisitions were based on what the American Alliance of Museums calls "coercive transfer," whereby the buyer takes advantage of the sellers' inability to get a fair price due to their dire need for basic necessities.[31] Here, for example, is Alfred Kroeber in 1909 instructing anthropologist Thomas Waterman how to hustle Native elders at least twice his age out of "old pieces that have seen use." Pay no more than one dollar for ceremonial feathers, he tells his protégée. "Two or three dollars should be high pay for this piece [a sweathouse door], as it is absolutely no more use to the owner. . . . The intrinsic value of an old house is practically nothing these days, and the people are attached to them for chiefly sentimental reasons." Waterman learned well from his cagey teacher. "Please buy Old Charley's house," he instructed an amateur anthropologist, "and ship it down to us by steamer. Say as little about it as possible and hire some Indian to fill his canoe full of planks." Decades later, Kroeber informed a go-between that he was still interested in buying "valuable objects which the old people used in dances and are like treasures."[32]

THE AMOUNT OF NEGLECT

Berkeley's unethical practices of procurement throughout the state were compounded by its longstanding, negligent steward-ship of human remains and artifacts inside the university. Two rationales guided the frenzy of collecting from the 1890s through most of the twentieth century: the scientific pursuit of knowledge about human origins and racial differences; and the preservation of an allegedly disappearing culture. In both cases, by its own standards and stated purposes, the university failed miserably.

The helter-skelter bundling of body parts and compulsive acqui-sition of artifacts without adequate documentary evidence and professional maintenance became a common practice at Berkeley, putting an almost impossible burden on descendants who, decades later, tried to identify their ancestors and possessions for purposes of repatriation claims under NAGPRA.

As early as 1895, the university curator was complaining to his boss that "the Ethnological collections belonging to the Museum [were] mixed together in the middle of the room . . . without notes or tags."[33] In 1902, an anthropologist ineffectually raised his con-cern that the department's collection of skulls was "accompanied only by loose labels and were for the most part unmarked for identification."[34] Frederic Putnam told President Wheeler that it had become impossible to keep up with an avalanche of archaeo-logical acquisitions. "It was only known in a general way what the boxes contained," making it impossible to unpack and care "for them in a proper manner."[35] In an exchange with a colleague in 1914, Edward Gifford noted that a record of some three hundred skeletal remains was of little scientific use. "There is usually no way of telling what is human and what is animal except by actual reference to the bones—a job which would take months."[36] In 1916, Alfred Kroeber admitted privately that Berkeley's growing collection of human remains was of minimal scientific value. "We have hundreds of Indian skeletons that nobody ever comes to study," Kroeber wrote Gifford in a personal letter.[37] Yet, the university continued to amass thousands more.

In 1931, H. H. Stuart, a Eureka dentist and self-trained archaeologist, sent Edward Gifford a gift of thirty-one skulls from various shellmounds in Humboldt. "They form a desirable addition to the collection of California crania," Gifford wrote Berkeley's president. Some seventy-five years later, in compliance with NAGPRA, the university repatriated thirteen of the skulls to the Yurok Tribe. There is no record of what happened to the missing eighteen skulls and "various human bones."[38] In 2005, the collections manager of the Phoebe A. Hearst Museum of Anthropology attributed this discrepancy to poor record keeping and the tendency of museums to "freely trade in crania."[39]

The pattern of systematic negligence continued throughout the twentieth century. A campus magazine reported in 1954 that the public was not able to see most of the museum's collection due to inadequate facilities. To illustrate storage problems, *California Monthly* included a photograph of the crowded basement of the forestry building, with boxes of crania and human bones on the floor.[40] Even after the Robert H. Lowie Museum of Anthropology (named after a leading anthropologist on the faculty from 1917 to 1950, and now known as the Phoebe A. Hearst Museum of Anthropology) was launched on the Berkeley campus in 1959, the collection's overflow was still stored in several buildings, including thousands of skeletal remains stacked in metal containers a few floors below the women's swimming pool.[41] In the 1980s, the director of the museum, James Deetz, reported that collections "were decaying due to neglect," conditions that continued for at least another two decades.[42] "When

I first saw the basement, I was horrified at the overcrowding, the general level of disorganization, the amount of neglect," said Rosemary Joyce, the museum's director in 1997. She allowed a reporter to document mousetraps in the aisles, dirty air ducts, and trash cans strategically placed to catch rainwater from a leak in the ceiling. "It will take decades to correct the storage problems."[43]

The university essentially ignored the enactment of global standards of museum care and protocols for the handling of human remains—such as a code of ethics first adapted by the International Council of Museums in 1986 and the Vermillion Accord on Human Remains issued by the World Archaeological Congress in 1989.

> Collections of human remains and material of sacred significance should be acquired only if they can be housed securely and cared for respectfully. This must be accomplished in a manner consistent with professional standards and the interests and beliefs of members of the community, ethnic or religious groups from which the objects originated, where these are known. (ICM)

> Respect for the mortal remains of the dead shall be accorded to all, irrespective of origin, race, religion, nationality, custom and tradition. (WAC)

In 1946, Kroeber had reported that the museum's collections "are probably the only ones of their quality and size in the country kept wholly in storage on account of lack of facilities to exhibit any of them."[44] "Sadly," concluded Lauren Kroiz, faculty director of the museum seventy-five years later, "such a statement could still be written about the museum today."[45]

It would take a decade after NAGPRA was legislated in 1990 before the museum's director could say that "the Hearst Museum is now in full compliance."[46] Yet, some twenty-one years later, the university's collection still included, according to its own count, 9,200 unrepatriated "ancestral remains," about 84 percent of the "osteological collection" that it reported in 1990.[47] In 2021, museum staff continued to painstakingly reassemble human remains, one ancestor at a time, from the thousands of bones and crania that had been routinely disassembled and sorted into discrete boxes of skeletal parts.

WHO COUNTS?

Over many decades, Berkeley has regularly and authoritatively announced the number of ancestral human remains in its museum collection. A close look at the evidence for these claims, however, reveals shaky math, selective data, arbitrary definitions, and unknown unknowns.

The university bases its count on record keeping that is filled with errors, inaccuracies, repetition, and unverified information. A chaotic data system was compounded by the shoddy, unprofessional, and disrespectful care of Native remains under its stewardship since the late nineteenth century. The university's unwillingness to provide sufficient funding and trained staff made it difficult for tribal representatives, Native organizations, and authorized researchers to access and make sense of archives.

The Hearst Museum significantly undercounts its collection of human remains by often counting multiple burials as a single individual or item; and by excluding from its count many fragments of skeletal remains that are mixed with funerary artifacts or considered too insignificant to enumerate. The actual count of Berkeley's collection of human remains is practically unknowable, comparable to the challenges faced by historians and scientists trying to estimate the number of people killed by atomic bombs in Hiroshima and Nagasaki in 1945.[48]

Nor will we ever know how many graves were desecrated in the process of excavations; nor how many graves were excavated by amateur archaeologists and civil organizations under the university's guidance, including information about the location of village sites; nor how donors of collections to the university acquired crania and body parts.

Part of the problem is shoddy record keeping and negligent stewardship, and part is the difficulty of figuring out how the university determined what constitutes human remains and what it decided to include in its inventory in the 1990s when required to do so by the federal government. Without context, definitions, and explanations, convincingly asserted numbers are like a Potemkin village—a facade of competence.

The first count appears in Frederic Putnam's annual report from the anthropology department in 1908. He speculated that the Berkeley's collection at that time included "nearly a thousand human crania and more or less perfect skeletons," excavated during archaeological expeditions in California, other parts of the United States, Mexico, and Peru. He did not include in this count the "many mummies in their cloth wrappings" brought back from Egypt.[49] Nor did Putnam enumerate the many imperfect skeletons and pieces of human bones that the university had excavated from graves in California, some of which were boxed and stored on campus, many of which were casually discarded on site.

For fifty years, between 1939 and 1989, Berkeley's anthropology museum routinely reported on the status of what it variously called "skeletal items," "skeletal material," "human skeletal material," "specimens of skeletal material," "osteological specimens," and "osteological materials." These data document a steady increase in the count: from 6,043 "skeletal items" in 1939 to 11,031 "osteological materials" in 1989.[50]

NAGPRA's requirement in 1990 that the university submit to the federal government an inventory of its collection of human remains, as well as "associated funerary objects" acquired in the United States, caused a panic, noted a campus administrator, putting Berkeley under a spotlight of "intense scrutiny from federal regulators, state politicians, Indian Tribes, the UC Office of the President, UC faculty, the media, and scientists across the U. S."[51] Two years later, the museum's director predicted that it would take twenty-five years to comply with NAGPRA given the inadequate level of staffing.[52] Moreover, the university could not rely for its inventory on the accuracy of pre-NAGPRA annual counts of "osteological materials."

Berkeley's first and lengthy response to NAGPRA was to stall by funding only one full-time staff person and expecting the museum to rely on students, interns, volunteers, and small grants to carry out a massive and complicated investigation. By late 1993, 90 percent of the inventory had *not* been completed. It was only in 1999, after the US assistant secretary for Fish and Wildlife, Department of Interior, informed Berkeley that it was the least compliant institution in the country and threatened the university with civil penalties, that serious work was begun on the inventory. With improved funding, new employees hired, and decent work-space made available, the museum began its review of 8,167 *"possible* catalogue records of human remains."[53]

The museum's staff faced several enormous challenges: trans-ferring a paper-based anarchy of data to a computerized system; searching for "basic descriptions" of about one-third of the collec-tion of human remains that lacked documentation; and trying to reunite human remains with their associated funerary artifacts, a "critical association between them [that] was often broken."[54] Rectifying more than a century of neglect, disorganization, and dismissal of Indigenous knowledge was a massive challenge, even if staffed adequately.

Fortunately, since the 1990s the Hearst Museum has compiled a digitized inventory that provides in one place all the information that it has scoured from paper records and index cards relating to, inter alia, its collection of human remains.[55] This catalogue draws upon work done in 1939 through a New Deal grant that funded the assis-tance of five untrained federal Works Progress Administration staff.[56]

Unfortunately, it would take a lengthy forensic investigation to vet a great deal of information that has not been verified, and to dis-entangle useful from confusing information, such as mistitled entries and inaccurate descriptions. Nevertheless, based on my selective survey of the catalogue, we can reach some tentative conclusions.

If you put "Human Remains" into the Hearst's search engine, up pop 25,054 entries, of which 22,261 are identified with California, more than twice the number in the university's NAGPRA inven-tory. What does this number mean?

On the one hand, the catalogue inflates the actual number of human remains by including mistitled faunal (animal) remains, repetitive entries, funerary and ceremonial artifacts, and human remains that have been deaccessioned—that is, repatriated or otherwise removed from the collection. In other words, there are many catalogue entries for "human remains" that no longer document human remains in the collection.[57]

On the other hand, the catalogue significantly deflates the actual number of actual human remains in the collection, as well as excludes many human remains from its NAGPRA-related count.[58] The Hearst, as is the case with several other museums, decides on what should be included in the count and for a long time has counted by "burial lots" rather than by individuals.[59]

For example, there are many single entries that reference multiple human remains and fragments of bone and crania. One such entry on an excavation in 1931 identifies human remains associated with eighteen different individuals;[60] another entry reports on the "comingled remains of a minimum of twelve individuals."[61] Other entries imply more than one skeleton.[62] A typical entry reports "47 bone fragments," another "34 bone fragments," with no indication of the number of burials.[63]

The practice of using one form to list multiple burials was so common that archaeologists created a special document: "Inventory Recording Form for Comingled Remains and Isolated Bones."[64]

There are also entries titled "Faunal Remains," "Abalone Shell with Soil," "Animal Tooth and Shell," "Awl or Punch," and so on that include information on human remains.[65] An entry labeled "Charcoal" refers to human detritus from a cremation; another on "Faunal Remains" notes "a few broken parts of a human skeleton from regions of hip and heel."[66] An entry titled "Asphalt" provides information on "asphalt adhering to rib fragment."[67] Another titled "Beads" includes a human tooth.[68]

When Edna Fisher was going through some thirteen thousand faunal specimens for the university's museum of zoology in the 1920s, she found human remains, some of which she sent to the museum of anthropology, some of which she "discarded."[69]

If we consider the multiple human remains listed as single entries and the untold pieces of human bone that are excluded from the NAGPRA-related inventory, an estimate of ten thousand to fifteen thousand individual human remains is not unreasonable. If we look beyond the legally defined boundaries of NAGPRA, the count is considerably larger.

NAGPRA only requires the university to publish evidence of human remains and related artifacts in its collections. The university's Standards of Ethical Conduct provide a broader framework for evaluating Berkeley's responsibility. It calls upon "members of the University community . . . to conduct themselves ethically, honestly and with integrity in all dealings," and to observe "principles of fairness, good faith and respect." Violation of these principles cannot be "justified on the basis of . . . achieving a *higher* purpose," such as excavating the Native dead in the name of science.[70] In addition, the Hearst Museum is bound by ethical guidelines issued by archaeological and museum associations that specify a code of conduct for relationship with tribes and Native communities, standards of care for collections, and the importance of accurate documentation.[71]

LIKE THE EARTH THEY ARE BURIED IN

Based on my review of hundreds of archeological reports and catalogue records maintained by the Hearst Museum, I conservatively estimate that for every skeletal remain excavated and preserved by the university, at least two were reinterred. This was done without ritual or any sense that the living and dead share a common humanity, or any effort to preserve the physical and spiritual integrity of corpses. It was a regular practice to remove and keep a piece of a skeleton, and unceremoniously dump the rest back into pits. Digging up "bone in great profusion" was commonplace.[72]

During an excavation in Emeryville in 1902, for example, Max Uhle reported that "none of the skulls could be secured intact."[73] A few years later at the same site, "a human skeleton was discovered," reported a graduate student. "We attempted to remove the skull whole by filling it with cotton, but upon lifting it, the bones fell apart."[74] While excavating the West Berkeley shellmound in 1904, Joseph Petersen reported that a child's bones "were greatly broken in removal."[75] That same year, Frederic Putnam supervised a dig in Delaware by Ernest Volk, who reported that "the bones of the skeleton are so soft that they are like the earth they are buried in and can't hardly be lifted without falling to pieces."[76]

A typical Berkeley-led excavation in the Carquinez Mound in 1912 uncovered burials "broken into fragments."[77] A year later, workers at a site of the First National Bank in Walnut Creek dug up twenty-five burials. By the time that Berkeley archaeologists showed up, "most of the skeletons had been dumped over the creek bank and buried." They recovered "portions of eleven individuals" to bring back to the museum.[78] Similarly, an archaeological team in Shasta County in 1935 packed several crates of human remains, most of which were missing crania. "Some bones have on them what appears to be dried flesh or skin," reported Waldo Wedel.[79] Robert Heizer dug up a corpse in San Jose in 1937: "condition good except feet lost in excavation," he reported.[80]

From its earliest years, the university encouraged collectors and amateur archaeologists to gift their collections, including human remains, to Berkeley or, as in the case of Philip Jones's buying spree (1900–02), to get a benefactor, such as Phoebe Hearst, to pay the bill. "Considerable number of skeletons have from time to time been unearthed," Jones reported to his patron.[81]

Donors regularly gifted human remains to the university from the 1890s through the 1980s: twenty-four human remains from Chumash territory between 1897 and 1902;[82] "skeletal material and prehistoric artifacts" from a Bay Area collector in 1919.[83] Digs were popular with high school students, who turned over a portion of their human spoils to the university, and provided local media with photo opportunities.[84] In the 1950s, a newspaper reported on "energetic University of California anthropology students" digging up burials in Berkeley. "First UC student to run across a skeletal form was Sally Foster, 20, of Claremont."[85]

Amateur archaeologists and friends of the university donated "skeletal material" from Lafayette and Mendocino in 1964; "skeletal fragments" from Alameda County in 1967; a "human skull" from Mountain View in 1970 and "human skeletal specimens from San Mateo in 1973; "one shrunken head from Colombia" in 1971; "miscellaneous osteological material" from West Berkeley in 1981; and "human osteological material" from Santa Cruz in 1987.[86]

There were many small gifts like these, and some huge ones. In 1942, the Sacramento Board of Education gave the university the "splendid Lillard Archaeological Collection," comprising of between fifteen thousand and twenty thousand items, including many human remains collected by the former president of Sacramento Junior College. In 1960, the State Indian Museum donated two thousand specimens of "skeletal material" to Berkeley.[87]

Until 1990 when NAGPRA was enacted, the university was eager to show off its spoils and boast in official publications about the size of its collections. After 1990, tribal activism put a halt to this widespread practice in universities and museums. Berkeley stored its vast collections underground and resisted accounting for how it had encouraged donations of human remains without verifying their provenience or demanding documentation or inquiring if they were ethically acquired. As an active collaborator in this process—not simply a passive, grateful recipient of gifts—the university played a leading role in providing nonprofessional collectors with expert advice, assistance, and legitimation.

ASSISTANCE IS NEEDED

For most of the twentieth century, Berkeley not only had the largest collection of human remains in the West; it also asserted hegemony over expertise on the subject.

From its founding in 1901, the Department of Anthropology took every opportunity to expand its sphere of influence. Each faculty member became a proselytizer promoting archaeology to a sizable constituency that ranged from boy scouts, country doctors, and men's clubs, to philanthropic women's organizations, local museums, and small and big-time collectors. In 1920, for example, Jesse Peter supervised an excavation by high school boys on the private property of a doctor "deeply interested in local anthropology." In the 1930s, two high school students turned over skulls and specimens to Berkeley archaeologists after completing a year-long dig in West Berkeley.[88]

The department took an interest in a wide variety of civic excavations, such as the San Mateo County Historical Society and San Mateo Junior College's joint exploration of local shellmounds; and a community service program organized by Santa Rosa Junior College to look for burials at Fort Ross. As late as 1967, primary school teachers were still bringing their classes to an excavation in Contra Costa, hoping "for some kind of portable exhibit of Indian life in this area."[89]

Exhumation of Native peoples' corpses and artifacts was a popular recreational fashion, driven partly by romantic nostalgia for the imagined past of a *disappearing race*, and partly by a mania for accumulating objects for prestige or profit. "White people came through this area in the 1920s and 1930s and took everything Indian they could get their hands on," recalled Yurok activist Joy Sundberg about northwest California. "Every college, every souvenir hunter wanted Indian artifacts. Back then there was no way to stop them."[90]

The work of gathering "knowledge of the first peopling of the Pacific Coast has been well begun," Frederic Putnam announced in 1905, "but assistance is needed for its rapid progress."[91] With assistance enthusiastically offered by would-be archaeologists all over the state, it became commonplace to send the fledging Department of Anthropology requests for guidance and information. Here are some typical inquiries during a single year:

> Several months ago, I found an old burial ground and dug up 3.... Skull is almost perfect with all teeth upper and lower.... Now if the remains are worth anything and are of any value to Science or Medical Study, I would appreciate hearing from you.

We members of the county historical society [San Rafael] here are interested in shell mounds, and Senator Rheindollar and Major Van Derbilt suggested that I write you for information.... Now if you can send me 2 or 3 maps of this county's shell mounds.

I and a friend of mine here made a discovery in which you may be interested viz the remains of an extinct race of people or tribe ... more than eight hundred years old.

I have read and read again every report on California archaeology I have been able to get. I am familiar with 'results' but have found very little on field technique.

I have been excavating indian skeletons and trinkets in an old burial ground on the campus of Marin Junior College in Kentfield.[92]

The university also cultivated relationships with wealthy private collectors, exchanging expert advice and endorsement for potential gifts. In 1914, Thomas Waterman catalogued J. McCord Stilson's private collection of 1,240 items in Chico, including "human teeth [and] fragment of human skull, very thick." Stilson acquired many items from other traders, making it impossible to verify provenance. In 1926, a visiting professor of anthropology from Sweden worked closely with San Joaquin Banker Elmer Dawson, owner of "8,000 specimens of great value," to excavate a site in Lodi.[93] In 1939, in exchange for advice about his collection and a set of museum publications, California automobile dealer E. B. McFarland donated skeletal material and artifacts to the university.[94]

The relationship between professionals and amateurs, academics and self-trained archaeologists was reciprocal. Berkeley received practical information about the location of burial sites, donations of human remains and funerary artifacts, and confirmation of its status as the final authority on Native history. In 1934, Gifford shared a map of shellmounds in Point Reyes with Lieutenant Commander Stewart Bryant, a lecturer in international relations at Stanford.

Bryant corrected some errors in Giddings's map, let him know that "human bones and artifacts [are] still available," and offered to deliver three skeletal remains when next in Berkeley.[95]

This cultivation of relationships with weekend archaeologists was routine in the 1930s and 1940s. A local archaeologist in Concord let Berkeley anthropologists know that he had dug up several burials: "The skulls and skeletons I took for you." While thanking a property owner in Walnut Creek for sending him two skeletons from his backyard, Robert Heizer encouraged him to keep digging because "accidental finds often turn out to be significant." Albert Mohr and David Fredrickson similarly appreciated a ranch owner's information about where to find Native sites in Glenn and Tehama Counties. A 1964 archaeological survey of excavations on Tuluwat Island (once known Indian Island) in Humboldt drew upon a map of burials made by a local dentist in the 1930s. "Altogether, for an amateur without a day's training," reported Albert Elsasser and Robert Heizer, "a remarkable job was done."[96]

In return, local collectors received expert advice and encouragement to go out and dig up burials. The Department of Anthropology readily sent out information and maps of Native sites. In 1910, "the ladies of the Mountain View Club" appreciated receiving a copy of Nels Nelson's report on the shellmounds of the Bay Area from John Merriam, Berkeley professor of paleontology. In 1933, students at Bakersfield Junior College "decided to look for U.C. number 32 burial ground" while excavating Pelican Island. "We are especially grateful to Dr. A. L. Kroeber," wrote the teacher in charge of a joint excavation by Fullerton Union High School and Junior College on Sunny Hills Ranch a few years later, "for his encouragement and friendly interest in our work."[97]

Mutuality of interests was exemplified in the university's relationship with Jeremiah Lillard, president of Sacramento Junior College. In 1933, Berkeley archaeologists supervised his students in a dig over several months, while Lillard took a field class from Berkeley's anthropology department during the excavation. "I've enjoyed the class greatly," he told his teachers.[98] He later supervised an excavation of 229 burials at another site. Lillard was "extraordinarily perceptive and energetic," recalled a deferential Robert Heizer, "and saw in some fashion which I could not, and can never divine, that one could recover the story of the Indian past by digging and studying the materials recovered."[99] After Lillard's death, the Sacramento Board of Education gifted his large collection to Berkeley.[100] Six years later, the collection had not been authenticated or catalogued.[101]

Some inquiries treated the university as a lending library of body parts. In 1949, the Department of Anthropology sent parts of a skeleton acquired in 1901 to UCLA "for teaching purposes."[102] As late as 1959, Robert Heizer received a request to borrow a skull. "Any Apache would do."[103]

The university's relationship with collectors and aspiring archaeologists played an important role in mapping burial sites and digging up human remains, some of which made their way to Berkeley, many of which were displayed as trophies in small museums or stashed in private collections in the style of cabinets of curiosities. Without the university's blessing and involvement, this network would not have flourished.

Today, Berkeley continues to be in violation of ethical standards established by the American Alliance of Museums: failing to ensure that its Indigenous collections "are lawfully held, protected, secure, unencumbered, cared for and preserved."[104] Given the state of misinformation, it is not possible to come up with an accurate count of the university's acquisition of Native human remains through its own excavations. Or to quantify its destruction of Native burial grounds, its accumulation of human remains through gifts, and its role as an adviser to hundreds of amateur archaeologists who dug up Native settlements throughout the state. It is clear, though, that the numbers estimated by the university at the time of its NAGPRA inventory represent only a small fraction of the suffering, havoc, and indignities that Berkeley wreaked on the survivors of genocide.

IN A DANGEROUS MOOD

The university's persistent failure to seek permission from relatives and descendants before digging up their ancestors is the ultimate ethical lapse. Guardians of the dead are a present absence. When asked in 1932 about the legalities of excavations, Kroeber replied that permission should be sought from the Smithsonian if federal land was involved and from the landowner if on private property. Otherwise, a permit might be needed from county officials, but a local ordinance "is not likely to be invoked unless someone takes offense at the digging." If in doubt, Kroeber advised, consult an attorney.[105]

The Hearst Museum archive is filled with gracious acknowledgement of benefactors who bankrolled expeditions, and documentation of archaeologists scrupulously requesting permission from the owners of land once occupied by murdered and displaced Native peoples, a procedure they meticulously followed until the late twentieth century.

In the 1890s, Stanford professor Mary Barnes "with the permission of the owner" took students to a nearby site where they dug up a "very old Indian."[106] Max Uhle's 1902 excavation of the Emeryville shellmound was made possible by Phoebe Hearst's "ample financial support."[107] In the 1930s, Edna Fisher thanked Del Monte Properties Company for permission to excavate a site in Monterey where "human bones and stone implements are said to have been found."[108] Robert Heizer "secured a permit to excavate from the University" and was in the field with a crew for three months thanks to the "generosity of Mr. and Mrs. Beverley Blackmer of Pyramid Lake, Nevada."[109] In 1946, Berkeley anthropologist John Merriam led a field trip to a dig in Mountain View where the owner, who sold soil from the shellmound on his land, "gave us all cooperation."[110] In the late 1950s, local businessman George Truitt allowed Berkeley archaeologists to excavate a West Berkeley shellmound on the property of his landmark business, which at the time of this writing still exists.[111]

Notably missing from the voluminous reports is any mention of archaeologists seeking approval of Native survivors or descendants before exhuming, crating, and disassembling their ancestors. Of course, they knew better and acted on an assumption they knew to be false: that there were no living or cultural descendants of the Native dead. More to the point, there were none who mattered to them.

Even the begrudging archive occasionally reveals evidence that archaeologists were well aware of the presence of biological and cultural descendants of the dead they exhumed.

When Paul Schumacher was surveying the California coast for the Smithsonian in the 1870s, he took time to pillage village sites. He was cautious around graves "as I did not wish to awaken the suspicion of the natives," he wrote in his report to the museum. This may have slowed him down but didn't stop him.[112] Similarly, during his "reconnaissance" of the Russian River area in 1909, Berkeley archaeologist Nels Nelson documented a cemetery that "is still used for burial by Indians living in the vicinity but," he added, "may be doubtless excavated with profit in the near future."[113] A Berkeley team excavating a site in Walnut Creek in 1913, with permission of the First National Bank, knew that Native descendants lived in the foothills of nearby Mount Diablo.[114] In 1937, Jeremiah Lillard's father worried that his acquisition of a Chumash pipe from a grave might get him in trouble with local descendants.[115]

Josephine Brown Marks, a Yurok woman with extraordinary knowledge about her tribe, chose not to share what she knew with anthropologist Thomas Waterman in the 1920s and stuck to her decision. "She says she knows many things about the old way of life," Robert Greengo reported on his visit to northwest California thirty years later, "which she has not told to anyone from the University." Harry Roberts, one of the few outsiders to be given a rigorous education in Yurok practices, explained: "There is so much that the early anthropologists could never get from the old-timers. When they realized that the anthropologists and psychologists couldn't understand them, they stopped speaking of personal things and only gave them what they could understand. That's the law: don't give people what they can't understand."[116]

Instead, tribes gave archaeologists what they could understand:

stubborn resistance that ranged from petitions and legal challenges to in-your-face confrontations.

In 1874, a Wintu woman, Matilda Charles Empire, petitioned a federal commissioner of Fish and Fisheries in Shasta County "not to disturb any of her friends and relatives who have gone the way of all flesh" and were interred "where the good Indians of the McCloud have been buried for centuries. The living members of the tribe," reported Commissioner Stone, "are in constant fear lest we should dig up their graves for relics."[117]

Berkeley archaeologists first encountered resistance to their collecting practices and met their match in 1906 when Kroeber sent anthropologist Samuel Barrett, who had grown up in Ukiah, to collect information for what would become a monograph on *The Ethno-Geography of the Pomo and Neighboring Indians* (1908). With the arrival of the railroad in 1889, according to Sherrie Smith-Ferri, Ukiah became a "hub of the early basket market," profiting off the obsession of middle-class consumers around the country with the "Indian basket craze." Before conquest and settlement, there were thousands of Indigenous people living in what are now Sonoma, Mendocino, and Lake counties, living in well-established "town-states," speaking seven distinct languages. "Their basketry is considered among the finest in the world."[118]

A few hundred Pomo survivors of massacres and dispossession stayed in the region, mostly working as migrant farmworkers. "Our people had to be tough to survive," said Tom Renick of the Yokayo Rancheria." They were ingenious, creative actors who, writes Smith-Ferri, "took a hand in shaping their own destiny through a combination of accommodation and resistance."[119]

When the federal government established reservations in Fort Bragg and Round Valley in the mid-1850s, many Pomoans escaped the roundup and stayed in the area. Some worked as indentured laborers, some squatted on the land of ranchers as payment for picking hops and beans, and some strategically married into white families. In the 1880s, a group calling themselves Yokayo—a Pomo word meaning lower valley—pooled resources, bought land, and produced their own crops. In 1905, following an internal dispute, the Yokayo Rancheria hired lawyers and successfully petitioned the Mendocino County Superior Court to create a tribal trust, a decision that was upheld by the California Supreme Court a few years later.[120] "Many of our Indians are becoming landowners," noted the *Dispatch-Democrat* in September 1878. "This speaks well of them."[121]

Samuel Barrett had deep knowledge about the brilliance of Pomo basketry, but he was out of his depth when, under orders from Kroeber, he dug up several ancestors and transported their remains to Berkeley. The Yokayo Rancheria hired the same high-powered local firm that had handled their trust. The lead lawyer, John Liddle McNab (who would later be appointed a US attorney by President Taft), fired off press releases and a letter to University President Benjamin Ide Wheeler, threatening criminal charges.

"Of course," McNab wrote Wheeler, "the persons who dug up the bodies may not have been aware that it is an offence under the penal code to remove a human body from a place of burial. I wrote to you knowing that you can refer this to the proper department and would suggest that if any information can be given upon this subject which would lead to a return of the bodies, it would be but the proper thing to do under the circumstances. The Chiefs of the tribe are men of considerable intelligence and our firm has represented them in some important litigation concerning their tribal relations, their right to hold lands, etc."[122]

Barrett told the excavation crew to keep quiet and "make no statements," and alerted Kroeber that "there is something in earnest meant and it would be my idea that something should be done about the matter." Kroeber took charge, reassuring McNab that "you will find it impossible for any claim to a body to be substantiated or for any location at the site to be identified. If we prove to be mistaken and have infringed upon anyone's rights, full restitution will of course be made. I am entirely responsible in the matter." McNab replied quickly and forcefully: "That the bodies were removed we, of course, have absolute proof from the owner of the property who was on the ground. Mr. Barrett, formerly of this county, is said to have been in charge of the expedition. Several parties know about the matter and it can be easily traced. . . . This graveyard is guarded very jealously by the Indian tribe and the tribe is in a dangerous mood [and] is not in a mood to be tampered with." To back up their case, the Yokayo Rancheria successfully lobbied what was then called the United States Indian Service (later known as the Bureau of Indian Affairs) to investigate "some grave robbing operations by scientists in the vicinity of Ukiah."[123]

As Kroeber played for time, McNab threatened to file criminal charges against the excavation team and to send the press more details of the case. "We do not believe that it will be at all conducive to the advancement of the investigations of your department to have this matter become public any more than it is." Immediately, Kroeber returned "twelve remains" to the Yokayo Rancheria.[124]

The Rancheria put a stop to Berkeley's expeditions to Pomo country, but most California tribes and rancherias did not have the necessary economic resources or legal acumen to take a grievance to the courts. Kroeber's crews shifted their attention to other parts of the state.[125]

In 1931, the US Indian Service located on the Hoopa reservation noted that "some of the Indians are making very vigorous complaint against excavations at Indian burying grounds along the coast."[126] In 1949, local Yurok women harassed a Berkeley crew trying to excavate a site in Tsurai (Trinidad). "My mother Georgia, her mother Minnie Shaffer, and another family remember, Olive Frank," recalled Axel Lindgren, "were there each day, raising havoc over this grave-digging project by the University boys."[127] A local columnist, in consultation with Robert Spott, reported that "desecration of the graves of their ancestors is, in the minds of the Yurok people, the final word in depravity. Perhaps the greatest cause for the lingering bitterness against the invading whites has been the utter disregard displayed for the sacredness of these family and tribal shrines."[128] Continual protests and complaints forced Heizer and colleagues in 1964 to cancel excavations in Trinidad "in deference to the request of local Indians."[129]

These early challenges had some success in putting a brake on archaeological excavations, but not stopping them. It took a decade

of militant activism coast to coast, accompanied by grassroots organizing and political lobbying before the struggle over Native ancestors and artifacts achieved results. The Red Power Movement—as
expressed in the organization of the American Indian Movement in
1968, the publication of Vine Deloria Jr.'s manifesto *Custer Died For
Your Sins*, the occupation of Alcatraz in 1969, and First Convocation
of American Indian Scholars in 1970—made cultural patrimony
and repatriation central issues. Deloria compared anthropologists
to missionaries who were "intolerably certain that they represent
ultimate truth." Singer Floyd Red Crow Westerman popularized
Deloria's message in an album: "And the anthros still keep coming
like death and taxes to our lands / To study their feathered freaks
with funded money in their hands."[130]

California was the first state in which a Native-led organization was formed to focus on halting the desecration and looting of
cemeteries. The intertribal Northwest Indian Cemetery Protection
Association (NICPA), created in 1970, physically confronted archaeologists and put a stop to unauthorized excavations, setting a precedent for national legislation twenty years later.[131]

"There was just a few of us when NICPA started," recalled Joy
Sundberg. "We had to pound on doors, talk to organizations, get
up and speak in front of politicians. I didn't give up. It was hard,
but we had to do it. I learned that a ragtag group of folks can defeat
the big guys."[132] The University of California stopped digging up
graves in Yurok country in 1970 after NICPA scared off a Bay Area
expedition that was attempting to carry out "salvage archaeology"
at the village site of Tsahpekw. "I was totally intimidated," said the
lead anthropologist. "I was shell-shocked for several days."[133] By the
early 1980s, NICPA's major demands—protection of Native cultural
sites, respectful partnerships between anthropologists and tribes,
and public condemnation of looting—began to receive recognition
in law and legislation, and to be practiced in the emerging field of
"compliance archaeology."

Meanwhile, the Hearst Museum encouraged excavations state-
wide, continued to accept human remains until 1987, and for years
did its best to undermine implementation of legislation that was

designed, in the words of Senator Daniel Inouye, to restore the "civil rights of America's first citizens."[134]

Without having to face NICPA, which dissolved in the early 1980s, or reckon (yet) with Native political clout in the legislature, or respond to a movement for reparative justice on campus, Berkeley begrudgingly complied with the narrowest interpretation of NAGPRA while attempting to extinguish its spirit. It took the university until 2000, ten years after passage of NAGPRA, to complete its inventory of "one of the largest collections of human remains in the world."[135] Even article 12 of the 2007 United Nations Declaration on the Rights of Indigenous People—"Indigenous peoples have the right to the repatriation of their human remains"—did not prompt urgent action or ethical introspection, thus putting Berkeley in the same company as the United States and three other countries that voted against ratification.[136] By 2021, thirty-one years after passage of NAGPRA, the Hearst Museum had, by its own generous estimate, repatriated only 16 percent of Native human remains.[137]

Meanwhile, the university's involvement in crafting and distributing eugenic ideas and a racial discourse of Progress had more enduring consequences than its obsession with hoarding.

The refusal of Berkeley anthropologists, for example, to speak out against the myth of "the disappearing Indian" echoed Kroeber's unwillingness to publicly express his horror at the California genocide. They could have pushed back against disinformation that was widely believed, despite the presence of survivors of genocide and their descendants and families who worked throughout the state; despite the persistence of Native ceremonial life; despite relentless resistance; and despite the availability of several Native elders to anthropologists eager for interviews and photographs. Kroeber traveled the state collecting information from his contacts about languages; Gifford's book on anthropometry included close to one hundred images of adults and elders from all over the state, all appearing seriously alive.[138]

IV

MISEDUCATION

EIGHT

Misanthropology

They had no names for themselves,
no traditions and no religion.

—JOHN MCGROARTY, 1911[1]

There isn't much Native American culture in
American Culture. . . . We birthed a nation
from nothing—I mean, there was nothing here.

—RICK SANTORUM, 2021[2]

THEIR CALIFORNIA

IN 2009, IN RESPONSE to a suit filed by the American Civil
Liberties Union of Northern California, the Del Norte County
Unified School District in northwest California acknowledged
institutionalized discrimination against its Native American students—including a climate of racial harassment and disproportion-
ate use of suspensions and expulsions—and agreed to implement
a series of remedies over the following five years. As part of this
settlement, I was invited by school officials to lead a workshop for
some twenty-five elementary school teachers who were grappling
with how to make their curriculum respond to charges of racism.

As I drove from the San Francisco Bay Area a few hundred miles
north up the California coast, through sites of memory where the
genocide had raged, to hardscrabble Crescent City—the once thriving and long abandoned fishing and logging town, now home to
one of the most notorious supermax prisons in the United States—I

recognized the same kinds of absences that hover over the Berkeley campus. There are no plaques or markers in the public squares and along the state's "Redwood Highway" that provoke travelers to consider the thousands of Native people who lost their lives, lands, and then their dead; no public memorials or annual rituals that ask us to reconcile a place of extraordinary beauty with the horrors of history; nothing to disturb the public image of northwest California as an "outdoor paradise" and "ecotourist's heaven." Searching California for public recognition of its foundational injustices was as frustrating as searching Lisbon, during a visit four years later, for public recognition of the central role of the transatlantic slave trade in Portugal's glorious past.

The Del Norte County schoolteachers were particularly exasperated with how the state-authorized textbook for fourth graders—*Our California: History–Social Science for California*, originally published in 2006 and still being used three years later—did injustice to history. Given the large number of Native families in the region, the resurgence of traditional cultural practices during the last thirty years, and the region's history as an epicenter of mass extermination policies and land grabs in the wake of the Gold Rush, socially responsible teachers want to do the right thing by their students. And *Our California*, they told me, gets in their way.[3]

At first glance, the book seems sensitive to issues of class, gender, and race. There are pictures of Japanese farmworkers, an African American mayor of San Francisco (Willie Brown), and the first woman in space (Sally Ride); acknowledgment of the "unfair treatment of migrant workers" (with images of Cesar Chavez and Dolores Huerta); and a paragraph on tribal government in a chapter on politics. But below the multicultural gloss, there is historical misinformation and casual intolerance, as well as a heavy dose of amnesia regarding California's Native past and present. By page two the rewriting of history is underway: "Our story of California begins hundreds of years ago with the California Indians." This sentence manages to both reduce multilinguistic and diverse tribal communities to a generic Indian and diminish their histories of thousands of years.

A well-meaning effort to portray the daily lives of four tribal groups (Cahuilla, Chumash, Miwok, and Hupa) "long ago" is undermined by the assumption that they were static and homogenous, with no changes over time. Accompanying an illustration of a swashbuckling and no doubt studious Spaniard on horseback is a reassuring take on colonialism as an exercise in broadening one's mind. The vocabulary word for this lesson is *explore*. Accompanied by an image of now four swashbuckling Spaniards on horseback, the next lesson asks the question, "How did the Spanish change how California Indians lived?" And "died" would have been appropriate since Native populations declined by about one-third in the period of Spanish rule. This time, the vocabulary includes *colony*, ever so euphemistically defined as "a settlement of people who come from a country to live in another land." Another key term, *mission*, becomes "a settlement set up by a religious group to teach their religion and other ways of life to native people." The assumption that Native peoples are godless heathens is reinforced by an image of Chumash on their knees before a padre and giant cross.

The missions, which figure prominently in California's iconography, get five images in the book, all of unpeopled buildings, including an illustration of a "Spanish Mission" that resembles a contemporary Napa Valley spa, complete with "guest rooms," "workers' housing," and "pottery shop and oven." Not an enslaved Indian in sight.

While the textbook acknowledges that "some California Indians" were "forced to give up their way of life" and that "many died from diseases brought over by Europeans," the overall impression of Spanish colonialism is positive. Presumably incapable of change for ten thousand years, "California Indians learned how to farm and make new things."

We also learn that under Mexican rule "many California Indians had no land or money," so ended up working on ranches. But after the US war against Mexico in 1848 (described as a "gain" in territory), Native peoples disappear from history, only to be reincarnated eighty-two pages and more than a hundred and fifty years later in a section on "tribal government."

Meanwhile, *Our California* sidesteps the challenges of teaching young children the history of genocide, extermination campaigns, human trafficking, and cultural erasure in the aftermath of the Gold Rush. Out of curriculum, out of mind.

No wonder teachers feel frustrated, families are angry, and Native kids rebel against a curriculum that whitewashes their California.

To understand how this obliviously crafted propaganda posing as history was still being promoted in required textbooks in the 2000s requires an investigation into the origins and development of what I call *The California Story*—a semiofficial, public narrative of the state's past—and into the role of the scribbling class, prominently represented by Berkeley academics, who converted an imagined past into taken-for-granted truisms.

Long after nineteenth-century genocidal violence subsided, venomous ideas took root in its ashes and flourished throughout the twentieth century.

CULTURAL FIREWALL

The catastrophes that were imposed on Native communities in California were well known and publicized in the late nineteenth century. Reformers who advocated forced assimilation over physical destruction spoke out against the "sin" of the "brutal treatment" of California tribes. "Never before in history," wrote a popular journalist in the early 1870s, "has a people been swept away with such terrible swiftness or appalled into utter and unwhispering silence forever and forever."[4] By the early twentieth century, however, explicitly racist views about Native peoples predominated, and the savage brutalities of a colonial regime were retrospectively justified.

The "astonishing social energy" of multinational, post–Gold Rush California, observed journalist Carey McWilliams, generated a vigorous publishing industry. San Francisco produced more books than the rest of the western United States, and by the 1850s equaled London in the number of its newspapers.[5] The publication in 1884 of Helen Hunt Jackson's novel *Ramona* propagated a nostalgic, imagined past in which courageous Spanish missionaries did their best to uplift backward Indians, and blue-blooded Californios left a legacy of genteel living and Old World romance. Utopian images of California as a tourist destination and real estate paradise made the California Story into a topic of national curiosity.[6]

Primers on California history for children and students were first produced in the 1860s.[7] The earliest travel guides included capsule histories, just as they do today.[8] Widely read magazines such as *The Land of Sunshine* (founded in 1894) and *Sunset* (1898) regularly carried memoirs and first-person accounts of times gone by. Henry Norton's *The Story of California*, published in 1913, went through twelve editions by 1934. It took a while for historians and other academics to produce California's textbooks: the first one-volume history of California was published in 1921; the first college-level text in 1929.[9]

The California Story was a popular enterprise, regularly incorporated into grandly produced "theatres of memory," such as world fairs and local spectacles, and into travel books, memoirs, adventure stories, textbooks, and magazines that exported its appeal far beyond the state, long before Hollywood entered the picture.[10] It was not the work of handpicked professional historians or a master political authority, but rather the creative invention of writers, journalists, boosters, academics, and businessmen who served on the ideological frontlines dispensing the cultural equivalent of poison gas.

Berkeley's faculty and patrons did much more than respond to the prevailing politics of conquest and modernization. As authoritative intellectuals, they were resourceful innovators who played a critically important role in shaping the state's public identity. The university also gave popular writers a stamp of legitimacy and platform from which to spout unabashedly racist ideas.

Hubert Bancroft (1832–1918), California's most recognized historian and a prolific publisher, as well as a benefactor of the university's Bancroft Library, popularized all kinds of derogatory insults about the Northern California Indian: "He was not such a bad specimen of a savage, as savages go, but filthiness and greed are not enviable qualities, and he has a full share of both."[11] Herbert Bolton, longtime chair of the history department and first director of the Bancroft

Library, wrote a forward for Phil Hanna's *California Through Four Centuries* (1935)—gushing about the author's "penetrating interpretation," "fine literary style," and "brilliant Introduction"—in which Hanna contrasted the civilized Spaniards with "the Indians [who] were a debased race, little advanced from the anthropoid ape. It is doubtful if more primitive savages existed at that time on the face of the earth."[12]

Anthropologist David Barrows, president of the university from 1919 to 1923, was a public expert on the racial superiority of white Europeans. "The black lacks an inherent passion for freedom," he wrote in his 1927 book on North Africa.[13] The University of California Press published the work of Berkeley's leading eugenicist Samuel Holmes, including a racist screed in which "American Indians" are written off as a "sort of foreign element in our population."[14]

Popular writers and journalists consulted Berkeley academics for their books and articles on California and Native histories and were invited to speak on campus.[15] Kroeber and other anthropologists were regularly cited by the press. They must have known that their work was being boiled down by popular writers into predetermined nuggets of colonial ideology, yet many engaged in "passive resistance and passive collaboration," not raising a fuss, keeping their silence.[16] Kroeber insisted on fencing off anthropology from the contemporary world for most of his career until it was too late to repair the damage, thus depriving the profession of an influential public voice when it was desperately needed.

Some crossed the line and took initiative. Kroeber entrusted the university's public educational programs in anthropology to his mentee Edward Gifford, who taught tens of thousands of schoolchildren essentialist quackery about how "the living aborigines of California fall into two groups, one low-faced, the other high-faced."[17]

Attorney Theodore Hittell drew upon lectures he gave at Berkeley in 1893 on the *History of California* to write his multivolume history of the state that depicted the region's tribes as "low-grade in the scale of humanity" and "equally stupid and brutish . . . to be regarded like the bears of the mountains and the coyotes."[18] Rockwell Hunt's textbook, in which he characterized California's tribes as "in reality only barbarians" and "wild and ignorant savages," was used in 1912 by Berkeley's museum of anthropology in its classes on history and geography offered to local public schools.[19]

Herbert Bolton had a significant impact on the popular and academic shaping of California history. Recognized for challenging Anglo-centric histories of the United States and elevating the importance of Spain's "frontiering genius," he trained many borderland historians whose ideas permeated school textbooks and pushed back against critics of the mission system.[20] "In the English colonies," Bolton wrote in an influential essay for the *American Historical Review*, published in 1917, "the only good Indians were dead Indians. In the Spanish colonies, it was thought worthwhile to improve the natives for this life as well for the next. . . . If the Indian were to become either a worthy Christian or a desirable subject, he must be disciplined in the rudiments of civilized life"— the *raison d'être* of the missions, argued Bolton. As he explained in a coauthored textbook for children, "the wild Indians were gathered into villages. They were taught the Christian faith and how to do useful things in the white man's way. . . . The friars treated the Indians kindly."[21]

In recognition of his defense of Spanish and Catholic colonialism, the King of Spain made Bolton a commander of the Royal Order of Isabella the Catholic in 1925, and Pope Pius XII named him Knight of St. Sylvester in 1949.[22]

Throughout the twentieth century, architects of the California Story built a cultural firewall that insulated generations of young people from the horrors of the genocidal past. Their Orwellian efforts to "make lies sound truthful and give an appearance of solidity to pure wind" is comparable to how the Nazi regime promoted cultural stereotypes of partisans in Eastern Europe as inherently barbarous. "The struggle we are waging there," Hitler said in August 1942, "resembles very much the struggle in North America against the Red Indians."[23] It is comparable to how the Argentinian military command, from the 1950s through the 1970s, inculcated in rank-and-file soldiers "a negative conception of otherness" that prepared them for the work of assassination and disposal of bodies during the "dirty war." And how instruments of genocide in Rwanda were shaped by demonic images of the Tutsi body as foreign and unnatural.[24]

THE CALIFORNIA STORY

The California Story refashioned the complex history of Native peoples in the region to suitably fit the state's racially sanitized origins story and narrative of relentless Progress. Dodging California's Indigenous and Mexican roots, the state's earliest textbooks and popular histories located the mythic idea of California in Castilian Spain, transported to the New World via religious missions from the 1770s through the 1820s. It was this origins story that motivated the California State Society Daughters of the American Revolution (DAR) in 1978 to erect a plaque on campus where the Pedro Fages military expedition had supposedly camped in 1772. At this high point in multicultural education during efforts to diversify the curriculum in the 1970s, the university and right-wing DAR were eager to trace Berkeley's provenance to an imagined aristocratic Spain rather than to its Indigenous and Mexican roots.[25]

As Max Oelschlaeger has noted, advocates of modernization regarded the previous caretakers of now occupied land as either generically invisible or not up to the job; and the land itself as "a stockpile of resources, lifeless matter-in-motion, a standing reserve for human appropriation."[26]

A master narrative of Progress, *fiat lux*—bringing light to the darkness, supplanting the deficiencies of predecessors with the ingenuities of settlers, replacing aimlessness with purposefulness— permeates the California Story that was told and retold until it assumed the status of indisputable facts, succinctly summed up in the title of a 1946 textbook: *From Wilderness to Empire: A History of California, 1542–1900.* The advocates of *fiat lux* were not so much propagandists as true believers and utopians who imagined themselves as shining beacons of light in the darkness and creating a new

Enlightening a Wilderness
"Fiat Lux," December 19, 2022, photograph by Semantha Raquel Norris

world out of the corpses of the old. "When I think . . . of the law," wrote Supreme Court Justice Oliver Wendell Holmes Jr. in 1934 in a statement engraved over the entrance to Berkeley's law school, "I see a princess" who represents how "mankind has worked and fought its way from savage isolation to organic social life."[27]

The narrative of the California Story typically emphasizes three interrelated components. I use the present tense here because the story's underlying assumptions have an impressive staying power, as I've discovered in my conversations with thousands of students.

First, that Native peoples are unrecognizable as members of the civilized human race. This depiction takes various forms: from the Agassiz tradition of polygenesis that promoted the idea of multiple human races, with "the Indian more like the slow, inactive, stout Orang";[28] to nostalgic exoticization that evokes ancestors entrenched and rooted in Nature, such as an observation by a popular writer in 1914 that "the bucks basked in the sun for eight months in the year."[29]

These views were mainstream, not at all exceptional. Racist and racialized caricatures and invectives routinely persisted into the late twentieth century, articulated by politicians, popular writers, and historians who made the troubled past palatable to several generations of teachers and schoolchildren. As I waded through a mound of textbooks, popular histories, and memoirs, I needed to take breaks to brood about the cumulative impact of this barrage of humiliations aimed at generations of Native families—such as the residents of Crescent City—and to recover my own equilibrium, just as I had done when researching the university's archive of death.

"Our American experience," said Governor Peter Burnett in his address to the legislature in 1851, "has demonstrated the fact that the two races cannot live in the same vicinity in peace." Moreover, he continued, California Indians are "from habit and prejudice, exceedingly averse to manual labor. . . . The inevitable destiny of the race is beyond the power or wisdom of man to exert."[30] To Theodore Hittell, an authority on California history writing more than forty years later, Native peoples in California were "all equally stupid and brutish,"[31] a view endorsed by the widely read *Land of Sunshine* magazine in 1894: "There are some forms of savage life we can admire. There are others that can only excite our disgust. Of the latter was the Californian Indian."[32] Before California was conquered, according to a popular historian, Indian tribes were "so stupid that they rarely learned one another's language, so lethargic that they rarely fought."[33]

"After sleeping and eating, the principal amusement of this primitive people was gambling," observed Henry Norton sixty years after Governor Burnett had identified sloth as a character flaw. "Everywhere the most prominent characteristic was laziness," concurred Norton.[34] Almost a century after Burnett's dire prediction about inevitable extinction, Robert Glass Cleland, who taught for many years at Occidental College before joining the Huntington Library where he significantly shaped California's historiography, endorsed what was now historical orthodoxy: "They were great thieves, wore little or no clothing, and loved music and dancing."[35]

To Rockwell Hunt, the former dean of the University of Southern California's graduate school, California Indians were an "inferior race," unworthy of inclusion in the state's historiography.[36]

Berkeley anthropologist Max Uhle's observation that many tribes represented "a low grade of civilization" resonated in popular accounts.[37] Not surprisingly, this kind of nonchalant racism permeated newspapers' reporting and students' field notes. In 1897, a Stanford professor titled her published essay "Some Primitive Californians"; a 1923 article in the *Los Angeles Examiner* announced, "Aborigine of State Had Few Clothes and Looked Like a Gorilla," illustrated with images of a gorilla and skulls; "Boning in History" was the headline for a local story about high school students digging up graves in Berkeley in 1931. "The early Indians," wrote a community college student after participating in an excavation in San Mateo, "were ugly looking. The almost black, dark mahogany complexion and heavy ugly features made them resemble the African Negro type more than the Indian type."[38]

California's anthropologists played a significant role in allowing a racist narrative to prevail. Of course, they knew about the catastrophes that accompanied the missions and Gold Rush, but they chose public silence and stayed within Kroeber's injunction to stick to the "purely aboriginal" and "uncontaminatedly native." It is rare to find in our textbooks, classrooms, and public places a reckoning with our nineteenth-century catastrophe: dispossession and massacres of Native communities; breakup of Native families, including a commercial trade in enslaved women and children; organized efforts to erase thousands of years of cultural experience; and systematic looting of Native graves and artifacts to benefit collectors, museums, and universities.

Beyond academia, writers were not constrained by disciplinary boundaries. "With race attitudes in America," wrote Carey McWilliams in 1944 in a chapter pointedly titled "The Non-Vanishing Indian," "one must begin at the beginning." The "Indian problem," he continued, "is central to the whole question." Along with "our treatment of the Negro," they are "the skeletons in the closet so far as American democracy is concerned." Berkeley academics paid no attention to McWilliams, and he paid no attention to them.[39]

An emphasis on the failure of Indigenous peoples, in the words of Hunt, to keep up with the "stern march of progress" permeates the California Story.[40] The alleged failure of the region's first inhabitants to thrive in the nineteenth century was explained not by conquest and terror, but by an inherent inability to create prosperity. "They were so ignorant and barbarous," observed Louise Heaven in 1867, that they could not "use or appreciate the blessings by which they were surrounded."[41] They were "as savage in A.D. 542 as they were a thousand years later," wrote John Hittell in 1878.[42] Their lack of civilization, noted a 1910 civics textbook issued by the California Board of Education, was evident in their incapacity to develop "the fixed and permanent character of their communities."[43] A book for young children published in 1941 instructed them that "the Indians did not learn to make better tools than the first Indians had made."[44] The teachers with whom I met in Crescent City in 2009 were supplied a textbook that similarly reduced colonial regimes to an educational self-help project: "In the 1500s, European countries wanted to learn about new places."[45]

In the 1930s, a popular textbook could relegate the ruin of California's Native peoples to a footnote.[46] By the mid-twentieth century, the argument about regressive Indians had become a fixture of potted histories. A booklet for "newcomers and tourists" explained that

> the Indians made no effort to develop the fertile interior valleys or rich coastal plains. . . . In fact, aside from dancing around a campfire, staging an occasional battle, and once in a while going fishing or hunting, the men did practically nothing. . . . In the matter of clothing, the early Indians were slightly less casual than the modern Nudists. . . . Religious sanctions encouraged the eating of a piece of flesh of any brave enemy killed in battle.[47]

As late as 1984, an elementary school textbook transformed the bloody horrors of the 1850s into a mild case of culture conflict: "The people who came to look for gold and to settle in California did not understand the Indians. They made fun of the way the Indians dressed and acted."[48]

Popular writers could confirm their prejudice about backward Indians by relying on Edward Gifford's prejudice that California's tribes had proved their inability to innovate change and were ahistorically frozen in time, "from the remote past down to the time of Caucasian settlement."[49]

The second standard component of the California Story is that Indigenous peoples are a *disappearing race*. The logic of late nineteenth- and early twentieth-century scientific racism was central to framing the near extermination of Native peoples in the imagery of natural rather than social history, subject to inevitable processes of erosion, decline, and biological weaknesses rather than the result of human intervention and genocide. Slaughter and contagious diseases were not something done to them, but something they did to themselves. This abdication of responsibility was widespread in colonizing regimes, such as Australia where Aboriginal peoples in nineteenth-century Australia were similarly portrayed as a "doomed race."[50]

Journalist John Hittell's observation in 1878 that a "physical weakness in the Indian blood" caused their supposed extinction became a maxim by the early twentieth century.[51] The Europeans no doubt hastened the demise of California's Indians, observed Phil Hanna in 1935, but they "would have perished just the same had the Spaniards not come to these shores [because] within them was the ineradicable germ of disintegration."[52]

Native peoples, with very few exceptions, are portrayed as passive and compliant, and therefore complicit in their own demise (comparable to 1940s and 1950s representations of Jews during the Holocaust as sheep submissively led to their slaughter), despite a long history of resistance, from guerilla warfare in the mid-nineteenth century, to young men and women in boarding schools at the turn of the century plotting what would become a pan-Indian movement, to political organizing against looting of graves and "land back" campaigns throughout the twentieth century and into the present.

Any popular writer looking for confirmation of assumptions about *disappearing Indians* had no trouble finding verification from experts. In 1906, Ales Hrdlička's research, published by University of California Press, reported that "numerous groups [of California Indians] are rapidly nearing extinction and of not a few . . . there are no longer any living representatives."[53] Zoologist Samuel Holmes blamed the victims: "Primitive peoples . . . never really incorporated into our social life. To the whites, they were simply in the way—and they disappeared."[54] Even Berkeley demographer Sherburne Cook, who had documented how California's tribes had been subjected "not to invasion but to inundation," speculated that "their possibly inferior physique" predisposed them to disease and premature death.[55]

"The Cahuilla Tribe will soon be gone," Berkeley anthropologist David Barrows lamented in 1900. "So perishes a tribe."[56] Some three decades later, a University of Southern California archaeologist reported that there were "no living Chumash Indians of pure strain in any part of Santa Barbara County."[57] Both would no doubt be greatly surprised to learn that the Agua Caliente Band of Cahuilla Indians is the largest landowner in today's Palm Springs, and that close to a quarter of a million Native Americans currently live in California, second only to Oklahoma.[58]

The third component of the California Story emphasizes that a minority of Indigenous people—those who do not disappear—are salvageable if they can be made to assimilate and surrender cultural and political sovereignty, first via the Spanish missionaries and then via American do-gooders in the wake of genocide.

This idea of culling Indigenous communities for potential converts has religious roots. George Berkeley (1685–1753), Berkeley's patron bishop, believed that the best way to rescue the "continent of America" from "ignorance and barbarism" was to recruit "by peaceable methods," or force if necessary, "such savages as are under ten years of age, before evil habits have taken a deep root, and yet not so early as to prevent retaining their mother tongue," so that they "might make the ablest and properest missionaries for spreading the gospel among their countrymen."[59]

Spain's visionaries put Bishop Berkeley's dream into practice by creating a system of missions that became, in Malcolm Margolin's words, "places of defeat and death"—colonial outposts and forced labor camps for some fifty-four thousand Native neophytes and perhaps as many as eighty thousand baptisms between the 1770s and 1830s. "Nowhere in the United States," concludes anthropologist Russell Thornton, "was there such a blatant, systematic destruction of American Indian peoples by Euro-Americans as in California."[60]

In the California Story's makeover version of this history, the missions are transformed into a "fairy tale, wonderful and unreal," an oasis of civilization in a "wilderness inhabited only by savage men and wild animals."[61] A 1915 textbook for children reported that "for a long time, our government has been trying to educate and civilize the Indians," and that "our government does all it can to make the Indians useful citizens."[62] A typically sunny version of California history, written in 1962, described Spain's mission policies as designed to keep the Indians "contented with food and with cloth for clothes or else they would go off to live as they pleased."[63]

Such a benign view of what were essentially carceral institutions was reinforced by Berkeley academics. Herbert Bolton affirmed in the *American Historical Review* that the missions "taught the Indians the Spanish language, and disciplined them in good manners, in the rudiments of European crafts, of agriculture, and even of self-government."[64] Samuel Holmes conceded that

> the white man has wrought frightful havoc among many primitive peoples [but there was an upside that was] decidedly beneficial. If he has introduced disease, he has, through hygiene and sanitation checked the spread of epidemics and greatly reduced the death rate among native peoples. . . . [W]ith the advent of industrial development, the improvement of political administration, the education of native children, and better hygiene and sanitation, the natives come to reap many advantages from the presence of the whites.[65]

When newly independent Mexico abandoned the missions in the 1830s, it was retrospectively blamed by California writers for the degeneracy of Native peoples: "Free from restraint, they soon sank to a low depth of barbarism and vice," observed a writer in *Land of Sunshine* in 1894.[66] It was a "sad" day, noted a 1922 textbook, when the survivors of the missions were prematurely propelled into freedom. "They still needed care as a child needs careful watchfulness and training."[67] Robert Cleland observed that "the depressing story began with the secularization of the missions."[68]

This defense of the mission as a civilizing institution echoes how the defeated Confederacy blamed Reconstruction for the premature liberation of African Americans from slavery. "The sudden enfranchisement [after the Civil War] of the negro without qualification was the greatest political crime ever perpetrated by any people, as is now admitted by all thoughtful men," argued Berkeley geologist Joseph LeConte in 1892. "Wherever the Negroes are in excess, [they] are rapidly falling back into savagery and even resuming many of their original pagan rites and superstitions." The LeConte brothers, Berkeley professor and president who had managed a Nitre and Munitions Bureau during the Civil War, remained Jim Crow enthusiasts long after the Civil War. "The Negro race is still in childhood," said Joseph in 1892. "It has not yet learned to walk alone in the paths of civilization."[69]

American boarding schools for Native children, the United States' modern version of the missions, similarly combined strategies of conversion with the coercive powers of the state.

In the late nineteenth century, the United States Indian Service promoted policies that separated Native children from their families in an attempt to break the bonds of tribal cultures and convert a new generation into a workforce on the lowest rung of capitalism. The residential reformatory combined the worst elements of a forced labor camp and orphanage, with harsh punishments for infractions such as "talking Indian" and going barefoot. At the Sherman Institute in California, the lesson plan included unpaid backbreaking labor harvesting melons and oranges for local farmers. "Our girls learned to sew and set Emily Post's table," recalls a Yurok-Karuk activist and poet, "while our boys were taught to weed and manicure lawns to prepare for great futures in menial labor." In 1928, a national survey of boarding schools reported "unmistakable evidence of malnutrition" and so-called teaching programs geared "for production and not for education." In some schools, noted the Meriam Report, "the child must maintain a pathetic degree of quietness."[70]

By the early 1900s, there were several boarding schools throughout the country, committed to stamping out Native languages, customs, clothing, and beliefs. It was not in any way a benign operation: marching out of time, walking on the grass, and "talking Indian" were harshly punished. Yet, it was not a very effective form of repression: it was here that young people from disparate tribes plotted their united resistance.[71]

Young Native people found all kinds of ways to subvert and disrupt the authorities. When roundups took place on reservations, they would hide or leave the area, often with the complicity of their families. Once in the schools, they had, in the words of a superintendent in 1886, a "pernicious habit of running away" and heading home. Mysterious fires were so commonplace that arson, as well as shabby construction, was suspected. Passive resistance in the form of work slow-downs, silence, and pranks drove some teachers away. In violation of regulations, students secretly spoke their birth languages and passed on stories and folktales. What teachers considered to be non-responsiveness actually disguised active efforts at cultural preservation, as revealed in a poem by Navajo students: "Maybe you think I believe you / That thing you say, / But always my thoughts stay with me / My own way."[72]

The campaign to forcibly erase Native cultures was implemented by white, female social workers and field matrons, who paradoxically discovered their own personal and professional fulfilment outside the stifling confines of the middle-class, patriarchal family by intervening without permission in the lives of Native women. In the guise of offering "help," they removed children from Native families and homelands; trained young Native girls to become servants of the urban gentry; and attempted to regulate the most intimate spaces of Native women—how they cared for and raised their children, the organization of their dwellings, their sexuality and marriage practices, and how they adorned their bodies and styled their hair.[73]

In the period between the World Wars and again in the 1960s to 1970s, subsequent generations of social workers, field matrons, and public health workers would be involved in the forcible sterilization of an estimated two hundred thousand poor women— disproportionately Indigenous, African American, Puerto Rican, and Mexican American.[74] Prior to the 1950s, California led the nation in the number of involuntary sterilizations, a practice that continued in state prisons until 2010. Sterilization without consent was not repealed in California until 1979 after it was revealed that 140 women, mostly of Mexican background, had been involuntarily sterilized at LA County/USC Medical Center.[75]

The sterilization campaign was carried out in the name of eugenics, a global movement in which Berkeley academics played active and influential roles, from endorsing the work of Nazi racial scientists to articulating biologically based theories of social inequality. The university's devastating practices and attitudes towards Indigenous peoples were embedded in a larger racial discourse.

NINE

Sorrow Songs

Through all the sorrow of the Sorrow Songs
there breathes a hope—a faith in the
ultimate justice of things. . . .

I sit with Shakespeare, and he winces not.
Across the color line I move arm and arm with
Balzac and Dumas. . . . So, wed with Truth,
I dwell above the veil. Is this the life you
grudge us, o knightly America?

—W. E. B. DU BOIS, 1903[1]

UNFIT HUMANITY

IN MARCH 1909, during a visit to San Diego, University President Benjamin Ide Wheeler met with publisher E. W. Scripps for an interview that covered several topics. "The conversation," recalled Scripps, "took a sudden dash into the subject of eugenics." Wheeler expressed his concern that "the population of the world is growing so fast that all the waste [i.e., uninhabited] places are being taken by unfit humanity." The absence of war and developments in medicine "are causing families to multiply so rapidly that it is only a question of time, when the race, or when its various governments will be absolutely compelled to take up the subject of eugenics and regulate the birth rate, particularly with a view to restrict the breeding of some people and encouraging the breeding of others."[2] Wheeler was one of the cofounders in 1903 of the Commonwealth Club of California, a fraternal civic club that endorsed eugenics policies and welcomed right-wing civic activists and academics who promoted "dreams of Aryan and Nordic supremacy that crested to popularity in the 1920s."[3]

About the same time that Wheeler was advocating state-regulated population control, Jacques Loeb, who taught at Berkeley from 1903 to 1910, was developing his critique of "eugenics—or rather a caricature of eugenics." A German-Jewish immigrant to the United States, whose career as a distinguished biologist later blossomed at the Rockefeller Institute for Medical Research, Loeb did not hesitate to express his contempt for what he called "racial biology." In a 1914 paper, he argued that mental ability and moral traits are not genetically transmitted, that genetics is not linked to intelligence, and that intermarriage does not lead to degeneracy. Unable to attend the NAACP's meeting in Baltimore, he sent a paper on "Heredity and Racial Inferiority" that was read at the conference and published in *Crisis*. "I do not need to assure you of my deep interest in the problem concerning heredity and the so-called racial inferiority," he wrote W. E. B. Du Bois, "and my best intentions to help your cause."

In a letter to a colleague in France in 1918, he singled out Benjamin Ide Wheeler for becoming an "agent" of the emperor by spreading German "race propaganda in America, of course in a quiet way." Loeb had no patience for the "false biological assumptions [of] war enthusiasts" who think that war is good for preserving the "virile virtues" of a nation, and that "superior races" have the right to "impress their civilization upon 'inferior races.'" Good thing he left Berkeley when he did—before the university turned itself into a military camp—because no doubt he would have been fired for his anti-war pacifism and active support of W. E. B. Du Bois's politics.[4] Two years after his departure, the university's matter-of-fact racism was on full display in a marching band, its musicians smartly outfitted for Labor Day in blackface.

Loeb's uncompromising critique of eugenics was rare in academia. As a science-based discourse and practice of governance forged in the nineteenth-century metropole, many intellectuals embraced eugenics to explain socially created inequalities as biologically and culturally fixed. Berkeley professor Susan Schweik's

Cal Band in Blackface, 1912

"Labor Day, February 29, 1912," photographer unknown, courtesy of the Bancroft Library, University of California, Berkeley (UARC PIC 04:107)

description of eugenics as a process—designed to sort out "people deemed fit or who fit in" from "people who are deemed unfit or who misfit"—captures its ambitious and flexible scope.[5] A line needs to be "drawn between the capables and the incapables," as Berkeley geologist Joseph LeConte asserted in his discussion of the "race problem" in the South in 1892.[6]

Eugenics, like race, is not a stable entity, but constantly in motion, depending on historical context, national variations, and the state of politics. In the nineteenth and twentieth centuries, eugenics was embraced by a wide political spectrum, by conservatives and liberals, by powerful nations worried about degeneracy and overpopulation, and by new nations committed to pronatalist policies. Today, in the United States, eugenic assumptions are apparent in policy debates about crime, welfare, citizenship, ableism, and reproductive technologies.[7]

A predominant American strand of eugenics is rooted in nationalism. Its enthusiasts legitimated conquest of tribes in the name of

Progress, rejected socialist explanations of inequality, and served the state with ideas about who makes the best citizens and workers— what constitutes fitness and capability; how to limit the reproduction of the unfit; and what to do with those determined to be unfit, abnormal, and unsalvageable.

The eugenics mainstream in the United States stressed that social success and failure can be traced to inherited attributes associated with "racial temperament," national origins, gender, sexuality, and ability/disability. For many eugenicists, compulsory sterilization, restrictions on immigration from what Donald Trump candidly referred to as *shithole countries*, and measurement of physical and cognitive ability are designed to cleanse the body politic of impurities that have accumulated due to the high birthrate of the "socially inadequate," the declining birthrate of white middle-class families, and the "evil of crossbreeding"—the kind of concern about "unfit humanity" raised by Berkeley's President Wheeler in 1909.[8]

You can hear strong echoes of this reactionary angst in the "Great Replacement Theory" that today is a foundational tenet of right-wing ideology.[9]

This tendency found a hospitable home in California during its formative decades when eugenics as science, policy, and discourse was truly interdisciplinary.[10] Nowhere was this more evident than at Berkeley, where from the late nineteenth century through the 1970s, many departments—anthropology, archaeology, anatomy, paleontology, zoology, political science, education, soil science, physiology, history, public health, and museum education—were curious about what could be learned about civilizational progress from the bodies of the Native dead, about racial hierarchies from the families of living Mexican immigrants, about innate pathologies from African Americans, and about intellectual ability from class background. In 1975, a fund of $2.4 million was bequeathed to the School of Public Health to establish "The Genealogical Eugenic Institute," which continued to make grants until exposed by faculty protests in 2018.[11]

Eugenics at Berkeley was not a fringe science. It was popular. And it was institutionally driven, beyond individual faculty members. The university itself was a bastion of uncritical race theory—from

1872, when Regent Edward Tomkins endowed a chair of oriental languages and literature in honor of Louis Agassiz, who emphasized "how deeply seated are the primary differences between the pure races,"[12] to the 1970s, when Arthur Jensen (1923–2012), an educational psychologist in Berkeley's Graduate School of Education, made a case that genetics are a determinative factor in intelligence.

In 1906, the fledgling University of California Press published a research report by the Smithsonian's Ales Hrdlička that documented physical and mental differences between Native and European Americans.[13] In the 1920s, the president's office funded, and the University of California Press published, an extensive *Bibliography of Eugenics*, compiled by zoologist Samuel J. Holmes. The press also published his book on race relations, in which the author commended the Ku Klux Klan for promoting the health and welfare of Negroes in the South, no irony intended.[14] Holmes represented the university at the Third International Congress of Eugenics, held in New York in 1932.[15]

Two members of the Berkeley faculty—Holmes and Herbert Evans—were charter members of the Human Betterment Foundation (HBF), the West Coast's leading eugenics organization from its founding in 1929 to its dissolution in 1942. The foundation's board included members of the intellectual elite throughout the state, including a Nobel Prize–winning physicist from Caltech, directors of the Huntington Library, and well-known academics. Members of the foundation led the campaign for the forced sterilization of some twenty thousand women in the state, and supported restrictions on immigration from Mexico, racial property covenants, and segregation in education.[16]

The HBF's publications on sterilization were translated and circulated in Nazi Germany, a source of great pride to the organization. A close colleague of Holmes and Evans at the Foundation was impressed by how quickly Hitler's regime had created the legal and medical bureaucracy to sterilize two hundred thousand women within three years. Germany, according to Charles M. Goethe (1875–1966), demonstrated a determination to "eliminate all low-powers to make room for high powers."[17] Three months before his death, Goethe sent money to the Northern League, a white supremacist organization in the Netherlands working to build "cooperation between all the Nordic peoples—the best, most intelligent and highest cultured Peoples of the world." The league's secretary thanked Goethe for his donation. "We would wish that we had some more men like you among our members."[18]

Herbert Evans (1882–1971) was appointed chair of the Department of Anatomy at Berkeley in 1915 and during his career made "a monumental contribution to the field of endocrinology."[19] Evans's official biographical record is scrubbed clean of his involvement in the Human Betterment Foundation, yet he remained for thirteen years on the governing board of an organization that enjoyed a relationship of mutual admiration with Nazi racial scientists, promoted the involuntary sterilization of thousands of "unfit" women, and supported nativist immigration policies. Holmes and Evans signed off on HBF's decisions until its dissolution in 1942, nine years after the Nazi government enacted the Law for the Prevention of Genetically Diseased Offspring (Sterilization Law) and seven years after the publication of the first American Edition of *Mein Kampf.*[20]

By contrast, Samuel Holmes was not at all reticent about his involvement in the Human Betterment Foundation or his admiration for Hitler's racial scientists. "There is a good deal of discussion in Germany over the curtailment of the increase of Poles, Jews, and other elements not in the good graces of the present régime," wrote Holmes in 1937, two years after the Nazis enacted the Nuremberg Laws, two years before Hitler authorized the murder of thousands of disabled children. "What the Germans may accomplish—and many of their best minds are giving serious thought to the problem—remains to be seen."[21]

Holmes put his best mind to work in the United States by lobbying for a quota on Mexican immigrants—"the least assimilable of foreign stocks"—and advocating financial incentives for white female students and faculty wives to procreate.[22] When it came to debates about nature versus nurture, Holmes sided with an unforgiving Nature. "As a result of numerous investigations in educational psychology, it is coming to be pretty clearly established that

environment has its very distinct limitations as a means of developing intellectual power. Or, in other words, if brains are not inherited," he wrote in 1933, "there is small chance of acquiring them."[23]

Holmes predicted that "American Negroes are coming into a
period of highly dysgenic propagation. . . . There will probably be
a continued infusion of white blood into the blacks which might
counteract their dysgenic breeding, but this infusion is growing less
in amount and probably poorer in quality."[24]

Both Holmes and Evans were outspoken in their prejudices
about Jews, which were mainstream in academia between the
world wars. Evans, recalled a colleague, was "an unabashed, vocal
anti-Semite. Once, sitting at the same table with him at lunch at
the Faculty Club, with others present, he suddenly said in a distinct
voice, anent nothing I had been aware of in the conversation, 'I have
never liked or trusted Jews.'"[25] Holmes published his antisemitic
bigotry, accusing "intellectuals of Jewish extraction [of] racial bias"
against "Nordics." Despite "their own claims to racial superiority,
the Jews evince a decided leaning toward egalitarianism." He was
particularly hostile to "Jewish anthropologists—and anthropology
has come to be largely a Jewish science"—because they "love to
pitch into the 'Nordic myth,' and a number of them seem to find
much satisfaction in the doctrine that the mental endowments of
the African Negroes are on the same level as those of the whites,
even the much-extolled Nordics. If this doctrine could only be
clearly established!"[26]

Some thirty-six years later, Berkeley psychologist Arthur Jensen
took up Holmes's argument about the relationship between genetics
and intelligence, albeit in a less flamboyant tone. "How much can we
boost IQ and scholastic achievement?" asked Jensen in his influential
1969 *Harvard Educational Review* article. Not much, if at all, he replied,
and certainly it was not worth the social investment trying to do so.

> It seems not unreasonable, in view of the fact that intelligence
> variation has a large genetic component, to hypothesize that
> genetic factors may play a part in this picture. But such a
> hypothesis is anathema to many social scientists. The idea that

the lower average intelligence and scholastic performance of Negroes could involve not only environmental, but also genetic factors has indeed been strongly denounced. But it has been neither contradicted nor discredited by evidence.[27]

Jensen's critique of the "social deprivation hypothesis" and federally funded "compensatory education programs" was incorporated into neoconservative attacks on the welfare state. His research boosted the popularity of Richard Herrnstein and Charles Murray's proposal in *The Bell Curve* that "it is time for America once again to try living with inequality, as life is lived."[28]

Holmes represented Berkeley's most outspoken proselytizer of the scientific value of eugenics, but many faculty members shared and circulated its assumptions, helping to turn a particular worldview into common sense.

The LeConte brothers, John and Joseph, never surrendered their belief in the inherent inferiority of African Americans, even after they assumed leadership roles at Berkeley. In his family biography, published posthumously in 1903, Joseph LeConte fondly recalled growing up on a plantation where preachers, supplemented by "mounted police," kept some two hundred slaves in line. "There never was a more orderly, nor apparently a happier working class than the negroes of Liberty County as I knew them in my boyhood." This happy order, recalled LeConte, was upended when Reconstruction unleashed "the intolerable insolence of the negroes set free with all their passions not only uncontrolled but often even encouraged. As I cannot speak of these matters with any calmness, I forbear to speak of them at all." Joseph had no trouble, though, speaking out rather passionately in favor of Herbert Spencer's social Darwinism and Louis Agassiz's idea that human evolution developed according to an "intelligent plan without" (that is, creationism) and "by substitution of one species for another," as nations inevitably advanced from "barbarism to civilization." To LeConte, racism was God-given and good science.[29]

There was a possibility, Joseph argued in 1892 in his capacity as president of the American Association for the Advancement of

Science, for civilizing "The Negro [who] has many fine and hopeful qualities." He is "plastic, docile, imitative, and therefore in a high degree improvable by contact with a superior race and under suitable conditions. It is doubtful if any other race could have so thrived and improved under slavery as the Negro has done." But the improvement of African Americans, Joseph continued, would only be possible under the careful supervision of "the white race. . . . Although the Negro by means of slavery has been raised above slavery, it would be a great mistake to suppose that he has yet reached the position of equality with the white race, that unassisted he can found a free civilized community." Moreover, "what is the best legal device for this purpose is just the problem to be worked out by the Southern people, and they will work it out if left alone."

Honoring the LeConte Brothers, 1898
"LeConte Plaque," December 19, 2022, photograph by Semantha Raquel Norris

As for the American Indian, concluded Joseph LeConte, there is little hope of successful "subordination." The "inevitable result is . . . extermination."

The LeContes were not the only ones who imported hereditarian ideology to Berkeley. Bernard Moses, who taught social sciences from 1875 to 1911 and created and chaired the department of history and political science, was a resolute eugenicist. In several books and articles, he warned that the "mingling [of] the blood of the white and colored races produces a mongrel people." Indigenous peoples, in his view, ranked the lowest in a hierarchy of civilizations. "Indians, like all savages, lacked the habit of consecutive work. . . . Neither the Indian nor the mestizo was capable of originating or carrying on great enterprises."[30]

Moses mentored anthropologist David Prescott Barrows, who completed his dissertation at the University of Chicago in 1897 on the ethnobotany of a "developing barbarism" before being appointed general superintendent of public education (1903–9) in the Philippines, where he became convinced that Filipinos had an "intrinsic inability for self-governance" and that "the white, or European race, is above all others the great historical race." Returning to California, his academic career at Berkeley flourished: professor of education, chair of political science, and president of the university (1919–23). He remained a public figure all his professional life, working his way up to major general in the National Guard. He led troops against the Maritime Strike of 1934, served as a consultant to the Department of War regarding the imprisonment of Japanese Americans during World War II, and became a staunch anti-communist.[31]

August Vollmer, Berkeley police chief (1905–32) and leading advocate of police professionalization—colloquially known as "the father of modern policing"—taught the university's first criminology classes as part of the political science curriculum after World War I. Vollmer, who had also participated in the military occupation of the Philippines, brought home not only expertise in counterinsurgency—what Aimé Césaire and later Michel Foucault referred to as the "boomerang effect"[32]—but also eugenic assumptions about "racial types" and "race degeneration" that he introduced into police training programs.[33] "A constitutionally defective individual will always be defective," wrote Vollmer in 1949. "As a general rule, brilliant and talented persons usually are descendants of people of superior qualities while the stupid and insane are descendants of dull or defective forbears."[34]

It was in anthropological theory and university-backed archaeological expeditions that eugenics found much more than individual supporters. It found a home. It was here that the university
significantly contributed to the science and discourse of eugenics.
President Wheeler demonstrated his appreciation for the department's anthropometric research by joining the department's executive committee in 1903.[35]

TO DESPISE NOT JUSTICE

In his theoretical work, Alfred Kroeber identified with Franz
Boas's cultural relativism and didn't jump on the eugenics band-
wagon that was so popular among his colleagues. He did not
associate, for example, with a leading faction of sociologists and
experts on race relations in early twentieth-century academia
that claimed African Americans were either inherently or culturally incapable of being assimilated into "Western Civilization."
Frederick Hoffman noted that "neither religion nor education"
had appreciably influenced "the moral progress of the race."
William H. Thomas denounced their "moral putridity." Joseph
Tillinghast argued that legacies of the West African family structure made African American parents incapable of "systematically
correcting and training" their children.[36] The sociologist Howard
Odum—whose *Social and Mental Traits of the American Negro*
Kroeber promoted in his anthropology syllabus—characterized
"the Negro [as] destitute of morals as any of the lower animals."[37]

During 1914–15, Kroeber gave talks at Berkeley—"What is the
Matter with Eugenics?"—that were reported with sensational
headlines in newspapers from Florida to Australia: "Eugenics
Condemned," "Eugenics a Snare," "Eugenics a Joke." In an unusually
blunt style, he dismissed eugenics as appealing only "to long-haired
men and short-haired women," arguing that "what is commonly
attributed to heredity has nothing to do with it. The men of the Ice
Age possessed the same mental capacities as the Anglo-Saxons of

today." Human progress is not inherited "from inside," he said, but "from outside," from the environment and "civilization."[38]

In a syllabus prepared in 1920 for teaching anthropology at Berkeley, Kroeber warned students that "the literature on eugenics or the artificial control of heredity and race is abundant, controversial, and propagandistic."[39] A few years later, he dismissed biologically based arguments about racial difference. "Racial inferiority and superiority are by no means self-evident truths," he wrote in his groundbreaking 1923 textbook. "It is a difficult task to establish any race as either superior or inferior to another, but relatively easy to prove that we entertain a strong prejudice in favor of our racial superiority." As for "claims sometimes made that eugenics is necessary to preserve civilization from dissolution, or to maintain the flourishing of this or that nationality, [they] rest on the fallacy of recognizing only organic causes as operative, when social as well as organic ones are active—when indeed the social factors may be much the more powerful ones."[40]

But Kroeber didn't close the door on eugenics. Perhaps some human traits, he hedged in 1923, are "the result of a blending of nature and nurture."[41] Whether out of a sense of political shrewdness or opportunism, Kroeber made sure that eugenics had a respectable place in the department and that his students studied "some of the best works" by leading eugenicists, such as Francis Galton, Karl Pearson, H. H. Goddard, R. L. Dugdale, and C. B. Davenport.[42]

Moreover, racialized attitudes and imagery permeated Kroeber's writings. "By temperament," he observed in a speech to the Commonwealth Club of California in 1909, "the California Indian is docile, peaceful, friendly, sluggish, unimaginative, not easily stirred, low-keyed in emotion, almost apathetic." He made a case to his audience that land, "not advice, not even education," was the best solution to Native poverty, but couldn't resist reinforcing the myth of docility. "When the priest came to transport him to the mission, he went; when the pioneer came to mine the ground on which stood his ancestral cabin, he retreated; unresistingly in one case as in the other."[43] In his textbook, while exploring "why a Louisiana negro is black and thick-lipped [and] sings at his corn-hoeing more frequently than the white man across the fence," Kroeber speculated that his "sloth and inclination to melody" resulted from both "social environment" and "inborn biological impulse. . . . There is room here for debate and evidence."[44]

In his public statements on eugenics, for the most part Kroeber played it safe. Unlike University President Benjamin Ide Wheeler, Kroeber did not advocate limiting the reproduction of the "unfit." Unlike geologist Joseph LeConte, social scientist Bernard Moses, anthropologist David Barrows, and zoologist Samuel Holmes, he did not publicly condemn African Americans who did not accept their subordinate place in the world, or denounce miscegenation as diluting the white race, or claim that Filipinos were incapable of self-governance, or join an organization that lauded the efforts of Nazi racial scientists. Nor, however, did he follow the courageous lead of biologist and former colleague Jacques Loeb who publicly expressed his contempt for eugenics as scientific racism.

Instead, Kroeber stayed within the guardrails of academic discourse, sticking to commonsense banalities about how "it is easier to talk of breeding improved human beings than to begin by improving oneself—training one's children. The future of the human race can be enhanced only through character building by individuals and courageous adherence to ideals by nations."[45] In his anthropology textbook he asked himself, "What may be the best attitude toward 'Jim Crow' cars and other forms of segregation?" and then ducked the answer.

> The belief in race inequalities is founded in emotion and action and then justified by reasoning. . . . It may be true, but it is not proved true. . . . Of course, the fact that a belief springs from emotion does not render that belief untrue, but does leave it scientifically unproved, and calling for investigation. . . . Scientific inquiries into race are for the present best kept apart from so-called actual race problems.[46]

Yet, some four hundred pages later, Kroeber concludes *Anthropology* by articulating a biocultural expression of eugenics. No longer is human ability and disability "inherently constituted" in biology; now it is "inherently constituted" in the "producers and dispensers of civilization." Kroeber came to the same conclusion as the one-dimensional eugenicists that he ridiculed: "On the whole, the greatest share of culture production has fallen to Caucasians. . . . [M]ost of the advances of the last twenty-five hundred years all fall to the account of the white race." Kroeber made no mention of the downside of colonialism and imperialism. There is not even a hint of the possible relationship between "culture production," slavery, and military conquest.

As for "Negroids," notes Kroeber, their "consistent failure to accept the whole or even the main substance of the fairly nearby Mediterranean civilization, or to work out any notable sub-centers of cultural productivity, would appear to be one of the strongest arguments that can be advanced for an inferiority of cultural potentiality on their part."[47] Kroeber's students would have learned that anthropological science confirmed deeply held, racist emotions.[48]

Thomas Waterman, described by his mentor as "brilliant" and "extraordinarily stimulating," was twenty-two years old in 1907 when he started working for Kroeber as a museum assistant. Kroeber steered him to Columbia University where he received his Ph.D. in anthropology under Boas in 1913. The next year, Kroeber hired him at Berkeley and trained him in research and theory. You can see Kroeber's imprint on his disciple in a paper published by Waterman a year after *Anthropology* was published, albeit with racism that was less varnished. "Nuances were not for him," as Kroeber observed in an obituary.[49]

Differences in human behavior, echoed Waterman, are the result of culture and training. In the 1920s, two "great groups"—Mongolians and Caucasians—were crowding "the platform" and "pushing out into the periphery," while "all Negro peoples are in process of being crowded into more and more restricted areas. Every presumption exists that they have been for long ages behaving in the same way." Waterman, like Kroeber, is silent on the impact of colonial violence and the slave trade on "the dark-skinned types [who] have in the long run allowed themselves to be pushed off the platform." Maybe the explanation for the Negroes' stagnant performance is that they were "notoriously poor sailors, and their ancestors must have been worse ones." Maybe "the Negro has been successful in propagating himself, as time has passed, only in areas further and further removed from the center." A clear indication of why Negroes are "a more primitive (i.e., less developed) type" is that they failed to learn the alphabet, but a generation after the distribution of tobacco, they were "smoking their heads off." Waterman deduced that "there is something distinctly the matter with a folk who in five thousand years do not acquire an alphabet, but who appropriate a bad habit overnight. They seem to resist advancement. They seem to me to be an older evolutionary form, and from their distribution and history, a vanishing one." In the "age-long struggle" for survival, the Negro is 'out of it' almost completely at the present time. He is an anachronism, like the kangaroo and the ornithorhyncus."

Waterman concludes his article with a one-line paragraph: "We ought to save out a few good Negro types before he becomes extinct."[50]

Kroeber and Waterman included W. E. B. Du Bois's *The Negro* in their anthropology syllabus, but it clearly did not impress them. A cursory reading of Du Bois's works available in the early twentieth century—*The Philadelphia Negro* (1899), *The Souls of Black Folk* (1903), or *The Negro* (1915)—would have given them very different ways of thinking about civilizational superiority and inferiority. It is worth quoting Du Bois at length in order to make clear that, just as the university made choices about what to learn or ignore from the past, so too Kroeber and his colleagues could have chosen a different conceptual framework and, with it, an antiracist morality.

"What is the Negro problem?" asked Du Bois. Unlike Kroeber, he didn't skirt its implications:

> We grant full citizenship in the World Commonwealth to the "Anglo-Saxon" (whatever that may mean), the Teuton and the Latin; and then with just a shade of reluctance we extend it to the Celt and Slav. We half deny it to the yellow races of Asia,

admit the brown Indians to the ante-room only on the strength of an undeniable past; but with the Negroes of Africa we come to a full stop, and in its heart the civilized world with one accord denies that these come within the pale of nineteenth-century Humanity. This feeling, widespread and deep-seated, is, in America, the vastness of the Negro problems.[51]

"I feel," proclaimed Waterman unscientifically, "that the Negro is inferior to us." No matter their best qualities, "they are going to disappear in time from off the face the earth, leaving it to the Mongolians and to us."[52] By contrast, Du Bois had "faith in the ultimate justice of things" and in the triumph of knowledge and struggle. "Your country? How came it yours?" he asked in *The Souls of Black Folk*:

> Actively we have woven ourselves with the very warp and woof of this nation—we fought their battles, shared their sorrow, mingled our blood with theirs, and generation after generation have pleaded with a headstrong, careless people to despise not Justice, Mercy, and Truth, lest the nation be smitten with a curse. . . . Would America have been America without her Negro people.[53]

Kroeber-the-anthropologist-academic was ready in 1923 to affirm the cultural inferiority of African peoples, while Du Bois-the-activist-sociologist said such a conclusion was premature because "archaeological research in Africa has just begun, and many sources of information in Arabian, Portuguese, and other tongues are not fully at our command; and, too, it must frankly be confessed, racial prejudice against darker peoples is still too strong in so-called civilized centers for judicial appraisement of the peoples of Africa. Much intensive monographic work in history and science is needed to clear mooted points and quiet the controversialist who mistakes present personal desire for scientific proof."[54]

Kroeber and Waterman were eager to consecrate the "failure of the Negro race," while to Du Bois it was the beginning of a golden age:

Already in poetry, literature, music, and painting the work of Americans of Negro descent has gained notable recognition. Instead of being led and defended by others, as in the past, American Negroes are gaining their own leaders, their own voices, their own ideals. Self-realization is thus coming slowly but surely to another of the world's great races, and they are today girding themselves to fight in the van of progress, not simply for their own rights as men, but for the ideals of the greater world in which they live: the emancipation of women, universal peace, democratic government, the socialization of wealth, and human brotherhood.[55]

Kroeber could have engaged Du Bois in a dialogue about why the "color line" and not the "Negro Problem" was the global crisis of the twentieth century. He could have crossed the racial divide "all graciously with no scorn or condescension" to join Du Bois's conversation with Shakespeare, who "winces not."[56] Instead, he kept his public silence on the horrors of racism and the humanity and tenacity of African Americans and Indigenous peoples.

▼

TEN

Making History

If not here before, not here now.

—ROBERT SPOTT, YUROK SAYING

*I'm a big believer in narrative, and how import-
ant narratives are. I think Berkeley needs to be
spending a lot of time thinking about its story.*

—UC BERKELEY CHANCELLOR CAROL CHRIST, 2019[1]

A SUITABLE PAST

IN ADDITION TO a hoarding problem, Berkeley also has a
self-imposed, long-term memory problem. Its landmark culture
exemplifies wishful remembrance, systematic amnesia, and quarter-
truths. Its official historical narrative is a model of active forgetting
and selective recollection.

If you put on your cultural blinders, it's a delight to walk through
the Berkeley campus. Its manicured lawns, pruned and shaped
trees, spaciousness, and extraordinary views of the San Francisco
Bay measure up to the landscapes of Princeton and Cornell and
exude, in the words of a faculty member in the 1930s, "an air of the
private."[2]

It's a delight until you know what the university's built environment represents and omits. Then, in the same way that conceptual
artist Fred Wilson experienced the "raw material" of American
museums, you might feel "a kind of tension" in your body between
attraction and revulsion. "It was a physical experience," recalled
Wilson.[3] It is for me too.

In the 1860s and 1870s, California's emerging ruling class pitched in a few million dollars—which served as the precedent for Berkeley's institutionalized public-private partnership—in the hope that Berkeley would become what boosters dubbed the "New Athens of the Far West."

During a visit to Greece in 1896, Benjamin Ide Wheeler imagined that one of its ancient buildings would look impressive in Berkeley. As president of the university three years later, he raised funds from the Hearst family and hired architect John Galen Howard to design what the *San Francisco Chronicle* heralded as "a great walled amphitheater such as scarcely existed in the world since the memory days of Greece." The William Randolph Hearst Greek Theatre premiered in 1903 with Aristophanes's *The Birds*, performed in Greek.[4]

The architectural design of the Greek Theatre, as urban historian LaDale Winling has pointed out, symbolized the "democratic promise of higher education" with its invitation to community participation and civic duty.[5] "It's an embodiment of the California ideal that life and culture can be enjoyed outdoors and democratically," said local historian Steve Finacom on the occasion of the theatre's one hundredth anniversary.[6] It was here in December 1964, during a convocation about the Free Speech Movement, that as a recently arrived graduate student I watched campus police drag activist leader Mario Savio off the stage when he tried to speak about why the university should protect free speech.

Berkeley's earliest buildings are examples of "recollective architecture"—a repository of history, meaning, and longing.[7] Before you get to the campus, you can see—even from San Francisco on a clear day—the university's "trusty landmark," the Campanile. It is "a symbol of the university's lofty vision and enduring contribution to California and the world," said President Wheeler at the tower's cornerstone-laying ceremony on March 18, 1914.[8] Like many of the university's original buildings, its Beaux-Arts design evokes European provenance. If you've visited Italy, you might recognize a resemblance to the Campanile di San Marco in Venice.

Another prominent building on campus, the Doe Memorial

The Berkeley Brand
"A View from the Berkeley Hills," photograph by Steve McConnell, courtesy of University of California, Berkeley

Library (1911), with its statue of Athena, Greek goddess of wisdom, at the library's entrance, suggests a "neo-classical temple of higher learning."[9] The oldest surviving building on campus, South Hall (1873), with its ornate ironwork, mansard roof, and gargoyles, reflects the influence of Napoleon III's Second Empire style (1852–71). One of the university's most splendid edifices, the Hearst Memorial Mining Building (1907), combines the Beaux-Arts tradition with Spanish mission architecture. The impressive entrance hall was modelled on France's Bibliothèque nationale.

John Galen Howard looked to another classical source—Rome's Colosseum—as inspiration for a mammoth football stadium that, nestled in the hills overlooking the city, impressed Robert Nisbet as "remarkably graceful for something that seated seventy thousand people" in the 1920s.[10]

The campus's "historic esplanade"—variously identified in university press releases as "a sacred landscape space" and "campus shrine"— is named after a French term for the area in front of a fortification.[11]

If you enter the campus through its main entrance on the west side and look behind Arnaldo Pomodoro's bronze of a fractured globe, you will find what appears to be an ancient plaque, mottled by age. In fact, it's less than fifty years old. The Don Pedro Fages Expedition Historical Marker commemorates the place where an expedition "under the auspices of the Empire of Spain" camped on Strawberry Creek in 1772.[12]

The Faculty Club, constructed in the heart of the campus in 1901, is one of the university's showplaces—an "architectural gem of Craftsman design" that reflects "a special northern California aesthetic."[13] Its design signals a link to late nineteenth-century, quintessentially English artistry that suggests the masculine clubbiness of a British university. To underline the point, women were refused membership and founded their own club in 1920.

On the east-side boundary of the campus is Founders' Rock where, as the story goes, a group of trustees from the College of California met in April 1860 to survey land that would become a "Seat of Learning" known as the University of California. "There is not another college site in America, if indeed anywhere in the world," editorialized the *Pacific*. "It is the spot above all others we have yet seen or heard of where a man may look in the face of the nineteenth century and realize the glories that are coming on."[14] The rock was inscribed and dedicated by the graduating class of 1896. It was here too that trustee Frederick Billings, inspired by a poem written by Bishop George Berkeley, an eighteenth-century Irish philosopher, proposed calling the new town *Berkeley* where "There shall be sung another golden age, / The rise of empire and of arts."[15]

These important material and symbolic landmarks of Berkeley's origins story are rooted in an idealized European past of Italy, Greece, Spain, England, France, and Ireland, while its actual Mexican history and much longer Native histories are reduced to spectral traces. The physical environment, as architectural historian Dolores Hayden has observed, contains "potent memories in its streets and sidewalks" that tell stories of the past. "We might even say that memory is naturally place-oriented or at least place-supported."[16]

There are no memorials to the Ohlone who lived for thousands of years on and around Strawberry Creek long before Don Pedro Fages hoisted Spain's flag. Or that mark how the University of California came to life in an era of rampant death. In an otherwise exhaustive architectural survey of the campus, a university planner trivializes longtime Ohlone homelands as "camping grounds."[17]

Berkeley's aspiration to a global reputation required more than impressive buildings, distinguished faculty, and professional landscaping. As one of the "world's top universities" and a "leading public university," it also had to craft a narrative about itself that imagines a heroic, shared, and cohesive identity,[18] as suggested by the following synthesis promoted on the university's website: "From a group of academic pioneers in 1868 to the Free Speech Movement in 1964, Berkeley is a place where the brightest minds from across the globe come together to explore, ask questions and improve the world."[19] The university's "milestones and discoveries" go from "earthquake science" in 1887 to "treating global malaria" in 2013.[20] Note the appropriation of the Free Speech Movement that the university did its best to suppress.

These themes—the university as an agent of civilization bringing rationality and modernity to the wilderness, and the university as social reformer—are central to Berkeley's brand as reflected in its slogans, choice of architecture, and memorials to "a suitable historical past."[21] The biblically inspired catchphrase *fiat lux*—a regional expression of manifest destiny—has endured for over a century, from its inscription on an arch that greets students at Sather Gate, to its use as a sign-off in the chancellor's messaging today. Like the God of *Genesis*, the university imagined itself bringing coherence to an "earth without form, a void."

PLANNED OBLIVIOUSNESS

Berkeley's plaques and other signifiers of the memorial landscape represent a who's who of money and power: military men, forward-looking financial and commercial capitalists, local and global politicians, respectably published eugenicists, and architects of regional imperialism.

"Deep rooted in the eternal hills, this memorial to the honored dead, here devoted to the service of the living," said Robert Gordon Sproul, the university's future president, at the dedication of the football stadium in 1923, "raises its noble crown into the clear California sky and stands in simple dignity, beauty and strength." At the ceremony for Memorial Stadium, named in honor of those who died during World War I, Sproul made no mention of the honored Ohlone dead, some of whose remains were dug up during the building's construction.[22]

A wall text in South Hall informs us that the building once housed the University Herbarium in the 1890s, but there is no mention of the Museum of Ethnology, opened in 1873, that displayed skeletons and skulls. A 2014 university press release draws attention to a granite drinking fountain erected in 1905 near the Campanile in a prime location to honor John Mitchell, a Congressional Medal of Honor recipient, but does not include information about why he received the award: "Gallantry in engagement with Indians" during the Red River War, 1874–85.[23]

Similarly, a text accompanying a portrait in the Doe Library of Bishop George Berkeley (1685–1753), after whom the city and university are named, describes him as a "renowned scholar and social thinker," but skips over the fact that his social thinking included endorsement of slavery and forcing Indigenous children to convert to Christianity.[24]

The university's indebtedness to Native histories is mostly erased or degraded in its visual culture. A tribute to the "visionary" Phoebe Apperson Hearst in the Bancroft Library emphasizes her feminism at the expense of her maternalistic racism. A wall text lauds her "philanthropic and academic spirit that forged Berkeley into the leading research university that it is today," but omits from "the excavated objects brought to Berkeley as a result of Mrs. Hearst's patronage" the hundreds of Indigenous human remains that were plundered from graves in several countries by expeditions that she funded.[25] The Phoebe A. Hearst Museum of

Anthropology's website includes information about its research on Bay Area shellmounds, "where people gathered for ceremonies and feasts, [and] where they buried their dead," but says nothing about how Berkeley archaeologists routinely dug up the dead from the mounds. The website includes a photograph of amateur archaeologist Philip Mills Jones "standing on an ancient mound" in 1901, but none of the crude selfies he produced that displayed his haul of skulls.[26]

These omissions happen so regularly that they constitute planned obliviousness rather than carelessness.

It takes a persistent search to find the occasional visual reminder of the Indigenous presence on the Berkeley campus, other than in the anthropology museum. The courtyard in Dwinelle Hall is named, without visible explanation, Ishi Court, after the Yahi survivor of massacres, bounty hunts, and starvation, whom the university housed and displayed in San Francisco in the tradition of human zoos from 1911 to 1916. We are not told anything about Ishi's identity nor about how the university reflects on its own responsibility for displaying him as "the most uncivilized man in the world" and, after his death, sending his brain to the Smithsonian.[27] Is the courtyard an honor or an apology or a somber reminder? A gesture of remembrance for what?

A painting of a generic Native woman hangs in the corner of a dining room in the Faculty Club. The painting is one of four in the room, done by well-known artist and faculty member Perham Nahl around 1917. The theme is food preparation prior to and after the founding of the university. According to in-house histories of the Faculty Club, it "represents an Indian squaw grinding corn in a stone mortar." The portrait evokes an "aboriginal Indian [who] probably" lived on the "the banks of Strawberry Creek," which used to flow copiously from the Berkeley hills to the bay, and "have for centuries been the gathering-place and eating-place of local inhabitants."[28] The painting and texts abstract the Indigenous woman from history, making her anonymous and tribeless, a relic of a *disappearing race*, while the artist communicates romanticized backwardness by depicting her semi-naked.

The recently opened mak-'amham / Café Ohlone, created by two Ohlone entrepreneurs in the courtyard of the Phoebe A. Hearst Museum of Anthropology, features Indigenous foods served with cultural information and brings life to an institution so associated with death and misery.[29] Overall, though, the campus landscape has failed to remind us that the Ohlone are a living, political, and cultural presence in the region.

Berkeley's official timeline of milestones includes "linguistic survey of native languages (1952)," but omits the predatory plundering of thousands of Native grave sites that the university and Department of Anthropology enthusiastically authorized.[30]

Celebrating the Federal Land Grab, 1909
"Bust of President Abraham Lincoln," December 19, 2022, photograph by Semantha Raquel Norris

President Lincoln's role in financing Berkeley as a land grant college through the Morrill Act is honored in a sculpture by the Campanile, while the Indigenous peoples whose stolen lands made the university's founding possible are symbolically vanished. The university purchased the bust of Lincoln in 1909, not in solidarity with the Emancipation Proclamation, but as a "reminder of Lincoln's role" in signing the Morrill Act that dispossessed tribes of their home-lands.[31] The original amnesia was compounded at an anniversary ceremony in 2012, when University President Mark Yudof praised the legislation as "a game-changer in social mobility and economic prosperity."[32] Moreover, it apparently didn't matter that John Gutzon de la Mothe Borglum, the sculptor who created the Lincoln bust, had close ties with the Ku Klux Klan and Confederate organizations.[33] Berkeley continues to enshrine the Morrill land grab as an example of the democratization of higher education. As a recent report under-states, "Native Californians are notably absent from the narrative."[34]

The Botanical Garden, with its impressive collection of native plants, begins its timeline in 1890, ignoring the Native communities who lived on its land for many previous generations and whose "sophisticated and complex harvesting and management practices . . . achieved an intimacy with nature unmatched by the modern-day wilderness guide, trained field botanist, or applied ecologist."[35]

Given how the university is rooted in land appropriated from tribes, these particular failures of memory are the most egregious, but they are not the only ones.

The south-side entrance to the university leads to the most visited site on the Berkeley campus, Sproul Plaza, where countless generations of activists have assembled in protest, listened to politi-cal speeches, and staffed information tables. The plaza is associated with the Free Speech Movement. It was here that Mario Savio urged us to grind the university machine to a halt by putting our "bodies upon the gears and upon the wheels, upon the levers, upon all the apparatus."[36]

The university may now claim the Free Speech Movement as its own, but let's not forget that administrators collaborated with J. Edgar Hoover's FBI and the CIA's John McCone, after whom a building is still named, to try to derail the FSM. Despite a prohi-bition against involvement in domestic intelligence, as enacted by the National Security Act (1947), CIA Director McCone passed confidential FBI reports about the movement's leadership to Edwin Pauley, one of the most right-wing members of the Board of Regents.

In January 1965, McCone requested a meeting with Hoover to discuss his concern about "communist influence" at Berkeley and the need for "some corrective action."[37] After resigning from the CIA, McCone was appointed by Governor Pat Brown to investigate the 1965 Watts riots, in which hundreds of African Americans were killed. "Maintenance of law and order is a prerequisite to the enjoyment of freedom in our society," concluded McCone.

The university's McCone Hall on the Berkeley campus houses departments of earth sciences, including geography.[38]

In 1989, on the occasion of the twenty-fifth anniversary of the FSM, the university reluctantly installed a memorial in the center of Sproul Plaza: a six-inch-deep circle of soil framed by a granite circle on which is inscribed: "This soil and the air space above it shall not be a part of any nation and shall not be subject to any entity's jurisdiction." Most people walk over this memorial without seeing it. Those who do stop to look might be puzzled because they will not find a rationale, historical context, or provenance. The university apparently agreed to its installation only if there was no mention of the Free Speech Movement.[39] Thus, it fails the most basic requirement of a memorial: reminder of an historical event. It would take until 2000 before the university approved an appropriate commemoration—the Free Speech Movement Café in Moffitt Library where you can eat, drink, and learn about the struggle—after philanthropist and FSM sympathizer Steve Silberstein made it a condition of a large donation.[40]

Berkeley eventually acknowledged Mario Savio's leadership in the FSM by naming the Sproul Steps after him and installing a bronze plaque on the steps in his honor in 1997.[41] But there is no information about Savio on the plaque, despite Savio's many memorable comments on the topic. Instead, there is a quote from a Greek philosopher about the importance of free speech. The university expelled Savio for his role in the FSM.

Meanwhile, a few yards from the Free Speech Movement's cryptic inscription in Sproul Plaza is one of the university's best-known memorials: Ludwig's Fountain. Here a visible, explanatory plaque, authorized by "Act of the Board of Regents" and dedicated in 1988, honors "Ludwig Von Schwarenburg Campus Canine."

A dog gets the respectful treatment that a movement for freedom of political speech is denied.

AMNESIA

Throughout the twentieth century, the university built solemn memorials to students, alumni, faculty, and staff who died and served in wars, from the 1870s "Indian Wars" to 9/11.

A recent survey of close to half a million public monuments throughout the United States found that the commemorative landscape is dominated by war and conquest; and that the tragedies of war, the victims of conquest, anti-war activism, and social justice leaders are rarely commemorated.[42] In this respect, Berkeley follows the norm.

The Civil War is unevenly remembered on campus. In 1933, the Daughters of Union Veterans of the Civil War planted a tree, marked by a small plaque, in memory of the Grand Army of the Republic vets who fought against the Confederacy. By contrast, the university elevated the reputation of the LeConte brothers, former owners of enslaved Africans and arms manufacturers for the Confederacy.

The John Mitchell fountain, erected on the Esplanade in 1905 with funds provided by university cadets, glorifies the campus armorer for his role in military campaigns against tribes in South Dakota and Texas. The armory was housed in North Hall, supervised by the gallant John Mitchell who "thrilled students with tales of Indian battles."[43] There are no comparable monuments on campus to California tribes who were victims of mass slaughter and displacement, or to those who resisted and survived genocide.

From the early twentieth century through the war in Vietnam, the university chose not to emphasize its long tradition of anti-war activism. Berkeley replicates a national trend in which "violence is the most dominant subject of commemoration," while the personal, social, and environmental costs of warfare are ignored; and the victims of domestic massacres are rarely acknowledged.[44] In the case of the University of California, not at all.

In the 1950s, the University of California allowed the Manhattan Project in New Mexico to establish a museum in its name without any curatorial oversight and without any content that might challenge official accounts of the decision to use atomic bombs against civilian populations. Meanwhile, the Berkeley campus avoids the topic altogether in its commemorative landscape. The university's involvement is the subject of books, plays, and memoirs, even an opera, but not of public debates within the university. A former Berkeley chancellor, elevated to secretary of the Smithsonian, got cold feet when he had an opportunity to disrupt the official mantra that killing Japanese civilians saved American lives.

There are glimmers of peace and social justice movements on campus.

In 1969, the celebrated artist Alexander Calder gave as a gift to the University Art Museum a full-size stabile of painted steel. Originally titled "Hawk" by Calder to suggest its bird-like image, the museum staff worried that it might be associated with pro-war sentiment and changed its title to "The Hawk for Peace." This was quite consistent with the artist's politics. He had publicly opposed the Cold War, signed anti-war petitions, and supported the McGovern campaign for the presidency.[45] When the Berkeley Art Museum and Pacific Film Archive (BAMPFA) moved to a new location, the anti-war sculpture was disappeared into storage for several years.[46] In 2022, BAMPFA returned it to its rightful public space on campus.

Four disturbing paintings of the US military torturing Iraqi prisoners at Abu Ghraib, donated to the university by artist Fernando Botero, can be seen by those who navigate to an out-of-the-way corridor in the law school's maze-of-a-building. The paintings are on loan from BAMPFA where the other twenty-eight images are stored, not displayed.[47]

When the university acknowledges social justice issues in its landscape, it does so reluctantly and often in response to an initiative by students and activists.

The name of the student union was changed to honor Martin Luther King Jr. at the urging of Ethnic Studies students in 1985. Students also led the campaign to commemorate Cesar Chavez at the Student Center; and friends of the Free Speech Movement successfully lobbied for the oddly unnamed tribute on Sproul Plaza in 1991. The AIDS Memorial Courtyard in the Doe Library that doubles as a "Quiet Study" area is a halfhearted gesture: there are no names to remember, no personal stories, and no information about the federal government's homophobic negligence in treating the disease.

For the most part, amnesia reigns.

EPILOGUE

Reckoning

*If no dialogue arises, then to me
the work is not so successful.*

—FRED WILSON, 1994[1]

DISCONNECTIONS

THERE ARE SIGNS of the university's ambivalence about its commemorative landmarks. Lincoln's bust that celebrates the grab of Native lands shows signs of neglect. Graffiti announcing that *ALL COPS ARE BASTARDS* remained for months until it faded on a bench erected by Naval ROTC to honor classmates killed during World War II. Following student complaints about the name of Berkeley's most prestigious library, a bust of Hubert Bancroft was removed from the foyer to a shelf in the reference center, partly obscured by a life-size photograph of an African American athlete on the Berkeley track team in 1976.[2]

In 2017, in the wake of global and local movements to dismantle public symbols of the colonial past, Berkeley's chancellor commissioned a Building Name Review Committee (composed of faculty, staff, students, alumni, and administrators) to make recommendations about unnaming buildings that violate the university's "Principles of Community."[3] The committee generated engaged discussions within departments, the first time such conversations had taken place at the university. As of spring 2023, the University of California had unnamed five buildings on the Berkeley campus: the law school's Boalt Hall, named after John Boalt, nineteenth-century advocate of Chinese exclusion; the physics department's LeConte Hall, named after the virulently racist LeConte brothers; social sciences' Barrows Hall, named after David Prescott Barrows, who thought that Filipinos could not govern themselves; anthropology's Kroeber Hall, named after Alfred Kroeber, who oversighted the plunder of Native graves; and governmental studies' Moses Hall, named after Bernard Moses, who embedded colonial ideology into the university's first social science curriculum.

Reckoning with the Past

"LeConte sign removal (November 2020)," photograph by Irene Yi, courtesy of University of California, Berkeley

In January 2022, members of Berkeley's student government and Black Student Union pointed out that a plaque honoring the LeConte brothers, located by a well-traveled path on campus, had not been removed.[4] "The university's dedication to anti-racism is only performative," noted student Senator Gabbi Sharp. As if to underline her critique, the university's public relations flak-catcher responded that the Building Name Review Committee's mission unfortunately only covered buildings, not plaques.[5]

The fiasco of the LeConte plaque is not an isolated example of the university's halfhearted gestures. It continues a long-standing practice: a plaque to Mario Savio that tells us nothing about Mario Savio; an AIDS Memorial Courtyard that does not explain how the federal government's deliberate negligence contributed to untold deaths; an exhibition on Japanese American students at Berkeley during World War II that studiously avoids Hiroshima and Nagasaki.

So many teaching moments evaded.

Kroeber's name is gone from the anthropology building, but Edward Gifford—his right-hand man in eugenics research—is still honored inside the building. The anti-Chinese John Boalt is banished, while the consistently racist George Hearst is ubiquitous.

In November 2020, University of California President Michael Drake authorized removal of Barrows's name from Barrows Hall. "The historical record provides ample evidence of intolerable racist beliefs and biases that are profoundly contrary to what we know, believe and stand for," said Chancellor Carol Christ.[6] Less than a year later, in celebration of Filipino Heritage Month, Berkeley's Doe Library exhibited copies of Barrows's *History of The Philippines* and a typed manuscript of his memoirs as evidence of the university's exemplary faculty. Students organized a spirited demonstration in protest of the university's hypocrisy.

Protesting Amnesia
Photograph by Tony Platt, October 28, 2021

The university's slothful pace of unnaming (five buildings in almost six years) is one indication of its unserious response to Berkeley's record of honoring the dishonorable. The Building Name Review Committee is only authorized to react to petitions, with the burden on students, faculty, and staff to make a case for unnaming. The committee is not empowered to be proactive, or to investigate the interrelationships of various "bad actors," or to consider who should be symbolically memorialized.

Thus, so far, *Hearst* is off limits.

UPHILL STRUGGLE

Achieving structural changes in academia is an uphill struggle. Berkeley has a long tradition of student activism matched by the university's long tradition of trying to repress, regulate, and co-opt activism.

"Sometimes," recalled former Berkeley Chancellor Albert Bowker (1971–80) in a candid moment, "you have to crack a few heads."[7] Actually, quite a lot of heads.

The university's brand as "one of the world's great public universities" committed to social justice prevails, despite its foundational and ongoing reliance for a large part of its budget on private funding, and its proven hostility to progressive activism. It takes persistent grassroots activism and social movements to make the university live up to its reputation, often at great human cost.

In particular, whenever land is at issue—from the Morrill Act's land grab and occupation of Ohlone homelands, to the seizure via eminent domain of Pueblo lands in New Mexico and Berkeley's People's Park—the university exercises its power like an avaricious landlord, eager to expand its holdings and quick to call out the police in defense of property rights or to deal with troublesome tenants.

The cops hauling Mario Savio off the stage of the Greek Theatre in 1964 during a debate on free speech was not a one-off. Benjamin Ide Wheeler's vision at the end of the nineteenth century of the Greek Theatre as a democratic space was accurate in one respect:

both classical Athens and contemporary Berkeley have excluded the majority of its residents from power—women and the enslaved in the former, and students and staff in the latter.

When students took over Sproul Hall in an act of nonviolent civil disobedience to support the Free Speech Movement, the university mobilized hundreds of police (including 150 California Highway Patrol officers), who carried out some 800 arrests. "They are learning," lectured President Clark Kerr, "that the community is no more sympathetic with anarchy than the university they so violently condemn. When patience and tolerance and reasonableness and decency have been tried, yet democratic processes continue to be forsaken by the FSM in favor of anarchy, the process of law enforcement takes over."[8]

The university made clear that demands by students for self-determination or to expand the boundaries of democracy would be met with bureaucratic finesse and, if need be, by force.

It took until the 1960s and some eighty years of organized protests and grumblings to get the university to abandon obligatory military service and end the censorship of political speech. It took another decade before the university's overwhelmingly white and male faculty and administration conceded to student demands to begin to diversify itself and the curriculum. In 1976, in the aftermath of the Civil Rights Movement, there were only twenty-six African Americans hired as full-time faculty at Berkeley; and it was not until two years later that the first African American woman, Barbara Christian, received tenure.[9]

In 1969, the Board of Regents mobilized the National Guard, Alameda County Sheriff's Department, and Highway Patrol to unsuccessfully stop community and student activists from transforming unused land, owned by the university, into a "people's park." In disorderly encounters—what sociologists dubbed a *police riot*—more than four hundred arrests were made, an onlooker (James Rector) was killed, another blinded (Alan Blanchard), and many were injured on the streets or while incarcerated. A municipal judge dismissed all charges. A few months later, a federal grand jury indicted twelve sheriff's deputies for abusing their authority—from firing at unarmed demonstrators to beating prisoners in custody.[10] "In war you are allowed to retaliate," said Sheriff Frank Madigan in defense of his deputies. Juries agreed, acquitting all the defendants.[11]

Again in 2022, campus authorities ordered the police to clear squatters and protesters from now fifty-year-old People's Park, an established public space that the university wants to convert into housing for its students.[12]

In the 1970s, despite massive demonstrations and an extensive lobbying campaign, the university closed down its School of Criminology on the grounds that a small group of faculty, including myself, and many students actively supported campaigns to civilize the police and significantly reduce the carceral state.[13] The school's pluralistic faculty, from radicals and liberals to hardline conservatives, created a lively, contentious exchange of ideas that academia is supposed to nourish.[14] Berkeley Chancellor Bowker was particularly agitated that our activism disturbed the university's cozy relationship with local police, contributing to their "decline in morale and reduction in size."[15]

In 1985, students organized a sit-in in Berkeley's Sproul Hall, demanding that the University of California divest billions of dollars invested in South Africa's apartheid regime. The campaign lit a spark, with hundreds of students sleeping overnight on the steps, and thousands participating in rallies during the day. The university responded by sending in riot police to arrest 158 students and clear the building, and eventually to establish a committee to study the issue. In response to the university's delaying tactics, students built a small shanty town outside the chancellor's office, chanting "Apartheid kills while UC counts its dollar bills." When the university ordered the police to tear down the structures and make arrests, dozens of activists were injured. As the movement gained political allies, including the governor and faculty, the regents relented and withdrew $3.1 billion from South Africa, the largest divestiture of any university in the country. On a visit to the Bay Area a few years later, Nelson Mandela thanked "our comrades in the struggle" for their contribution to dismantling apartheid. "Remember that we respect you. We admire you. And above all, we love you all."[16]

STUBBORN RESISTANCE

Native resistance to the accumulation of ancestral remains and cultural patrimony is testimony to the kind of determination, organizing, and stamina that is required to break through the university's stonewalling of repatriation claims. A turning point occurred in April 2017, twenty-seven years after passage of the Native American Graves Protection and Repatriation Act (NAGPRA), when more than seventy representatives of fifty tribes participated in the California Indian Tribal Forum at Berkeley to speak bitterness about the university's history of heartless inactions and malign neglect. University representatives listened to a litany of complaints: "delays and excuses," "stubborn resistance to respecting and implementing NAGPRA," and failure to "establish positive collaborative relationships with Native Americans that acknowledge and remedy the devastation wrought by early Berkeley anthropologists and researchers through the unethical collection of archival material and human remains."[17]

The forum sparked a series of actions and political pressures on the university. "Our history as a university is deeply flawed and overly technical and dehumanizing," commented University of California Regent John Perez in September 2018, as Governor Jerry Brown signed legislation that recognizes "repatriation of human remains as a fundamental human right for all California Native American tribes."[18] The following year, newly elected Governor Gavin Newsom acknowledged "over a century of depredations and prejudicial policies against California Native Americans." Newsom apologized on behalf of the state for "many instances of violence, maltreatment and neglect," including genocide. His executive order created a Truth and Healing Council to "bear witness" to the "historical relationship between the State of California and California Native Americans."[19]

Finally, the University of California got the widely publicized message. President Janet Napolitano, a former secretary of Homeland Security, apologized to tribes and pledged that the university would comply with the "spirit as well as the legal requirements" of

NAGPRA.[20] A campus committee called upon the university "to acknowledge its participation in a system that damaged and extracted Indigenous people's cultural heritage, to listen to those who have been harmed, and to take actions to help repair the harm."[21]

On January 30, 2020, thirty years after Congress passed NAGPRA, I sat in on another listening session with tribal representatives at which Berkeley Chancellor Carol Christ apologized "for the pain our actions have caused for the local tribes and the other tribes whose ancestors are still held at the Hearst." The atmosphere was formal and tense. "We are eager," Christ continued, "to initiate conversations with tribes about how we can return these ancestors as swiftly and respectfully as possible to their descendants for reburial. . . . I believe strongly that the time is right for change, that the time is right for us to correct historical wrongs."[22] Participants at the meeting said that the time will be right when the university implements its promises.

In October 2022, thirty-two years post-NAGPRA, university administrators say that they are only now beginning to implement a repatriation strategy to return nine thousand ancestors, most of whom were taken from graves in nearby tribal homelands.[23] Moreover, most Bay Area tribes are not federally recognized and therefore do not have land in which to re-bury their ancestors. So far, the University of California, which is one of the largest landowners in the state, does not intend to repatriate homelands or, in the words of the Sogorea Te' Land Trust, to engage in a process of "rematriation," namely "restore sacred relationships between Indigenous people and our ancestral land, honoring our matrilineal societies, and in opposition of patriarchal violence and dynamics."[24] According to an in-depth investigation by ProPublica and NBC News, "a small group of institutions," led by the University of California, "has played an outsized role" in failing to comply with NAGPRA. As of January 2023, the university has "the largest collection of unrepatriated Native human remains in the US," of which it has only made 22 percent available for return to tribes. "Our implementation plan," a "university spokesperson" responded to the exposé, will take up to ten years.[25]

BEYOND GESTURES

To take responsibility for the distant present, in a way that isn't simply a gestural performance, means tackling issues that are deep-rooted and institutional, not attributing them to the efforts of a few rotten apples or writing them off as the ancient history of "men of their times."

It means acknowledging—again and again—that the past bleeds into the present, that damage done decades ago has long-term consequences.

It means recognizing that responsibility for this weighty history is shared by a wide variety of participants, from the university's governing body to those who silently assented:

Regents who appropriated long-inhabited lands and unilaterally asserted their God-given ownership, celebrated the university as the rightful spoils of war, welcomed white supremacists to Berkeley, made extreme wealth a measure of honor, and promoted the age of atomic warfare and weapons of mass destruction.

Administrators who looked for architectural inspiration everywhere but here to create an "Athens in the West," erased the land's Indigenous past and present from the university's origins stories, encouraged the plunder of Native graves and homelands in order to aggrandize the university's global reputation, made George Hearst into an honorable person, and cracked down on movements that tried to make Berkeley live up to its social justice aspirations.

Faculty who represented Native peoples in popular literature and educational texts as biologically destined to extinction, and whose embrace of eugenics had devastating consequences for millions of people—the nonconsensual sterilization of poor women, racialization of Mexican immigrants, tracking of families of color into segregated housing and substandard education, and denial to people with physical and intellectual disabilities of a right to full lives.

Faculty who stomached colleagues spouting racist venom, stayed within the intellectual confines of academic specialization, kept their heads down when they knew much better, and tolerated a discourse that legitimated conquest and genocide. *Fiat lux*? More like *Fiat obscurum*.

The width and depth of participation indicates how, in the phrase of historian Maile Arvin, a "logic of possession"—possessing the land, possessing the people, possessing History—is deeply etched into the institution.[26] Berkeley's corporate model of governance is built to sidestep, deflect, and minimize controversial issues that might disrupt inspirational narratives. Its "brand management team"[27] adopts tactics honed in boardrooms and political think tanks—damage control, procrastination, and diversion of system-wide issues into bureaucratic silos—that for so long effectively disconnected my efforts "to know the place" and make connections between past and present. The university cultivates an upbeat culture of forgetfulness reminiscent of Turkey's officially mandated amnesia about the genocide of Armenians in the early twentieth century, post–Second World War Yugoslavia's reticence about massacres in Croatia, and Spain's "collective pact of forgetting" after the death of Franco.[28]

Silence is habit-forming.

SETTLING UP

It will no doubt be a difficult undertaking for the university to honestly face its responsibilities, especially the central part it played in the dispossession of Indigenous lands, bodies, and artifacts, followed by the cultural production of knowledge that helped to establish, in the words of Philip Deloria, "the rules of the game for empire, expansion, and a distinct species of white supremacy."[29] Fortunately, we can learn from other institutions and movements about what it takes to undertake a serious reckoning with the past.

Land acknowledgements and apologies at public events do not need to be rote rituals. The University of California, says its president in a typical passive voice, "is committed to recognizing and acknowledging historical wrongs endured by Native Americans."[30] This absolves the university of any specific responsibility and says nothing about how and why the university considered it good scientific practice to extract thousands of Native bodies from their graves and reduce them to dismantled specimens without the permission of their biological or cultural descendants. As Joseph Pierce points out, "The problem with land acknowledgments is that they are almost never followed by meaningful action. Acknowledgment without action is an empty gesture, exculpatory and self-serving. What is more, such gestures shift the onus of action back onto Indigenous people, who neither asked for an apology nor have the ability to forgive on behalf of the land that has been stolen and desecrated. It is not my place to forgive on behalf of the land."[31]

In July 2022, Pope Francis's "penitential pilgrimage" to Canada promised more than a symbolic performance. He offered a personal regret for the Catholic Church's involvement in the residential schools that inflicted enormous physical and cultural damage on First Nation communities. "I humbly beg forgiveness," said the Pope, "for the evil committed by so many Christians against the Indigenous peoples." Moreover, he committed the church to "conduct a serious investigation into the facts of what took place in the past and to assist survivors of the residential schools to experience healing from the traumas they suffered." Francis's visit potentially represents a tentative first step in acknowledging the vitality of Indigenous ways of knowing. It remains to be seen whether or not this will lead to what Robin Wall Kimmerer in *Braiding Sweetgrass* calls a "moral covenant of reciprocity" between tribes and the church.[32]

The unnaming of a building should be the beginning of a process of truth and justice, not its end result. We can learn from Pasadena's Neighborhood Unitarian Universalist Church that has been meeting since 2017 to practice accountability for the realization that one of its founders, Robert Millikan, was a core member of the Human Betterment Foundation. In addition to organizing a study group about the history of eugenics and planning a "renaming ritual," the church's Truth and Reconciliation Committee actively supported legislation to provide reparations to the survivors of forced sterilizations. "The activities of our committee are systemic justice work," says chairperson Donna Perkins. "We've become a conscious model of reparations to counteract the fact that Millikan supported an organization which prided itself on being a conscious model to the Nazis."[33]

A memorial does not need to be a perfunctory gesture, such as a soon-to-be-forgotten plaque. The subjects of memory and their biological and cultural descendants should be active partners in how and where commemoration takes place. Memorial artwork offers a model, such as Phung Huynh's steel installation "Sobrevivir" in the courtyard of a Boyle Heights hospital in Los Angeles, which marks the experience of more than two hundred women, including many immigrants from Mexico, who were involuntarily sterilized at the LA County/USC Medical Center between 1968 and 1974. The artwork is site-specific, highly visible, and engages visitors both soulfully and cognitively. "If you don't speak English, they treat you another way," instructs a text around the installation.[34]

Regarding Berkeley's long history of forced sales of Indigenous artifacts, we should draw upon the experiences of organizations that track and account for works of art that were taken from Jewish families in Europe during the Nazi regime. "Good title," concluded the Clinton Commission on Holocaust Assets in the United States, "cannot be conveyed to stolen property." The commission emphasized the importance of a serious investigation into the historical evidence. "Such an accounting is consistent with the moral imperative to remember and learn from the darkest period in modern times."[35]

Berkeley also has a great deal to learn from several universities that have been wrestling for at least a decade with the paradox of enlightened knowledge coexisting with the trade in enslaved Africans. In April 2022, Harvard's administration, for example, announced that it would commit $100 million to repairing "the harms of the university's ties to slavery."[36] By contrast, Berkeley's investment is a pittance.[37] According to California's Acting State Auditor, thirty-two years after enactment of NAGPRA the University of California has neither required Berkeley to set a deadline for completing "timely repatriation," nor dedicated "adequate funds" for completing the process.[38] As of late 2022, according to the Office of the President, there are no plans for reparations in the form of land back or financial restitution. In 2021, 27 Native

Americans (out of an incoming class of 6,931) were admitted to Berkeley's undergraduate program.[39]

Whatever steps are taken to do justice to history, the process must involve the active, substantial, and equitable involvement of tribes and Native organizations whose ancestors' lives and deaths are inseparable from the university's material and cultural foundations. As Yurok elder Walt Lara Sr. points out, the method of "settling up" a dispute is as important as its outcome.[40] It should be a public, transparent process, similar to how students and faculty during the Vietnam War interrupted business-as-usual through teach-ins that equipped the anti-war movement with important information about the history of American imperialism.

Academia does not have a good record of respectful collaboration with tribes, but there are some positive signs of change. Anthropologist Jennifer Raff says that any research involving genetics should only be conducted in partnership with "Indigenous descendant communities."[41] A recent study of genomic data from the Muwekma Ohlone Tribe, published in the prestigious *Proceedings of the National Academy of Sciences*, was a joint effort of tribal members and researchers—from the conceptualization of the project to analysis of data and its implications for policy. The eleven coauthors include members of the tribe.[42]

If the university is seriously committed, as its brand proclaims, to becoming "one of world's great public universities, asking questions and improving the world," it needs to put the "brightest minds" to work on excavating its own history. Instead of resorting to specialized task forces and subcommittees, it should take a bold approach along the lines of South Africa's Truth and Reconciliation Commission.

We need to ask big questions: What would it take for Berkeley to live up to its reputation as an agent of social change and a public trust? What would it mean to reconsider the purposes of a university from an Indigenous perspective? What would it mean to come to terms with how conquest, racial capitalism, a sense of Progress as entitlement, a refusal to learn from ancestors, the production and distribution of ideas about the inherent inferiority of a majority of the world's peoples, and the construction of California's color line are an essential part of the university's and therefore the region's history?[43]

As I recently walked through the Berkeley campus—past buildings, statues, and plaques that celebrate the appropriation of Native homelands to finance the University of California; that dignify entrepreneurs who built their fortunes from the plunder of war and conquest; and that enshrine academics who polished their careers by making white supremacy respectable—I was reminded of Yurok Judge Abby Abinanti's admonition that "the hardest mistakes to correct are those that are ingrained."[44]

To paraphrase Langston Hughes, our challenge is to make the university into a place "that never has been yet / And yet must be." How this will happen remains for us to determine.

Acknowledgments

I STARTED WORKING on the issues in this book late in life and at the end of my career, so I needed to catch up on a lot of learning about the centrality of Indigenous history in American history. Many thanks for the patience of many teachers, especially Jim Benson, Seth Davis, Janet Eidsness, Callie Lara, Walt Lara Sr., Malcolm Margolin, Nazune Menka, Bob McConnell, and Joy Sundberg.

This book originated in my work with Berkeley's Truth and Justice Project. The project was formed in December 2019 to investigate the history of Berkeley's role in the accumulation of Native ancestors and cultural artifacts. The original organizers of the Truth and Justice Project were Phenocia Bauerle, Seth Davis, Tony Platt, and Carolyn Smith. Seth Davis, Nazune Menka, and Tony Platt currently lead the project. I have been responsible for its research, made urgent by the project's commitment to praxis.

The project moved forward with the participation of law students in a federal Indian law seminar, cotaught with Seth Davis at Berkeley Law in the fall semester 2020; and with an undergraduate seminar in humanities, led by Susan Schweik in the spring semester 2022, on "Remembering Eugenics at Berkeley and in California." This was an unusually creative experience working with two generous and collaborative faculty members. Susan was also very generous with research funding. As a result, I broadened the inquiry into an investigation of the university's foundations and development.

Students played a key role in helping to carry out an ambitious agenda. Special thanks to Danielle Elliot, Grace Paine, and Victoria Sun—who understand what it means to do socially responsible research; and to Semantha Norris, who researched and assembled the images for the book, including her own. A team of students— Nahlee Lin, Tuli Ospina, and Victoria Sun—worked on the initial research on campus memorials. Emma City deepened my knowledge about Frederic Putnam; and Amy Reavis and Nora Wallace about Berkeley's land grab. Thanks to Jennifer Kerr for finding new stuff in old archives.

I appreciate the many engaged conversations about the project's framework and implications with colleagues near and far. Special thanks to Elisabeth Anstett, Eduardo Bautista, Miroslava Chavez-Garcia, Seth Davis, Marcy Darnovsky, Jean-Marc Dreyfus, David Edgar, Andrew Garrett, Isidro Gonzalez, Bob Gottlieb, Benedict Ipgrave, Waldo Martin, Ed McCaughan, Nazune Menka, Richard Perry, Jeannie Pfaelzer, Peyton Provenzano, Janelle Reinelt, Milton Reynolds, Victoria Robinson, Susan Schweik, Julie Shackford-Bradley, Jonathan Simon, Orin Starn, Alex Stern, Dick Walker, Vron Ware, and comrades in the Carceral Studies Working Group. Lynn Cooper not only spent many hours discussing the research but made me ride my bike while doing so.

Opportunities to present my research through a global project on eugenics (*From Small Beginnings*) and at conferences and seminars kept me on my toes and sharpened my wits: "Eugenics in California and the World: Race, Class, Gender/Sexuality, and Disability" (University of California, Santa Barbara, June 2011); "Battling Eugenics" University of Warsaw, Poland (April 2022); and "Managing Imperial Legacies," University of Edinburgh, Scotland (June 2022). At Berkeley, the Center for the Study of Law and Society welcomed me back from exile and gave me a forum to try out ideas for this book. Thank you also to the Native American Law Students Association (NALSA) at Berkeley for hosting a talk.

Sarah Chailan in Provence and Dick Walker in Burgundy provided wonderful spaces, surrounded by extraordinary beauty, in which to quietly think through and write the final draft in France in the summer of 2022.

Peter Callopy, Caltech University archivist, confirmed my suspicion that the records of the Human Betterment Foundation had been scrubbed clean. Linda Deck, director of the Bradbury Science Museum in Los Alamos, was very helpful in providing information about the museum's early history.

Several people at Berkeley welcomed my research and unconditionally gave me access to internal archives. Linda Rugg, associate vice chancellor for research, took a genuine interest in and encouraged the project. Tom Torma (NAGPRA liaison) shared his extensive knowledge with me, as did Sabrina Agarwal (chair of Berkeley's NAGPRA Advisory Committee). Thanks to the expertise of Susan McElrath (head of Bancroft Public Services) and Kathryn Neal (associate university archivist), I found my way into a mass of evidence.

I am especially grateful to Lauren Kroiz (director) and key members of her staff at the Hearst Museum (especially Ira Jacknis and Paolo Pellegatti) for opening up archival closets and letting out the truth.

Thanks to Don Fehr (Trident Media Group) for sage advice and keeping the faith.

Heyday was enthusiastic about this project from day one and engaged in its production every step of the way, from writing and rewriting to getting out the words. A pleasure to work with such a committed and engaged team, led by the bibliophilic Steve Wasserman. My special thanks to Emmerich Anklam for his sharp editorial insights; Terria Smith for her thoughtful advice; Kalie Caetano for envisioning a broad readership; Diane Lee for aesthetic and ethical advice about design; and Molly Woodward for close attention to both substance and detail.

Cecilia O'Leary and Dennis Sherman spent untold hours critically reading drafts of the manuscript. I hoped they would say, "Do not change one word," but fortunately they didn't.

I have had no contact with the artist Fred Wilson, but you might notice that his groundbreaking work on mining museums helped me to shape this project. I also tried to keep in mind Stuart Hall's advice about starting small and thinking big. And when things seem exceptionally bleak, I'm reminded of Mike Davis's parting words: "What keeps us going, ultimately, is our love for each other, and our refusal to bow our heads, to accept the verdict, however all-powerful it seems. It's what ordinary people have to do. You have to love each other. You have to defend each other. You have to fight."[1]

Tony Platt, Berkeley, California

Notes

A Note to Readers

1 Damon B. Akins and William J. Bauer Jr., *We Are the Land: A History of Native California* (Berkeley: University of California Press, 2021), 305.

Prologue: Connections

1 Eva Hoffman, *After Such Knowledge: Memory, History, and the Legacy of the Holocaust* (New York: PublicAffairs, 2004), 177.

2 In 2022, the Chancellor's Office created a "Berkeley/Cal Identity Task Force" and contracted with a branding agency to "develop a name framework for the campus." https://chancellor.berkeley.edu/berkeleycal-identity-task-force.

3 National Action/Research on the Military-Industrial Complex (NARMIC), *Police on the Homefront: A Collection of Essays* (Philadelphia: American Friends Service Committee, 1971), 31.

4 Alice Walker, "The Civil Rights Movement: What Good Was It?" *American Scholar* (Autumn 1967): 554.

5 Arthur M. Eckstein, *Bad Moon Rising: How the Weather Underground Beat the FBI and Lost the Revolution* (New Haven: Yale University Press, 2016), 128.

6 Memorandum from Berkeley Chancellor Albert H. Bowker to UC Berkeley Budget Committee, May 1, 1972. Author's personal copy.

7 Two of us, Barry Krisberg and myself, who taught this class, were denied tenure at Berkeley; the third, Paul Takagi, was ostracized by the university for his political activism. Barry Krisberg, "Teaching Radical Criminology," *Crime and Social Justice* 1 (1974): 64–66; Paul Takagi, "Growing Up a Japanese Boy in Sacramento County," *Social Justice* 26, no. 2 (1999): 135–149.

8 "Minutes of the Second Meeting of the Target Committee, Los Alamos, May 10–11, 1945," Washington, DC: US National Archives, http://www.dannen.com/decision/targets.html.

9 Tony Platt, *Grave Matters: The Controversy over Excavating California's Buried Indigenous Past* (Berkeley: Heyday, 2011; 2nd edition, 2021).

10 Martin Fackler, "At Hiroshima Ceremony, a First for a US Envoy," *New York Times* (August 7, 2010).

11 *UC Berkeley Tribal Forum Report* (August 2017), unpublished. Author's personal copy.

12 Yasmin Anwar, "UC Berkeley No. 1 US Public, 8th Best Globally in Times Higher Ed Ranking," *Berkeley News* (September 1, 2021), https://news.berkeley.edu/2021/09/01/uc-berkeley-no-1-u-s-public-8th-best-globally-in-times-higher-ed-rankings/; Yasmin Anwar, "UC Berkeley No. 1 on Forbes' List of America's Top Colleges," *Berkeley News* (September 8, 2021), https://news.berkeley.edu/2021/09/08/uc-berkeley-no-1-on-forbes-list-of-americas-top-colleges/.

13 I borrow this imagery from Max Sebald. W. G. Sebald, "An Attempt at Restitution: A Memory of a German City," *The New Yorker* (December 20, 2004).

14 Raphael Samuel, *Theatres of Memory*, vol. 1, *Past and Present in Contemporary Culture* (London: Verso, 1994), 430.

15 Saidiya Hartman, "Venus in Two Acts," *Small Axe* 26 (June 2008): 4.

16 W. E. B. Du Bois, *Black Reconstruction in America: An Essay toward a History of the Part Black Folk Played in the Attempt to Reconstruct Democracy in America 1860–1880* (New York: Atheneum, 1973; originally published 1935), 714.

17 Architect John Galen Howard quoted in Harvey Helfand, *University of California, Berkeley: An Architectural Tour and Photographs* (New York: Princeton Architectural Press, 2002), 1.

18 "Foreword" to Kishan Lara-Cooper and Walter J. Lara Sr., eds., *Ka'm-t'em: A Journey toward Healing* (Pechanga, California: Great Oak Press, 2019), xiii.

One: Ghosts of Forgotten Histories

1 Philip Deloria, "Defiance," *The New Yorker* (November 2, 2020): 76.

2 Twyla Tharp, *The Creative Habit: Learn It and Use It For Life* (New York: Simon & Schuster, 2003), 119.

3 Waldo R. Wedel, "Archaeological Notes on the Howell's Point Site, CA-Col-2 and CA-Sha-47, 1935," University of California, Berkeley, Phoebe A. Hearst Museum of Anthropology, Archaeological Archives (hereafter cited as PAHMA AA), #18.

4 Benjamin Madley, *An American Genocide: The United States and the California Indian Catastrophe, 1846–1873* (New Haven: Yale University Press, 2016); Damon B. Akins and William J. Bauer Jr., *We Are the Land: A History of Native California* (Berkeley: University of California Press, 2021), 300.

5 Robert F. Heizer, C. Chard, and Ernst N. Johnson, "The Archaeology of the Hotchkiss Site CA-Cco-138, 1937–1938," PAHMA AA #14.

6 Llewellyn Loud, "Half Moon Bay Mounds, General Notes, 1912," PAHMA AA #363.

7 Llewellyn Loud, "Carquinez Mound #236 (CA-Sol-236), 1912," PAHMA AA #364.

8 Akins and Bauer, *We Are the Land*, 327.

9 Letters from Kroeber to Loud (August 30, 1913) and from Loud to Kroeber (September 3, 1913), in Robert F. Heizer, ed., *An Anthropological Expedition, or Get It Through Your Head, or Yours for the Revolution* (Berkeley: University of California Department of Anthropology, 1970), 16–18.

10 Llewellyn L. Loud, "Ethnogeography and Archaeology of the Wiyot Territory," *University of California Publications in American Archaeology and Ethnology* 14, no. 3 (December 1918): 329–330.

11 Thomas R. Hester, "Robert Fleming Heizer, 1915–1979: A Biographical Memoir," *National Academy of Sciences* (1996).

12 See, for example, Robert F. Heizer, C. Chard, and Ernst N. Johnson, "The Archaeology of the Hotchkiss Site, CA-Cco-138, 1937-1938," PAHMA AA #14; Robert F. Heizer, Gordon H. Hewes, and James A. Bennyhoff, "Notes on the Excavation of CA-SJo-68, 1938-1950," PAHMA AA #66; Jeremiah B. Lillard, George Neitz, Franklin Fenega, and Robert F. Heizer, "Field Notes on the Archaeology of the Windmiller Site, CA-Sac-107, 1935-1937," PAHMA AA #68; Robert F. Heizer, "Notes on the Miller Mound, CA-Col-1, 1936," PAHMA AA #94.

13 Robert F. Heizer, ed., *They Were Only Diggers: A Collection of Articles from California Newspapers, 1851–1886* (Ramona, CA: Ballena Press, 1974), ix–x.

14 Theodora Kroeber and Robert F. Heizer, *Almost Ancestors: The First Californians* (San Francisco: The Sierra Club, 1968), 19.

15 Heizer, *They Were Only Diggers*, 148.

16 This confrontation is described in Platt, *Grave Matters*, 116–121.

17 Robert F. Heizer, "A Question of Ethics in Archaeology—One Archaeologist's View," *Journal of California Anthropology* 1 and 2, (1974): 145–151.

18 University of California Robert H. Lowie Museum of Anthropology, *Biennial Report for the Year Ending June 30, 1987*.

19 Philip M. Jones, "Original Photos and Diary, 1901," PAHMA Manuscript #43; Philip M. Jones, "Survey of the Tulare Valley Mounds, Buttonwillow and Adobe Holes (Kern County)," PAHMA Manuscript #42. Photographs of Jones draped in skulls are included in this archive. Out of respect for descendants, human remains are not displayed in photographs in this book.

20 "University of California, A Photographic Essay," *Life* (October 25, 1948): 96; University of California Museum of Anthropology, *Report to President Robert Gordon Sproul For the Year Ending June 30, 1948*.

21 Sherburne Cook, *The Conflict between the California Indian and White Civilization* (Berkeley: University of California Press, 1943), 255–263.

22 M. C. Bruner, *California—Its Amazing Story* (Los Angeles: Wetzel Publishing Co., 1949), 10.

23 Beth Ashley, "Retired Bishop Apologizes for Mistreating the Miwoks," *Marin Independent Journal* (December 26, 2007).

24 Presidential Advisory Commission on Holocaust Assets in the United States, *Plunder and Restitution: The US and Holocaust Victims' Assets*, Washington, DC: US Government Printing Office, 2000.

25 California State Legislature, 1868, quoted in University of California press release celebrating Charter Day, 2018, https://light.berkeley.edu/o/charter-day-a-university-is-born/.

26 Michel Rolph-Trouillot, *Silencing The Past: Power and The Production of History* (Boston: Beacon Press, 1995).

27 Rockwell D. Hunt, *Fifteen Decisive Events of California History* (Los Angeles: Historical Society of Southern California, 1959).

28 A. A. Gray, *History of California from 1542* (Boston: D. C. Heath, 1934), iii; Grace S. Dawson, *California: The Story of Our Southwest Corner* (New York: Macmillan, 1939), 169.

29 Hartman, "Venus in Two Acts," 1–14; Saidiya V. Hartman, *Scenes of Subjection: Terror, Slavery, and Self-Making in Nineteenth-Century America* (New York: Oxford University Press, 1997).

30 William J. Bauer Jr., *California through Native Eyes: Reclaiming History* (Seattle: University of Washington Press, 2016), 10, 121, 123.

31 Bauer, *California through Native Eyes*, 28.

32 Hartman, *Scenes of Subjection*, 10.

33 Beth Piatote, *The Beadworkers: Stories* (Berkeley: Counterpoint, 2019), 188.

34 Gretel Ehrlich, "Chronicles of Ice," *Orion Magazine* (November 1, 2004), https://orionmagazine.org/article/chronicles-of-ice/.

Two: Present Absences

1 Cutcha Risling Baldy, *We Are Dancing for You: Native Feminisms and the Revitalization of Women's Coming-of-Age Ceremonies* (Seattle: University of Washington Press, 2018), 152.

2 Quoted in Janice Thomas, "Strawberry Canyon, 'A Mountain Gorge,'" *Berkeley Landmarks*, September 2005, http://berkeleyheritage.com/berkeley_landmarks/strawbcanyon.html.

3 Verne A. Stadtman, *The University of California, 1868–1968* (New York: McGraw-Hill Book Company, 1970), 20.

4 Thomas, "Strawberry Canyon."

5 *Biennial Report of the Regents of the University of California for the Years 1872–3* (Sacramento: T. A. Springer, 1873), 7–8.

6 Peter Bacon Hales, *Atomic Spaces: Living on the Manhattan Project* (Urbana: University of Illinois Press, 1997), 9.

7 Christopher D. Dore et al., "Why Here? Settlement, Geoarchaeology, and Paleoenvironment at the West Berkeley Site (CA-Ala-307)," *Proceedings of the Society for California Archaeology* 17 (2004): 27–33.

8 "Red Men Lived on Campus," *The Daily Californian* (July 23, 1915).

9 Archaeologist Nels C. Nelson, who did extensive research on shellmounds in the Bay Area, thought that "large mounds" could be "anywhere from 3,000–4,000 years old." Nelson, "San Francisco Bay Mounds, 1907," UC Berkeley, PAHMA, AA #349.

10 Bauer, *California through Native Eyes*, 28.

11 Akins and Bauer, *We Are the Land*, 300.

12 Richard Levy, "Costanoan," in Robert F. Heizer, ed., *Handbook of North American Indians, California*, vol. 8 (Washington, DC: Smithsonian Institution, 1978), 485; Alan Levanthal, Les Field, Hank Alvarez, and Rosemary Cambra, "The Ohlone: Back from Extinction," in Lowell John Bean, ed., *The Ohlone Past and Present: Native Americans of the San Francisco Bay Region* (Menlo Park, CA: Ballena Press, 1994), 297–336.

13 Akins and Bauer, *We Are the Land*, 300.

14 Malcolm Margolin, *The Ohlone Way: Indian Life in the San Francisco–Monterey Bay Area* (Berkeley: Heyday Books, 1978), 8.

15 Malcolm Margolin, ed., *Life in a California Mission: The Journals of Jean François de la Pérouse* (Berkeley: Heyday Books, 1989), 64, 67.

16 Margolin, *The Ohlone Way*, 8, 169.

17 Leventhal et al., "The Ohlone: Back from Extinction."

18 A. L. Kroeber, *Handbook of the Indians of California*, Bulletin #78 (Washington, DC: Smithsonian Institution, 1925), 464, 466; Alfred L. Kroeber and Robert F. Heizer, *Continuity of Indian Population in California from 1770/1848 to 1955* (Berkeley: University of California Archaeological Research Facility 9, 1970), 2–3.

19 Leventhal et al., "The Ohlone," 312.

20 See, for example, Risling Baldy, *We Are Dancing for You*.

21 Shaunna Oteka McCovey, "Letter to a Young Native: Sovereignty is Action," in Lara-Cooper and Lara Sr., *Ka'm-t'em*, 274.

22 Cutcha Risling Baldy and Kayla Begay, "Xo'ch Na:nahsde'tl'-te: Survivance, Resilience and Unbroken Traditions in Northwest California," in Lara-Cooper and Lara Sr., *Ka'm-t'em*, 42.

23 Chris Peters and Chisa Oros, "Voices from the Sacred: An Indigenous World-view and Epistemology of Northwestern California," in Lara-Cooper and Lara Sr., *Ka'm-t'em*, 3.

24 Walt Lara Sr., "Closing Statement," *ibid.*, 314.

25 Alissa L. Severson et al., "Ancient and Modern Genomics of the Ohlone Indigenous Population of California," *Proceedings of the National Academy of Sciences* 119, no. 13 (March 2022), https://doi.org/10.1073/pnas.2111533119; Sabrina Imbler, "Validation for a Tribe That Lost Its Recognition," *New York Times* (April 19, 2022).

26 Marc Augé, "Planetary Landscapes," in Paul Virilio et al., eds., *Native Land: Stop Eject* (Arles, France: Actes Sud, 2009), 109.

27 Piatote, *The Beadworkers*, 8.

28 *Biennial Report of the Regents of the University of California for the Years 1873–5* (Sacramento: G. H. Springer, 1875), 108.

29 Helfand, *University of California, Berkeley*, 4, 230.

30 J. C. Merriam, accession file #305, Museum #12-3480 (August 2-3, 1907), University of California, Berkeley, PAHMA; J. C. Merriam, "Shellheap No. 308, August 3, 1907," in Nels C. Nelson's field notes, "San Francisco Bay Mounds," PAHMA AA #349.

31 N. C. Nelson, "Shellmounds of the San Francisco Bay Region," *University of California Publications in American Archaeology and Ethnology* 7, no. 4 (December 1909): 322.

32 Kroeber quoted in "Shell Mounds in Faculty Glade. Site of Club Where Professors Take Ease Was Aborigines' Home," *Oakland Tribune* (October 5, 1914). See, also, A. L. Kroeber, *Anthropology* (New York: Harcourt, Brace and Co., 1923), 320–323; and Dore et al., "Why Here?" 27–33.

33 "City Beneath Campus? Discover Indian Relics. Claim of Aged Scientist May Be Borne Out by Investigations," *Oakland Tribune* (August 22, 1914).

34 "Red Men Lived on Campus," *The Daily Californian* (July 23, 1915).

35 "Mongoloid Type Skeleton is Dug Up at Berkeley. Workmen Uncover Old Indian Burial Ground at Faculty Glade," *Oakland Tribune* (June 20, 1925); see, also, PAHMA, burial #12-3828.1, Acc. 609.

36 "Prehistoric Indian Skeleton Dug Up on University Campus. Bones Repose on Shell Bed. Scientist to Study Frame," *Oakland Tribune* (August 3, 1907).

37 Personal communication to author from Paolo Pellegatti, Research Archaeologist, PAHMA, May 31, 2020; and from Ira Jacknis, Research Anthropologist, PAHMA, May 31, 2020. As required by the California Environmental Quality Act, I do not include information about the exact location of specific sites: "Environmental documents must not include information about the location of an archaeological site or sacred lands or any other information that is exempt

from public disclosure. . . . Native American graves, cemeteries, and records of
Native American places, features, and objects are also exempt from disclosure."
Public Records Act. Cal. Code Regs. #15120 (d); Public Resources Code, #5097.9;
California Governor's Office of Planning and Research, *Technical Advisory: AB 52
and Tribal Cultural Resources in CEQA* (June 2017).

38 Northwest Information Center (NWIC), California Historical Resources,
Information System, Sonoma State University, P-01-000043, 19-2224 UC
Berkeley. The Northwest Information Center of the California Historical
Resources Information System is one of nine information centers affiliated
with the State of California Office of Historic Preservation.

39 Ira Jacknis, "A Museum Prehistory: Phoebe Hearst and the Founding of the
Museum of Anthropology, 1891–1901," in Roberta J. Park and J. R. K. Kantor,
eds., *Chronicle of the University of California* 4 (2000): 55.

40 *Annual Report to the Regents of the University of California, 1877* (San Francisco: John H. Carmany and Company, 1877), 15.

41 Smithsonian National Museum of Natural History, Division of Archaeology,
A97299-0, Accession #14244, 1884.

42 Smithsonian National Museum of Natural History, Division of Archaeology,
A200224-0, Accession #34809, March 29, 1899.

43 *Annual Report to the Regents of the University of California* (Berkeley:
University Press, 1878), 25; *Annual Report to the Regents of the University
of California* (Berkeley: University Press, 1879), 4; *Annual Report to the
Board of Regents of the University of California for Year Ending June 30,
1880* (Sacramento: J. D. Young, 1880); *Annual Report to the Regents of the
University of California* (Sacramento: James J. Ayers, 1884), 58; *Annual
Report to the Regents of the University of California* (Sacramento: J. D. Young,
1890), 125; *Report to the Regents*, 187 (San Francisco: John H. Carmany and
Company, 1877), 15; *Report to the Regents*, 1878, 25; *Report to the Regents*,
1880, 24; *Report to the Regents*, 1884, 58; *Report to the Regents*, 1890, 125;
Report to the Regents, 1892 (Sacramento: A. J. Johnston, 1892), 121–122;
Smithsonian National Museum of Natural History, Division of
Archaeology, A200224-0, Accession #34809 (March 29, 1899).

44 James Gilbert Paltridge, *A History of the Faculty Club at Berkeley* (Berkeley: University of California, The Faculty Club, 1990), 3. See, also, Edmond
O'Neill, *An Account of the Birth and Growth of the Faculty Club of the University of California*, privately printed, 1933, Bancroft Library. According to
O'Neill, the Berkeley site "was evidently a camp of some importance."

45 PAHMA 1-4738; PAHMA 1-6991; PAHMA 1-4506, Accession #166; PAHMA
12-3480.2, Accession #305; PAHMA 1-24306; PAHMA 12-2672 "burial number";
PAHMA 1-19444, Acc. 100HHH; PAHMA, Accession #10001, Museum #12-
3465A, CA-Ala-308; PAHMA 1-24109, Acc. 100DL; PAHMA, burial #12-3828.1,
Acc. 609; PAHMA 1-39719, Acc. 1938 AP; PAHMA 1-143011, Acc. UCAS-450.

46 University of California Robert H. Lowie Museum of Anthropology, *Annual Report for the Year Ending June 30, 1973*, 7.

47 PAHMA 1-25906 to 1-1259612.

48 William Roop, "Archaeological Reconnaissance of the Proposed Biological Sciences Construction and Alterations Project," University of California at Berkeley (September 28, 1982), NWIC S-005625, 19-2224 UC Berkeley.

49 William Roop, "Archaeological Survey of Underdeveloped Lands and Proposed Building Locations within the Lawrence Berkeley Laboratory, University of California Berkeley" (July 29, 1986), NWIC S-008719, 19-2224 UC Berkeley.

50 Robert Charbonneau, "Strawberry Creek Management Plan," UC Berkeley, December 1, 1987, https://creeks.berkeley.edu/sites/default/files /publications/scmp1987_chapter3.pdf, 9; personal communication to author from Robert Charbonneau, June 25, 2020.

51 Carol Kielusiak, "Archaeological Survey of 70 Acres of Land and Recordation and Evaluation of Four Historic Resources at the E. O. Lawrence Berkeley National Laboratory" (February 2000), NWIC S-028039, 19-2224 UC Berkeley.

52 David Buckley et al., William Self Associates, *Geoarchaeological Testing Report for the University of California, Berkeley, Student Athlete Performance Center, Alameda County, California* (December 2008).

53 UC Berkeley Press Release, "Assessment of Memorial Stadium Site by Independent Archaeologists" (September 6, 2007), https://www.berkeley.edu /news/features/stadium/archaeologists.shtml.

54 Max Uhle, "The Emeryville Shellmound," *University of California Publications in American Archaeology and Ethnology* 7, 1 (1907): 4.

55 "Burial and Feature Records from Ala-307, West Berkeley Mound, 1950," PAHMA AA #179.

56 "Reds Want Bones of Forefathers," *San Francisco Call* (August 23, 1906); "May Arrest The Professor," *Dispatch-Democrat* (August 24, 1906).

57 Stadtman, *The University of California*.

58 George R. Stewart, *The Year of the Oath: The Fight for Academic Freedom at the University of California* (New York: Doubleday, 1950), 65–66.

59 Paltridge, *A History of the Faculty Club*, 3.

60 https://www.berkeley.edu/map?facultyglade. Accessed August 2022.

61 Henry George, *Progress and Poverty: An Inquiry into the Cause of Industrial Depression and the Increase of Want with Increase of Wealth* (New York: D. Appleton and Co., 1881).

62 *Annual Report of the Regents of the University of California for Year Ending June 30, 1887* (Sacramento: J. D. Young, 1887), 51.

63 Donald R. Brown, "Jonathan Baldwin Turner and the Land-Grant Idea," *Journal of the Illinois State Historical Society*, 55 (1962): 378.

64 John Y. Simon, "The Politics of the Morrill Act," *Agricultural History*, 37 (1963): 110.

65 Justin S. Morrill, *Speech of Hon. Justin S. Morrill, of Vermont, on the Bill Granting Lands for Agricultural Colleges*, Washington, DC: Congressional Office (1858), S533. M74, https://lccn.loc.gov/44038936.

66 Mark Yudof, "For 150 years, UC science and agriculture transform California," *California Agriculture*, 66, 2 (2012), https://escholarship.org /uc/item/9gw5b2hq.

67 Mark Yudof, "Morrill Act Speech," April 30, 2012, https://video.ucdavis.edu /media/Morrill+ActA+SpeakerA+Mark+Yudof/0_fr3q7zjx/25823302.

68 Quoted in Hayden Royster, "This Land Is Their Land," *California* 133, 2 (Summer 2022): 37.

69 Robert Lee and Tristan Ahtone, "Land-Grab Universities," *High Country News* (March 30, 2020), https://www.hcn.org/issues/52.4/indigenous -affairs-education-land-grab-universities. See, also, the proceedings of a two-part conference organized at Berkeley on September 25 and October 23, 2020: Joseph A. Myers Center for Research on Native American Issues and Native American Student Development, *The University of California Land Grab: A Legacy of Profit from Indigenous Land—A Report of Key Learnings and Recommendations*, University of California, Berkeley (2021).

70 First Morrill Act, ch.130, 12 Stat. 503, 7 USCS § 301, 304.

71 *Report of the Regents of the University of California Relative to the Operations and Progress of the Institution* (Sacramento: T. A. Springer, 1872); "A Brief Historical Tour of the University of California," *University of California History Digital Archives*, https://www.lib.berkeley.edu/uchistory/general_ history/overview/tour1.html; Verne A. Stadtman, ed., *The Centennial Record of the University of California, 1868–1968* (University of California, 1967) https://oac.cdlib.org/view?docId=hb4v19n9zb&brand=oac4&doc.view =entire_text; Stadtman, *The University of California*, 27–34.

72 Amy Reavis and Nora Wallace, "*Entitled To Our Land*: The Settler Colonial Origins of the University of California," *California Law Review* 13, forthcoming 2023.

73 Clark Kerr, *The Uses of the University* (Cambridge: Harvard University Press, 1963), 47.

74 Lee and Ahtone, "Land-grab Universities." See, also, Margaret A. Nash, "Entangled Pasts: Land-Grant Colleges and American Indian Dispossession," *History of Education Quarterly* 59, no. 4 (November 2019): 437–467.

75 Davarian L. Baldwin, "Public University, Private Developer," *San Francisco Chronicle* (May 31, 2022).

76 Reavis and Wallace, "*Entitled To Our Land*"; LaDale C. Winling, *Building the Ivory Tower: Universities and Metropolitan Development in the Twentieth Century* (Philadelphia: University of Pennsylvania Press, 2018), 125.

77 "The Lost Island of Sandoval County," *The Atom* 1, no. 1 (January 1964), https://www.lanl.gov/library//find/lanl-publications-atom.php.

78 Hales, *Atomic Spaces*, 2–18.

79 Deloria, "Defiance."

80 Garrett et al., *Native American Collections in Archives*, 37.

81 Lee and Ahtone, "Land-Grab Universities," 36.

82 Josiah Royce, *California: From the Conquest in 1846 to the Second Vigilance Committee in San Francisco, A Study in American Character* (Boston: Houghton Mifflin Company, 1886), 2.

83 Donald L. Johns, Captain US Army, "Military Science," in Stadtman, ed., *The Centennial Record*.

Three: The Sound of History

1 Jim Harrison, "The Brand New Statue of Liberty," in *Jim Harrison: The Essential Poems*, ed. Joseph Bednarik (Port Townsend, WA: Copper Canyon Press, 2019), 118. Thanks to Peter Nabokov for bringing this poem to my attention.

2 The phrase is associated with Charles Tilly, *Coercion, Capital, and European States, A. D. 990–1992* (New York: Wiley-Blackwell, 1993).

3 Thomas Bender, *A Nation among Nations: America's Place in World History* (New York: Hill and Wang, 2006), 132.

4 Stadtman, *The Centennial Record*.

5 Madley, *An American Genocide*, 256, 334–335, 549. On the early history of the political and financial arguments concerning the University of California, see Stadtman, *The University of California, 1868–1968*.

6 Madley, *An American Genocide*, 334.

7 Jean Pfaelzer, *Driven Out: The Forgotten War Against Chinese Americans* (Berkeley: University of California Press, 2008), 54.

8 Pfaelzer, *Driven Out*, 74–75; Margaret Cahalan, "Trends in Incarceration in the United States since 1880: A Summary of Reported Rates and the Distribution of Offenses," *Crime and Delinquency* 25, no. 1 (January 1979): 40; Paul Takagi and Tony Platt, "Behind the Gilded Ghetto: An Analysis of Race, Class and Crime in Chinatown," *Crime and Social Justice* 9 (Spring–Summer, 1978): 10; John Helmer, *Drugs and Minority Oppression* (New York: Seabury, 1975), 18–33; Gary Y. Okihiro, *Margins and Mainstreams: Asians in American History and Culture* (Seattle: University of Washington Press, 1994).

9   Jacknis, "A Museum Prehistory," 55–56; *Biennial Report of the Regents of the University of California for the Years 1873–5* (Sacramento: G. H. Springer, 1875), 108.

10 Madley, *An American Genocide*, 345.

11 Stadtman, *The University of California*, 51.

12 Madley, *An American Genocide*, 276–280, 532–533; Frank H. Baumgardner III, *Killing for Land in Early California: Indian Blood at Round Valley, 1856–1863* (New York: Algora Publishing, 2006). See, also, Thomas Fuller, "He Unleashed a California Massacre. Should This School Be Named for Him?" *New York Times* (October 27, 2021). Following Fuller's reporting and a public outcry, in November 2021 the Board of Directors of the law school voted to remove Hastings's name.

13 John Walton Caughey, *California* (New York: Prentice-Hall, 1940), 391.

14 Byron Nelson Jr., *Our Home Forever: The Hupa Indians of Northern California* (Salt Lake City: Howe Brothers, 1978), 45.

15 Risling Baldy, *We Are Dancing for You*, 53–54.

16 *Convention on the Prevention and Punishment of the Crime of Genocide*, Adopted by the General Assembly of the United Nations, December 9, 1948.

17 Madley, *An American Genocide*, 358.

18 More than one-third of Madley's book consists of appendices that document every known massacre and military expedition against California Indians. Madley's comprehensive research leaves no source unexplored: state and federal archives, legislative reports, memoirs and manuscripts, and library collections. This is the foundational account of California's genocide on which all future studies will be based.

19 Hubert Howe Bancroft, *California Inter Pocula* (San Francisco: The History Company, 1888), 253.

20 Loud, "Ethnography and Archaeology," 306.

21 Kroeber and Heizer, *Almost Ancestors*, 18–20.

22 Claudia Koonz, *The Nazi Conscience* (Cambridge: The Belknap Press, 2003), 3.

23 Here I draw upon the insights of Zygmunt Bauman, *Modernity and the Holocaust* (Ithaca: Cornell University Press, 2000).

24 Madley, *An American Genocide*, 14, 178, 354.

25 Clyde A. Milner II, "National Initiatives," in Clyde A. Milner et al., eds., *The Oxford History of the American West* (New York: Oxford University Press, 1994), 183.

26 R. Gregory Nokes, *The Troubled Life of Peter Burnett, Oregon Pioneer and First Governor of California* (Oregon State University Press, 2018), 2, 65–66.

27 Governor Peter H. Burnett, "Governor's Annual Message to the Legislature" (January 7, 1851), *Journals of the Senate and Assembly of the State of California* (San Francisco: G. K. Fitch and V. E. Geiger, 1852).

28 Albert L. Hurtado, *Indian Survival on the California Frontier* (New Haven: Yale University Press, 1988), 1. For the various estimates of California's Indigenous population in the 1800s, see Russell Thornton, "Population History of Native North Americans," in *A Population History of North America*, eds. Michael R. Haines and Richard H. Steckel (Cambridge: Cambridge University Press, 2000), 9–50.

29 Bender, *A Nation among Nations*, 21.

30 Tony Platt, "The Result Would Have Been the Same," January 23, 2012, https://goodtogo.typepad.com/tony_platt_goodtogo/2012/01/the-result-would-have-been-the-same-.html.

31 Raymond H. Kévorkian, "Earth, Fire, Water: How to Make Armenian Corpses Disappear," in Anstett and Dreyfus, *Destruction and Human Remains*, 89–116.

32 Marianna Ferreira, *Sweet Tears and Bitter Pills: The Politics of Health among Yuroks of Northern California* (Ph.D. dissertation, University of California, Berkeley, 1996).

33 In some concentration camps, such as Majdanek in Poland, two-thirds died this way. Robert Jan Van Pelt, "*Sinnreich erdacht*: Machines of Mass Incineration in Fact, Fiction, and Forensics," in Anstett and Dreyfus, *Destruction and Human Remains*, 117–145.

34 David Graeber and David Wengrow, *The Dawn of Everything: A New History of Humanity* (New York: Farrar, Straus and Giroux, 2021), 493.

35 Margolin, "Introduction," *Life in a California Mission*, 458.

36 Tai S. Edwards and Paul Kelton, "Germs, Genocides, and America's Indigenous Peoples," *Journal of American History* (June 2020): 52–76.

37 Bender, *A Nation among Nations*, 163–202.

38 Hurtado, *Indian Survival*, 218.

39 James Rawls, *Indians of California: The Changing Image* (Norman: University of Oklahoma Press, 1984), 93; Tony Platt, "Bitter Legacies: A War of Extermination, Grave Looting and Culture Wars in the American West," in Anstett and Dreyfus, *Human Remains and Identification*, 14–33; Madley, *An American Genocide*, 146–147.

40 Madley, *An American Genocide*, 159.

41 Rawls, *Indians of California*, 93; Madley, *An American Genocide*, 162; Caughey, *California*, 391; Carl Meyer, *Bound for Sacramento: Travel Pictures of a Returned Wanderer*, trans. Ruth Frey Axe (Claremont: Saunders Studio Press, 1938).

42 Kévorkian, "Earth, Fire, Water."

43 Adams, *Education for Extinction*; Fear-Segal, *White Man's Club*; Cathleen Cahill, *Federal Fathers and Mothers: A Social History of the United States Indian Service, 1869–1933* (Chapel Hill: University of North Carolina Press, 2011); Peter Nabokov, ed., *Native American Testimony: A Chronicle of Indian-White Relations from Prophecy to the Present, 1492–1992* (New York: Viking Penguin, 1991), 216–217.

44 For biographies of regents, see University of California History, digital archives, "Regents of the University of California," https://www.lib.berkeley.edu/uchistory/general_history/overview/regents/biographies_b.html.

45 Benjamin F. Rush, Charles F. Reed, Richard P. Hammond, William H. L. Barnes, William S. Rosecrans, William T. Welcker, and George Stoneman attended military academies.

46 Bender, *A Nation among Nations*, 201; William D. Carrigan and Clive Webb, *Forgotten Dead: Mob Violence against Mexicans in the United States, 1848–1928* (New York: Oxford University Press, 2013).

47 *The Daily Californian* (January 26, 1898).

48 Stadtman, *The University of California*, 51.

49 For George Stoneman's military experience, see Madley, *An American Genocide*, 132.

50 https://chancellor.berkeley.edu/task-forces/building-name-review-committee/building-name-review-barrows-hall; https://prabook.com/web/david.barrows/3765274; Kenton J. Clymer, "Humanitarian Imperialism: David Prescott Barrows and the White Man's Burden in the Philippines," *Pacific Historical Review*, 45, no. 4 (1976): 495–517.

51 "John Franklin Swift," *University of California History: Digital Archives, Regents of the University of California*, https://www.lib.berkeley.edu/uchistory/general_history/overview/regents/biographies_s.html#swift_j.

52 Bonnie Azab Powell, "The Histories of Berkeley and the US Military Have Long Been Allied," *Campus News* (October 11, 2002), https://www.berkeley.edu/news/media/releases/2002/10/11_rotc_history.html.

53 *Biennial Report of the Regents of the University of California, 1872–1873* (Berkeley: University of California, 1873), 21; *Biennial Report of the Regents of the University of California, 1877–1879* (Berkeley: University of California, August 1879), 25. See, also, Stadtman, *The University of California*, 155.

54 Andrew J. Moulder, Secretary to the Regents of the University of California, *Report of the Regents of the University of California, Relative to the Operations and Progress of the Institution*, (Sacramento: T. A. Springer, 1872), https://oac.cdlib.org/view?docId=hb887008m3&brand=oac4&doc.view=entire_text.

55 Donald L. Johns, Captain US Army, "Military Science," in Stadtman, *The Centennial Record.*

56 "Elmer Reginald Drew Letters to Christopher Adam Elliott, 1884–1892," University of California Berkeley, Bancroft Library, CU610.

57 Daniel Coit Gilman, "University Commencement," *Biennial Report of the Regents of the University of California 1872–73* (Berkeley: University of California, 1873).

58 Powell, "The Histories of Berkeley and the US Military"; Donald L. Johns, Captain US Army, "Military Science," in Stadtman, ed., *The Centennial Record.*

59 "Faculty Members Meet and Offer Aid toward Preparedness," press release, Feb 7, 1917, Records of the Regents of the University of California, 1868–1933, Bancroft Library CU-1, Box 84, #32, "Faculty Club."

60 Ellen W. Schrecker, *No Ivory Tower: McCarthyism and the Universities* (New York: Oxford University Press, 1986), 20.

61 Cecilia O'Leary, *To Die For: The Paradox of American Patriotism* (Princeton: Princeton University Press, 1999), 241.

62 Stadtman, *The University of California*, 193–196.

63 There are two memorials (including the football stadium) to American soldiers who died in World I; a memorial glade and bench "in memory of our classmates who gave their lives for their country in World War II"; and a plaque "in memory of the classmates who gave their lives in the service of their country in the Korean War, 1950–1953."

64 O'Leary, *To Die For*, 129–149.

65 Richard Slotkin, *The Fatal Environment: The Myth of the Frontier in the Age of Industrialization, 1800–1890* (Wesleyan University Press, 1986), 7, 385, 409.

66 George Armstrong Custer, "The Red Man" (1858), quoted in Slotkin, *The Fatal Environment*, 410.

67 Andrew L. Yarrow, "Beneath South Dakota's Black Hills," *New York Times* (August 9, 1987); Gray Brechin, *Imperial San Francisco: Urban Power, Earthly Ruin* (Berkeley: University of California Press, 1999), 351, footnote 11.

68 Philip J. Deloria, *Playing Indian* (New Haven: Yale University Press, 1998), 104.

69 Nabokov, *Native American Testimony*, 110; Slotkin, *The Fatal Environment*, 431.

70 Slotkin, *The Fatal Environment*, 8, 531; William H. Truettner, ed., *The West as America: Reinterpreting Images of the Frontier, 1820–1920* (Washington, DC: National Museum of American Art, 1991), 297.

71 Walt Whitman, "A Death Sonnet for Custer," *New York Daily Tribune* (July 10, 1876), https://whitmanarchive.org/published/periodical/poems/per.00142. See, also, Slotkin, *The Fatal Environment*, 10–11.

72 "Josiah Royce, 1855–1916," SNAC (Social Networks and Archival Context), https://snaccooperative.org/ark:/99166/w6zg6v1d.

73 Royce, *California*, 2, 30, 222, 376.

74 Jacques Loeb, "Biology and War," *Science* (January 26, 1917): 73–76.

75 Risling Baldy, *We Are Dancing for You*, 67, 72.

76 Royce, *California*, 500.

Four: A Matter of Life and Death

1 Title of Wojnarowicz's exhibition at Whitney Museum of American Art, New York, July 13–September 30, 2018.

2 "Pinched: A Prison Experience" and "The Pen: Long Days in a County Penitentiary" were both published in *Cosmopolitan* magazine in 1907. Reprinted in H. Bruce Franklin, ed., *Prison Writing in 20th-Century America* (New York: Penguin Books, 1998), 37–57.

3 Jack London, *Martin Eden* (New York: Modern Library, 2002), 29. Originally published in 1909.

4 The phrase comes from Richard Hoggart's description of how working-class students felt at British universities in the 1950s. Richard Hoggart, *The Uses of Literacy* (Harmondsworth: Penguin Books, 1957), 302.

5 Mario Savio, "An End to History," in Michael V. Miller and Susan Gilmore, eds., *Revolution at Berkeley: The Crisis in American Education* (New York: The Dial Press, 1965), 239–243.

6 James Joyce's "I Hear an Army" was first published in 1907 in a poetry collection, *Chamber Music*.

7 Robert Duncan, *The H. D. Book* (Buffalo: Frontier Press, 1984), 14–20, http://ccca.concordia.ca/history/ozz/english/books/hd_book/HD_Book _by_Robert_Duncan.pdf.

8 Quoted in William Warren Ferrier, *Origin and Development of the University of California* (Berkeley: The Sather Gate Book Shop, 1930), 584.

9 "Cadet Corps," https://news.berkeley.edu/military-on-campus/.

10 Robert S. McNamara (with Brian VanDeMark), *In Retrospect: The Tragedy and Lessons of Vietnam* (New York: Times Books, 1995), 6.

11 Stadtman, *The University of California*, 301–305.

12 Robert Nisbet, *Teachers and Scholars: A Memoir of Berkeley in Depression and War* (New Brunswick: Transaction Publishers, 1992), 59.

13 Stadtman, *The University of California*, 303.

14 Nisbet, *Teachers and Scholars*, 200.

15 Stadtman, *The University of California*, 307.

16 Donald L. Johns, Captain US Army, "Military Science," in Stadtman, *The Centennial Record*; Powell, "The Histories of Berkeley and the US Military."

17 Stadtman, *The University of California*, 307–309; United States Atomic Energy Commission, "In The Matter of J. Robert Oppenheimer," Washington, DC, transcript (April 16, 1954), 757.

18 "Japanese cherry trees commemorate UC alumni," *Berkeley News* (April 9, 2013), https://news.berkeley.edu/2013/04/09/cherry-tree-grove/.

19 In 2009, the university, by way of apology, offered these former students the opportunity to receive their degrees. Kathleen Maclay, "Honorary degrees for students affected by World War II internment order," University of California Berkeley press release (September 8, 2009).

20 Stadtman, *The University of California*, flyleaf blurb.

21 "Uprooted: The Incarceration of Japanese Americans," The Bancroft Library Gallery, October 2021 to June 2022, visited October 25, 2021.

22 Yoshiko Uchida, *Desert Exile: The Uprooting of a Japanese-American Family* (Seattle: University of Washington Press, 1982), 3–4, 42–43, 58–62.

23 International Campaign to Abolish Nuclear Weapons, *Mass Destruction: American Universities in the US Nuclear Weapons Complex*, ICAN (November 2019). According to the US Department of Energy, "after the war, the University of California opted to maintain their relationship with the Los Alamos laboratory. University administrators saw their management of Los Alamos as a public service and an opportunity for valuable research opportunities. When the second weapons laboratory was established at Livermore, initially as an extension of the Rad Lab, the university became manager there as well. The University of California has served uninterrupted as manager or as part of a management team of the three laboratories, which are now part of the Department of Energy's national laboratory system: the Lawrence Berkeley National Laboratory (the direct descendent of the Rad Lab), the Lawrence Livermore National Laboratory, and the Los Alamos National Laboratory." US Department of Energy, "The Manhattan Project, University of California," https://www.osti.gov/opennet/manhattan-project-history/People /CivilianOrgs/university-of california.html.

24 Los Alamos Historical Society, *Los Alamos 1943–1945: Beginning of An Era* (Los Alamos: Los Alamos Historical Society, 2007).

25 Office of the President, University of California, "Los Alamos National Laboratory (LANL)," accessed March 19, 2022, https://www.ucop.edu/laboratory -management/about-the-labs/overview-lanl.html.

26 Personal communication to author by e-mail from Linda Deck, Museum Director, Bradbury Science Museum (February 2, 2022).

27 Hal K. Rothman, *On Rims and Ridges: The Los Alamos Area Since 1880* (Lincoln: University of Nebraska Press, 1997), 8, 73.

28 Veronica Taylor et al., "Native Americans and the Manhattan Project" (June 28, 2016), Atomic Heritage Foundation, https://www.atomicheritage.org /history/native-americans-and-manhattan-project.

29 Hales, *Atomic Spaces*, 25.

30 Hales, *Atomic Spaces*, 10.

31 Hales, *Atomic Spaces*, 17.

32 University of California Los Alamos Scientific Laboratory, "Science Museum" brochure, c. 1954.

33 Rothman, *On Rims and Ridges*, 208, 209, 318.

34 "Two Worlds and a Dream: Portrait of an Outstanding Young Man," *The Atom* 1, no. 7 (July 1964): 6–9, https://www.lanl.gov/library//find/lanl -publications-atom.php.

35 Quoted in Hales, *Atomic Spaces*, 206–207, 209.

36 Hales, *Atomic Spaces*, 209.

37 "History at Your Feet," *The Atom* 1, no. 2 (February 1964): 6–7.

38 Hales, *Atomic Spaces*, 208–210.

39 Alex Wellerstein, "Counting the Dead at Hiroshima and Nagasaki," *Bulletin of the Atomic Scientists* (August 4, 2020), https://thebulletin.org/2020/08 /counting-the-dead-at-hiroshima-and-nagasaki/.

40 United States Atomic Energy Commission, *In The Matter of J. Robert Oppenheimer*, 762–764.

41 A recent estimate suggests 214,000 died. Seren Morris, "How Many People Died in Hiroshima and Nagasaki?" *Newsweek* (August 3, 2020). For a thoughtful review of the evidence, see Wellerstein, "Counting the Dead."

42 United States Atomic Energy Commission, *In The Matter of J. Robert Oppenheimer*, 740, 761–764.

43 Ibid, 742.

44 US Department of Energy, "Radiation Accidents," The Manhattan Project, accessed March 18, 2022, https://www.osti.gov/opennet/manhattan-project -history/Science/Radioactivity/rad-accidents.html; Louis H. Hempelmann, Clarence C. Lushbaugh, and George L. Voelz, "What Has Happened to the Survivors of the Early Los Alamos Nuclear Accidents?" Conference for Radiation Accident Preparedness, Oak Ridge, Tennessee, October 19–20, 1979. See, also, T. L. Shipman, "A radiation fatality resulting from massive

over-exposure to neutrons and gamma rays," in *Diagnosis and Treatment of Acute Radiation Injury* (New York: International Documents Service, 1961), 113–133.

45 Thomas P. McLaughlin et al., *A Review of Criticality Accidents*, pdf, Los Alamos, New Mexico: Los Alamos National Laboratory, 2000.

46 Alex de Waal, "Lab Leaks," *London Review of Books* (December 2, 2021), 28.

47 Rothman, *On Rims and Ridges*, 322.

48 Kai Bird and Martin J. Sherwin, *American Prometheus: The Triumph and Tragedy of J. Robert Oppenheimer* (New York: Alfred A. Knopf, 2005), 329, 331–332.

49 Michael Heyman, "The Smithsonian: From the Spirit of St. Louis to Enola Gay" (Nov 10, 1994), quoted in Richard H. Kohn "History at Risk: The Case of the *Enola Gay*," in Edward T. Linenthal and Tom Engelhardt, eds. *History Wars: The Enola Gay and Other Battles for the American Past*, New York: Henry Holt and Company, 1996), 164–166.

50 Author unknown, notes on a class in "Museum Studies" taught by Lonnie Bunch, February 12, 1996. Author's personal copy.

51 Quoted in Edward T. Linenthal, "Anatomy of a Controversy," in Linenthal and Engelhardt, *History Wars*, 39.

52 Engelhardt & Linenthal, "Introduction: History Under Siege," in *History Wars*, 4.

53 Kohn, "History At Risk," 167.

54 Author unknown, notes on a class in "Museum Studies."

55 See, for example, John Mecklin, "The Energy Department's Fusion Breakthrough: It's Not Really About Generating Electricity," *Bulletin of the Atomic Scientists*, December 16, 2022.

56 Winling, *Building the Ivory Tower*, 123, 150.

57 Schrecker, *No Ivory Tower*.

Five: Berkeley, Inc.

1 "Principles for Naming," https://vpap.berkeley.edu/space-planning /policies-and-guidelines/principles-naming.

2 Quoted in Stadtman, *The University of California*, 108.

3 Stadtman, *The University of California*, 86, 107–109, 118.

4 Stadtman, "Early Benefactors," *The Centennial Record*. This assessment is repeated in another in-house history of the University, produced by Berkeley's Center for Studies in Higher Education. See Patricia A. Pelfrey, *A Brief History of the University of California* (Berkeley: The University of California, 2004), 16.

5 John Aubrey Douglass, "Creating a Fourth Branch of State Government: The University of California and the Constitutional Convention of 1879," *History of Education Quarterly* 32, 1, (Spring 1992): 72.

6 Reavis and Wallace, "*Entitled to Our Land.*" For brief biographies of regents, see https://www.lib.berkeley.edu/uchistory/general_history/overview/regents/biographies_b.html.

7 Robin W. Winks, *Frederick Billings: A Life* (Berkeley: University of California Press, 1991), 99.

8 Alexandra M. Nickliss, *Phoebe Apperson Hearst: A Life of Power and Politics* (Lincoln: University of Nebraska Press, 2018), 183.

9 Mining Foundation of the Southwest, "Donald H. McLaughlin, 1891–1984," https://www.miningfoundationsw.org/Donald_McLaughlin; Mario Sifuentes Briceño, *Cerro de Pasco: The Greatest Investment of the XXth Century* (Peru: Ludens Communicaciones, 2017), 140, https://online.flippingbook.com/view/155289001/.

10 Quoted in Helfand, *University of California, Berkeley*, 105.

11 Nisbet, *Teachers and Scholars*, 23, 25, 32.

12 Clark Kerr, *The Uses of the University* (New York: Harper and Row, 1966), 2, 45. The book is based on a series of lectures given by Kerr at Harvard in 1963.

13 For a full list of named buildings, see https://dac.berkeley.edu/navigating-cal/campus-buildings.

14 "Berkeley's Founders' Pledge," https://founderspledge.berkeley.edu/.

15 George Hearst appears as a character in season three of the HBO western drama *Deadwood*.

16 Nickliss, *Phoebe Apperson Hearst*, 187–188.

17 George Hearst obituary, *The City Argus* (March 7, 1891). George Hearst's "Senate Memorabilia and Personal Ephemera 1866–1891," George and Phoebe Apperson Hearst Papers, BANC MSS 72/204 c, reel 5, The Bancroft Library, University of California, Berkeley. Hereafter cited as "George and Phoebe Apperson Hearst Papers."

18 Judith Robinson, *The Hearsts: An American Dynasty* (New York: Avon Books, 1991), 22; Nickliss, *Phoebe Apperson Hearst*, 24; Matthew Bernstein, *George Hearst: Silver King of the Gilded Age* (Norman: University of Oklahoma Press, 2021), 7.

19　Quoted in Bernstein, *George Hearst*, 8.

20　Bernstein, *George Hearst*, 211.

21　Bernstein, *George Hearst*, 164; Nickliss, *Phoebe Apperson Hearst*, 148–151, 367–414.

22　Quoted in Robinson, *The Hearsts*, 47-48.

23　"Constitutional Amendment Abolishing Slavery: in Legislature of California, Sixteenth Session, 1865 and 1866," https://csl.primo.exlibrisgroup .com/discovery/fulldisplay?docid=alma990013690020205115&context =L&vid=01CSL_INST:CSL.

24　*Congressional Record*, House, 51st Cong., 1st sess. (26 June 1890): 6544.

25　"History, Art and Archives," *US House of Representatives*, Office of the Historian, *Black Americans in Congress, 1870–2007* (Washington, DC: US Government Printing Office, 2008); "Legislative Interests," https://history .house.gov/Exhibitions-and-Publications/BAIC/Historical-Essays /Temporary-Farewell/Legislative-Interests/ (March 21, 2022); "The Elections (or "Force") Bill," *HarpWeek*, https://elections.harpweek. com/1892/cartoon-1892-medium.asp?UniqueID=24&Year=1892; "Compromise of 1890," *encyclopedia.com*, https://www.encyclopedia.com/history /dictionaries-thesauruses-pictures-and-press-releases/compromise-1890.

26　"Senator's Hearst's Pluck," *San Francisco Examiner* (March 3, 1891), "George and Phoebe Apperson Hearst Papers."

27　Bernstein, *George Hearst*, 142, 191–192.

28　Quoted in Bernstein, *George Hearst*, 132.

29　John F. Dunlap, *The Hearst Saga: The Way It "Really" Was* (John F. Dunlap, self-published, 2002), 75–76.

30　Quoted in Gray Brechin, *Imperial San Francisco*, 351, footnote 11.

31　Bernstein, *George Hearst*, 119–120; Alexandra New Holy, "The Heart of Everything That Is: Paha Sapa, Treaties, and Lakota Identity," *Oklahoma City University Law Review* 23 (1998): 349–350.

32　Bernstein, *George Hearst*, 172; Ferdinand Lundberg, *Imperial Hearst: A Social Biography* (New York: The Modern Library, 1936), 19.

33　"S. 1260—50th Congress (1887–1889): A Bill to restore to the public domain a part of the Uintah Valley Indian Reservation in the Territory of Utah, and for other purposes" (January 9, 1888).

34　Briceño, *Cerro de Pasco*, 28.

35　John Ridge, ed., *Ore Deposits of the Park City District with a Contribution on the Mayflower Lode, in Ore Deposits of the United States, 1933–1967* (New York: The American Institute of Mining, Metallurgical, and Petroleum Engineers, 1968), 1102–1127; Briceño, *Cerro de Pasco*, 24.

36 Briceño, *Cerro de Pasco*, 36.

37 Dora Mayer De Zulen, President of the Press Committee of the Associación
    Pro-Indígena, *The Conduct of the Cerro de Pasco Mining Company* (Lima,
    Peru: El Progresso, 1913), https://archive.org/stream/conductofcerrode
    oomayerich/conductofcerrodeoomayerich_djvu.txt. See, also, Lundberg,
    Imperialist Hearst; Bill Harlan, "Homestake Hangs Up Pick for Last Time,"
    Rapid City Journal (December 14, 2001), https://rapidcityjournal.com
    /homestake-hangs-up-pick-for-last-time/article_593815fa-7473-5e5d-aaf2
    -7597d1034b28.html.

38 Max Uhle and Phoebe A. Hearst, "Package of Photographic Prints Cerro de
    Pasco and Environs," PAHMA Portal, Museum #13–477.

39 See, for example, https://hearstmuseum.berkeley.edu/about/; https://rac
    .berkeley.edu/phoebe/background.html; https://www.berkeleydailyplanet
    .com/issue/2011-04-20/article/37716.

40 Mary Jane Lenz, "George Gustav Heye," in Duane Blue Spruce, ed, *Spirit
    of a Native Place: Building the National Museum of the American Indian*
    (Washington, DC: National Geographic Society and National Museum of the
    American Indian, 2004), 87–115.

41 Curtis M. Hinsley, Jr., "Digging for Identity: Reflections on the Cultural
    Background of Collecting," in Devon A. Mihesuah, ed., *Repatriation Reader:
    Who Owns American Indian Remains?* (Lincoln: University of Nebraska
    Press, 2000,) 45.

42 Brechin, *Imperial San Francisco*, chapter 7.

43 Nickliss, *Phoebe Apperson Hearst*, 246–256.

44 Nickliss, *Phoebe Apperson Hearst*, 53, 257, 258.

45 Nickliss, 262–263; University of California Berkeley, Bancroft Library,
    Records of the Regents of the University of California, 1868–1933, Box 33,
    Anthropology, 1901–1904.

46 Kroeber to Boas in Ira Jacknis, "The First Boasian: Alfred Kroeber and Franz
    Boas, 1896–1905," *American Anthropologist* 104, 2 (2002): 524–525.

47 "George Andrew Reisner (1867–1942)," *Dictionary of Art Historians*, https://
    arthistorians.info/reisnerg; The Bancroft Library, "Foundations of Anthro-
    pology at the University of California," https://bancroft.berkeley.edu
    /Exhibits/anthro/6curriculum2.html; PAHMA, "Phoebe Hearst's Collections,"
    https://hearstmuseum.berkeley.edu/collection/phoebe-hearst-collections/.

48 Quoted in Nickliss, *Phoebe Apperson Hearst*, 263.

49 PAHMA Portal, Museum #12-5038(0), 1913.

50 PAHMA Portal, Museum #12-3062 and #4-4842a, 1903.

51 Max Uhle, "Rules for archaeological research and advice to the investigator," lecture delivered at Universidad Central del Ecuador, Quito, May 31, 1923, in John Howland Rowe, "Max Uhle, 1856–1944: A Memoir of the Father of Peruvian Archaeology," *University of California Publications in American Archaeology and Ethnology* 46, no. 1 (1954): 82, 90, 99.

52 Rowe's tribute to Uhle, published more than a decade after his death, damns him with very faint praise.

53 A search, for example, of the Hearst Museum's digitized database for "Uhle human remains Peru" results in 1,718 items; for "Peru human remains," the result is 2,237 items. PAHMA, Museum Portal, https://portal.hearstmuseum .berkeley.edu/.

54 Uhle, "The Emeryville Shellmound," 2; Max Uhle, "Original Copy of the First Emeryville Paper, CA-Ala-309, 1902," PAHMA, AA #20.

55 *First Quarterly Report of the Department of Anthropology of the University of California, November 30, 1901,* UC Regents Records, CU-23, Box 2, 1.

56 *The Report of the Secretary to the Board of Regents of the University of California for Year Ending June 30, 1906* (Sacramento: W. W. Shannon, 1907), 18.

57 Nickliss, *Phoebe Apperson Hearst,* 259, 274.

58 Nickliss, 273, 280.

59 Nickliss, 277–283; Frederic W. Putnam, "Department of Anthropology," in *Biennial Report of the President of the University on behalf of the Regents to His Excellency the Governor of the State, 1906–1908* (Berkeley: The University Press, October 1908), 91.

60 "Mrs. Hearst's Donation for the Department of Anthropology extracted from the President's Report," 1908, UC Regents Records, Box 55, #36, Anthropology.

61 Burton Benedict, "Anthropology and the Lowie Museum," *Museum Anthropology* 15, no. 4 (November 1991): 26–29.

Six: The Love of Possessions

1 *Sitting Bull: The Collected Speeches* (United States: Coyote Books, 1998), 75.

2 *Biennial Report of the Regents of the University of California for the Years 1873–5,* (Sacramento: G. H. Springer, 1875), 108; Gary J. Tee, "The Elusive C. D. Voy," *Journal of the Historical Studies Group* 39 (September 2010): 17–50; National Park Service, Department of the Interior, "Notice of Inventory Completion: University of California, Berkeley," *Federal Register* 84, 79 (April 24, 2019), 17191–17192.

3 Lee Davis, review of *Time's Flotsam, Journal of California and Great Basin Anthropology* 17, 1 (1995): 141.

4 Deloria, "Defiance," 76.

5 George Goodman Hewett, "Inventory of Vancouver Expedition Collection," c. 1800, Manuscript #1126, The Centre for Anthropology, British Museum.

6 Charles H. Read, "An Account of a Collection of Ethnographical Specimens Formed During Vancouver's Voyage in the Pacific Ocean, 1790–1795," *The Journal of the Archaeological Institute of Great Britain and Ireland* 21 (1892): 100.

7 George Vancouver, *A Voyage of Discovery to the North Pacific Ocean and Round the World, 1791–1795* (London: G. C. and J. Robinson, 1798).

8 Author's correspondence with Jim Hamill and research at the Centre for Anthropology, Department of Africa, Oceania and The Americas, British Museum, London (June 25, 2009); British Museum database, AN330699001.

9 Arnold Pilling, "The British Museum Collection from Avila, California, 1952," PAHMA AA #136.

10 Quoted in Thomas C. Blackburn and Travis Hudson, *Time's Flotsam: Overseas Collections of California Material Culture* (Menlo Park: Ballena Press, 1990), 120–128.

11 Hans-Ulrich Sanner, "California," in Peter Bolz and Hans-Ulrich Sanner, eds., *Native American Art: The Collection of the Ethnological Museum Berlin* (Seattle: University of Washington Press, 1999), 131–145.

12 Arnold Pilling, "The British Museum Collection from Avila, California."

13 Douglas Cole, *Captured Heritage: The Scramble for Northwest Artifacts* (Norman: University of Oklahoma Press, 1995); Joseph Roach, *Cities of the Dead: Circum-Atlantic Performance* (New York: Columbia University Press, 1996).

14 "Sir Augustus Wollaston Franks," *Encyclopedia Britannica Online*, www .britannica.com.

15 Sanner, "California."

16 Julia Hinde, "Invaluable Resource or Stolen Property?" *The Times Higher Education* (September 21, 2007); "Dutch Return Head of Ghana King," *BBC News* (July 23, 2009); Margaret Werry, "Moving Objects (on the Performance of the Dead)," Paper presented at conference of International Federation of Theatre Research, 2013; Margreth Nunuhe, "Cabinet Approves Return of Skulls." *New Era* (March 25, 2011); Elise Pape and Holger Stoecker, Editorial, special issue on "Human Remains from Namibia in German Collections," *Human Remains and Violence* 4, 2 (2018), 1–4; Constance Méheut, "France's Return of the Skulls of 24 Algerian 'Resistance Fighters,'" *New York Times* (October 18, 2022).

17 Thomas Jefferson, "Notes on the State of Virginia" (1787), in *Writings* (New York: The Library of America, 1984), 223–226; Douglas J. Preston, "Skeletons in Our Museums' Closets," *Harper's* (February 1989): 66–75.

18 Robert E. Bieder, *Science Encounters the Indian: The Early Years of American Ethnology* (Norman: University of Oklahoma Press, 1989) 79; Ann Fabian, *The Skull Collectors: Race, Science and America's Unburied Dead* (Chicago: University of Chicago Press, 2010).

19 Alês Hrdlička, *Directions for Collecting Information and Specimens for Physical Anthropology* (Washington, DC: Smithsonian Institution, 1904), 15–17.

20 Hrdlička, *Directions for Collecting Information and Specimens,* 4, 50.

21 Ales Hrdlička, "Contribution to the Physical Anthropology of California: Based on Collections in the Department of Anthropology of the University of California and in the U. S. National Museum," *American Archaeology and Ethnology* 4, no. 2 (June 1906): 4, 50.

22 Robert W. Rydell, *All the World's a Fair: Visions of Empire at American International Expositions, 1876–1916* (Chicago: University of Chicago Press, 1984), 221–223.

23 Alês Hrdlička, "Eugenics and Its Natural Limitations in Man," *Science* 42, no. 1085 (October 1915): 546.

24 Fabian, *The Skull Collectors,* 189; Robert F. Heizer and C. Hart Merriam, "Notes on CA-Ker-185, 1941," PAHMA AA #109.

25 Quoted in Bieder, *Science Encounters the Indian,* 67.

26 "Jacknis, "The First Boasian," 520–532.

27 Quoted in Orin Starn, *Ishi's Brain: In Search of America's Last "Wild" Indian* (New York: W. W. Norton and Co., 2005), 159.

28 Hrdlička, "Contribution to the Physical Anthropology of California," 49.

29 Quoted in Sanner, "California," 135; "Miscellaneous Information, Correspondence and Archaeological Data on Northwestern California Sites," n.d., PAHMA AA #398; Tracy Garcia, "Colonial Encounters with the Past: Paul Schumacher, the Smithsonian Institution and the Origins of Pacific Coast Archaeology," (Master's thesis, Department of Anthropology, University of Oregon, Spring 2010).

30 Frederic W. Putnam, *Reports upon Archaeological and Ethnological Collections from Vicinity of Santa Barbara, California, and from Ruined Pueblos of Arizona and New Mexico, and Certain Interior Tribes,* in George M. Wheeler, *Report upon United States Geographical Surveys West of the One Hundredth Meridian,* vol. 7, "Archaeology" (Washington, DC: US Government Printing Office, 1879), https://www.biodiversitylibrary.org/item/123729#page/25/mode/1up.

31 Putnam, "The Southern Californians," in *Reports,* 1–3, 30.

32 H. C. Yarrow, "Report on the Operations of a Special Party for Making Ethnological Researches in the Vicinity of Santa Barbara, Cal., with a Short Historical Account of the Region Explored" (1876), in *Reports,* 46.

33 Mark Sibley Severance and Dr. H. C. Yarrow, "Notes Upon Human Crania and Skeletons Collected by the Expeditions of 1872–74," in *Reports*, 391–397.

34 Yarrow, "Report on the Operations of a Special Party," in *Reports*, 32–47.

35 Clarence Ruth, "Research Among the Ancient Chumash Village Sites of Northwestern Santa Barbara County, May 1936," PAHMA AA #1.

36 David Prescott Barrows, *The Ethno-Botany of the Coahuilla Indians of Southern California* (Chicago: The University of Chicago Press, 1900, dissertation submitted 1897), https://archive.org/stream/ethnobotany00barr rich?ref=ol#page/82/mode/2up.

37 For examples of the routine exhumation of Native grave sites during construction projects and farming, see Jeremiah B. Lillard, "Notes of the Archaeology of Santa Barbara County, 1937," PAHMA AA #2; and Max Uhle, "The Emeryville Shellmound, 1902," PAHMA AA #20.

38 John C. Merriam, Arnold R. Pilling, and Franklin Fenega, "Archaeological Notes on the Castro Mound, CA-SCL-1, 1910, 1951," PAHMA AA #47.

39 Mary Sheldon Barnes, "Some Primitive Californians," *Popular Science Monthly* 50 (February 1897), 486–495.

40 "Mammoth Cave of Calaveras," *Daily Alta California* (December 7, 1851); untitled story, *Daily Alta California* (October 31, 1853); "The Calaveras Cave," *Daily Alta California* (November 16, 1853); "UC Anthropologists Unearth Mass Grave in Moaning Cave," *Berkeley Gazette* (December 25, 1950); Donald W. Lathrap and William J. Wallace, "Field Notes (Including Burial Records) for Moaning Cave, 1951," PAHMA AA #110.

41 Alexander S. Taylor, *The Indianology of California* vol. 1, ed. Ray Iddings (Three Rocks Research, 2015); Kroeber, *Handbook of the Indians of California*, 963.

42 Stephen Powers, *Tribes of California* (Berkeley: University of California Press, 1976).

43 National Museum of Natural History, Smithsonian Institution Archives, Record Unit 305, Accession #4856.

44 Ira Jacknis, "A Museum Prehistory: Phoebe Hearst and the Founding of the Museum of Anthropology, 1891–1901," *Chronicle of the University of California* 4 (2000); 55–56.

45 *Biennial Report of the Regents of the University of California for the Years 1873–5* (Sacramento: G. H. Springer, 1875), 108.

46 *The Daily Californian* (April 14, 1886).

47 *Annual Report to the Board of Regents of the University of California* (hereafter cited as *Report to the Regents*) (Berkeley: University Press, June 1879), 4; *Report to the Regents* (Sacramento: J. D. Young, June 1881), 21; *Report to the Regents* (Sacramento: J. D. Young, June 1882), 54; *Report to the Regents* (Sacramento: J. D. Young, June 1887), 55.

48 *Report to the Regents* (Berkeley: University Press, 1878), 25–16; *Report to the Regents*, 1879, 4; *Report to the Regents* (Sacramento: J. D. Young, 1880), 24; *Report to the Regents*, 1882, 54; *Report to the Regents* (Sacramento: James J. Ayers, June 1884), 58; *Report to Regents* (Sacramento: James J. Ayers, June 1885), 59; *Report to the Regents* (Sacramento: James J. Ayers, June 1886), 61.

49 *Report to the Regents* (Sacramento: J. D. Young, 1890), 125.

50 "The Philip M. Jones Collection," https://hearstmuseum.berkeley.edu /collection/phoebe-hearst-collections/, accessed October 2, 2020.

51 Philip M. Jones, "Original Photos and Diary, 1901," PAHMA Manuscript #43; Philip M. Jones, "Survey of the Tulare Valley Mounds, Buttonwillow and Adobe Holes (Kern County)," PAHMA Manuscript #42.

52 Records of the Regents of the University of California, 1868–1933, Bancroft Library, CU-1, Box 33, Anthropology.

53 "Mrs. Hearst's Donation for the Department of Anthropology extracted from the President's Report," 1908, Bancroft Library, Records of the Regents, Box 55, #36, Anthropology.

54 Yarrow, "Report on the Operations of a Special Party," 46.

55 Minutes of Department of Anthropology Executive Committee, September 1, 1903, Bancroft Library, Records of the Regents, Box 33, Anthropology 2A, 1901–1904.

56 Frederic W. Putnam, "A Problem in American Anthropology," *Science* 10, no. 243 (August 25, 1899): 235.

57 Robert W. Rydell, *All the World's A Fair: Visions of Empire at American International Expositions, 1876–1916* (Chicago: University of Chicago Press, 1984), 55.

58 "On an Indian Grave Opened on Winter Island, Salem," *Proceedings of the Boston Society of Natural History*, 10 (December 20, 1865), 246–247, https:// www.biodiversitylibrary.org/page/9492228.

59 See, for example, A. L. Kroeber, "The Languages of the Coast of California North of San Francisco," *University of California Publications in American Archaeology and Ethnology* 9, no. 3 (1911): 273–435.

60 Putnam, "A Problem in American Anthropology," 235.

61 A. L. Kroeber, "Progress in Anthropology at the University of California," *American Anthropologist* 8, no. 3 (July–September 1906): 483–492.

62 Quoted in Nickliss, *Phoebe Apperson Hearst*, 298–299.

63 Letter from Frederic Putnam to Alfred Kroeber, July 23, 1906, Bancroft Library, Records of the UC Berkeley Department of Anthropology, CU-23, Box 15, #17.

64 Kroeber, "Progress in Anthropology," 483–492.

65 Hrdlička, "Contribution to the Physical Anthropology of California," 51–52, 54.

66 Records of the Regents, Bancroft Library, Box 33, Anthropology, 1901–1904, Minutes of Department of Anthropology Executive Committee, September 1, 1903.

67 Frederic W. Putnam, "Department of Anthropology," in *Biennial Report of the President of the University on behalf of the Regents to His Excellency the Governor of the State, 1906–1908* (Berkeley: The University Press, October 1908), 89–109.

68 Frederic W. Putnam, "The Anthropological Department of the University of California," 5 typed pages, December 1902, *Last Quarterly Report of the Department of Anthropology of the University of California, November 30, 1901*; Frederic W. Putnam, *The Department of Anthropology of the University of California* (Berkeley: The University Press, August 1905), 4.

69 Putnam, "A Problem in American Anthropology," 234; Putnam, "Department of Anthropology," 89.

70 Pierre Bourdieu and Alain Darbel, *The Love of Art: European Art Museums and Their Public* (Stanford: Stanford University Press, 1990), 113.

71 *Annual Report to the Board of Regents of the University of California* (Sacramento: J. D. Young, June 1887), 55.

72 Graeber and Wengrow, *The Dawn of Everything*, 495–496.

73 *Annual Report of the President of the University on behalf of the Regents to His Excellency the Governor of the State, 1912–1913* (Berkeley: The University Press, 1913), 24.

74 "Indian Ethnology Ably Discussed," *The Daily Californian* (October 2, 1901).

75 Julian Lang, Introduction to Lucy Thompson, *To the American Indian: Reminiscences of a Yurok Woman*, originally published 1916 (Berkeley: Heyday, 1991), xx; Bauer, *California through Native Eyes*; Graeber and Wengrow, *The Dawn of Everything*.

76 *Report of the Secretary to the Board of Regents of the University of California for Year Ending June 30, 1907* (Berkeley: University of California, 1908), 3–4; "Mrs. Hearst's Donation for the Department of Anthropology Extracted from the President's Report," 1908, Records of Regents, Box 55, #36, Anthropology.

77 *Biennial Report of the President of the University on behalf of the Regents to His Excellency the Governor of the State, 1908-1910* (Berkeley: The University Press, 1910).

78 *First Quarterly Report of the Department of Anthropology of the University of California, November 30, 1901*, Records of the UC Berkeley Department of Anthropology, Bancroft Library Archives CU-23, Box 2, 1; Jacknis, "A Museum Prehistory"; "Workshop for the Study of Man," *California Monthly* XLV, September 1954.

79 University of California Robert H. Lowie Museum of Anthropology, *Report to Chancellor Glenn T. Seaborg For the Year Ending June 30, 1959*, 7–8.

80 Charles King, *Gods of the Upper Air: How a Circle of Renegade Anthropologists Reinvented Race, Sex, and Gender in the Twentieth Century* (New York: Doubleday, 2019), 13, 343.

81 Quoted in Jacknis, "Alfred Kroeber as Museum Anthropologist," 29.

82 A. L. Kroeber, "The Indians of California," *Transactions of the Commonwealth Club of California* 4 (December 1909): 437.

83 Arthur J. Ray, "Kroeber and the California Claims: Historical Particularism and Cultural Ecology in Court," in *Central Sites, Peripheral Visions: Cultural and Institutional Crossings in the History of Anthropology*, ed. Richard Handler (Madison: University of Wisconsin Press, 2006), 248–274.

84 Judith Dides, California Department of Parks and Recreation, Interview with Joy Sundberg (January 8, 1990). Author's personal copy.

85 Risling Baldy, *We Are Dancing for You*, 73–99.

86 Thomas Buckley, *Standing Ground: Yurok Indian Spirituality, 1850–1990* (Berkeley: University of California Press, 2002), 16.

87 Robert Spott and A. L. Kroeber, *Yurok Narratives* (Berkeley: University of California Press, 1942), vi.

88 Mary Gist Dornback, "Anthropologist, Educator—UC's Alfred Kroeber Dies," *Council of California Indians Newsletter* (December 25, 1960).

89 Richard Keeling, "Kroeber's *Yurok Myths*: A Comparative Re-Evaluation," *American Indian Culture and Research Journal* 6, no. 3 (1982): 72.

90 A. L. Kroeber, "Two Papers on the Aboriginal Ethnography of California," *Reports of the University of California Archaeological Survey* 56 (March 1, 1962): 58.

91 Personal communication to author, March 7, 2009.

92 A. L. Kroeber, "Yurok National Character," in *The California Indians: A Source Book*, eds. R. F. Heizer and M. A. Whipple (Berkeley: University of California Press, 1971), 387.

93 Lang, "Preface," xx.

94 Tony Platt, "The Yokayo vs. The University of California: An Untold Story of Repatriation," *News from Native California* 6, no. 2 (Winter 2012–2013), 9–14.

95 Kroeber, *Handbook of the Indians of California* (1925), 464, 466. *Costanoan* was a generic term used by anthropologists to define Native groups living on the Pacific Coast from the San Francisco Bay Area to Point Sur. *Ohlone* is the preferred term today.

96 Leventhal et al., "The Ohlone Back from Extinction," 298, 312.

97 Theodora Kroeber, *Alfred Kroeber: A Personal Configuration* (Berkeley: University of California Press, 1979), 57.

98 Alexandra Minna Stern, *Eugenic Nation: Faults and Frontiers of Better Breeding in Modern America* (Berkeley: University of California Press, 2005).

99 For example, in two years from 1915 to 1917, Gifford gave 246 public lectures. *Annual Report of the President of the University on behalf of the Regents to His Excellency the Governor of the State, 1915–1916* (Berkeley: University of California Press, 1916); *Annual Report of the President of the University on behalf of the Regents to His Excellency the Governor of the State, 1917–1918* (Berkeley: University of California Press).

100 E. W. Gifford, "California Indian Physical Types," *Natural History*, 26 (1926): 50–60, reprinted in Heizer and Whipple, *The California Indians*, 97–104.

101 Agassiz, "Permanence of Characteristics."

102 University of California Robert H. Lowie Museum of Anthropology, *Report to Chancellor Glenn T. Seaborg for the Year Ending June 30, 1959*, 7–8. Tribute to Gifford visited May 21, 2022.

Seven: Hoarding

1 Quoted in Stadtman, *The University of California*, 207.

2 *Biennial Report of the Regents of the University of California for the Years 1873–5* (Sacramento: G. H. Springer, 1875), 108; University of California Robert H. Lowie Museum of Anthropology, *Biennial Report for the Year Ending June 30, 1987–89*, 12.

3 Edward M. Luby, "Administrative Update on Compliance with the Native American Graves Protection and Repatriation Act (NAGPRA), January 1, 1999, through December 31, 2000," author's personal copy.

4 By 1989, Native American materials comprised more than 64 percent of the museum's total collection. University of California Robert H. Lowie Museum of Anthropology, *Biennial Report for the Year Ending June 30, 1989*.

5 "Desires Material on Californian Indians," *The Daily Californian* (October 7, 1903).

6 Joseph Peterson, "Excavations in the West Berkeley Shellmound, CA-Ala-307, 1904," PAHMA AA #33.

7 Nels Nelson, "Carbon Copies of N. Nelson's San Francisco Bay Mounds, 1907," PAHMA AA #384; Nelson, "Shellmounds of the San Francisco Bay Region."

8 Alfred L. Kroeber, "Progress in Anthropology at the University of California," *American Anthropologist* 8, no. 3 (July–September 1906): 487.

240 *Notes*

9   Burton Benedict, "Anthropology and the Lowie Museum," *Museum Anthropology* 15, no. 4 (November 1991): 26–29.

10 The secretary was later charged with a crime. At the time his embezzlement was discovered, the regents tried to restrict publicity. They reported the matter in their triannual report for 1901–1904, but only in a typewritten version, not in their usual published form. *Report of the Secretary to the Regents of the University of California for three years ending June 30, 1904*, typewritten, Records of the Regents of the University of California, Bancroft Library, Cal #308df.

11 University-led excavations took place in 1910, 1911, 1912, 1913, 1914, 1923, 1924, 1925, 1928, 1929, 1930, 1935, 1936, 1937–38, 1939, 1940, 1941, 1942, 1946, and 1947.

12 "Indian Coffins Dug Up," *The Daily Californian* (July 5, 1916).

13 John Howland Rowe, "Alfred Louis Kroeber, 1876–1960," *American Antiquity* 27, no. 3 (January 1962): 395–415.

14 Ira Jacknis, personal communication, April 1, 2010.

15 Letter from Dr. H. G. Chappel to Kroeber, December 18, 1911, UCB Anthropology Archives, CU-23, Box 211; letter from J. E. Depue to Kroeber, October 13, 1921, UCB Anthropology Archives, CU-23, Box 48; Kroeber, *Handbook of the Indians of California*, v.

16 Correspondence between Gifford and Golda Williams, October–November 1925, UCB Anthropology Archives, CU-23, Box 181.

17 Gifford, "California Anthropometry," 223.

18 "University of California: A Photographic Essay," *Life* (October 25, 1948): 96.

19 Jacknis, "The First Boasian," 524–525; American Museum of Natural History, Department of Anthropology, Ethnographic Collection, accession #s 50-3482 to 50-3833; Sanner, "California," 142; Blackburn and Hudson, *Time's Flotsam*, 97–98.

20 Letter from A. L. Kroeber to Victor H. Henderson, Secretary of the Regents, December 3, 1909, Records of the Regents of the University of California 1868–1933, University of California Bancroft Library, CU-1, Box 49, File #25, "A. L. Kroeber 1909."

21 Robert McConnell, personal communication to author, November 3, 2009.

22 Max Uhle, "Rules for Archaeological Research and Advice to the Investigator," 90.

23 Max Uhle, "The Emeryville Shellmound, 1902," PAHMA AA #20.

24 Philippe Ariès, *Western Attitudes toward Death from the Middle Ages to the Present* (Baltimore: Johns Hopkins University Press, 1974), 25.

25 Alfred L. Kroeber, *Yurok Myths* (Berkeley: University of California Press, 1976), 228.

26 Max Uhle, "The Emeryville Shellmound, 1902," PAHMA AA #20.

27 "Swedish Savant Discovers Relics of Prehistoric Indians of California Near Lodi," *San Francisco Chronicle* (October 12, 1926).

28 Stewart Bryant, "Notes on the Indian Shell Mounds, Point Reyes Quadrangle, 1934," PAHMA AA #25; Clarence Ruth, "Research Among the Ancient Chumash Village Sites of Northwestern Santa Barbara County, 1936," PAHMA AA #1; Robert M. Heizer et al., "The Archaeology of the Hotchkiss Site, CA-Cco-138, 1937-8," PAHMA AA #14; Robert M. Heizer, "Notes on the Excavation at CA-Sjo-142, 1937-8," PAHMA AA #69; Adan E. Treganza and Ernst N. Johnson, "Burial Data on Ca-Ccc-139, 1939," PAHMA AA #29; Adan E. Treganza, "Data on Soil Samples from Indian Village Sites, 1946," PAHMA AA #267; "The Cedric Thornton Collection from Potter Valley, Mendocino, 1960," PAHMA AA #293.

29 Thornton, "Population History," 27–28.

30 Robert Spott, "Address," *Transactions of the Commonwealth Club of California* 21, no. 3 (1926): 133–135.

31 American Alliance of Museums," Unlawful Appropriation of Objects During the Nazi Era," https://www.aam-us.org/programs/ethics-standards-and -professional-practices/unlawful-appropriation-of-objects-during-the-nazi-era/.

32 A. L. Kroeber, "Specimens," memo from Kroeber to Waterman, c. 1909, A. L. Kroeber Papers, 1869–1972, Bancroft Library, University of California, Berkeley, microfilm 2635, reel #130; letter from Waterman to Kittie Goodwin, August 19, 1915, UCB Anthropology Archives, CU-23, Box 64; correspondence between Kroeber and Rev. Eugene Williams, November 24 and December 8, 1944, UCB Anthropology Archives, CU-23, Box 181.

33 Letter from J. J. Rivers to Martin Kellogg, July 23, 1895, Records of the Regents of the University of California 1868–1933, University of California Bancroft Library, CU-1, Box 24, "Regents Correspondence and Papers," File #21.

34 Editorial footnote in Hrdlička, *Contribution to the Physical Anthropology of California*, 52.

35 Frederic W. Putnam, "Department of Anthropology," in *Biennial Report*. See, also, Frederic Ward Putnam, *The Department of Anthropology of the University of California*.

36 Letter from E. W. Gifford to Nels Nelson, June 16, 1914, PAHMA AA #348.

37 Letter from Kroeber to Gifford (March 24, 1916), quoted in Starn, *Ishi's Brain*, 47.

38 Letter from Gifford to Robert G. Sproul (April 7, 1931), Archaeological Archives, Manuscript Division, PAHMA. See, also, Platt, *Grave Matters*, 165–166.

39 Natasha Johnson, Collections Manager, PAHMA NAGPRA Unit, personal communication to author, April 28, 2008.

40 "Workshop for The Study of Man," *California Monthly*, XLV (September 1954), 15–18, 34.

41 University of California Robert H. Lowie Museum of Anthropology, *Report to Chancellor Glenn T. Seaborg for the Year Ending June 30, 1960.*

42 Quoted in Nickliss, *Phoebe Apperson Hearst*, 426.

43 Gretchen Kell, "Hidden Treasures," *Berkeley Magazine* (May 1997).

44 University of California Museum of Anthropology, *Report to President Robert Gordon Sproul for the Year Ending June 30, 1946*, 11.

45 Lauren Kroiz, "Report for Strategic Planning Conversation," unpublished memo, September 1, 2020.

46 University of California PAHMA, *Biennial Report for the Year Ending June 30, 2001*, 4.

47 The 2021 figure is based on personal communication from Lauren Kroiz, director of the Hearst Museum, February 17, 2021.

48 Alex Wellerstein, "Counting the Dead at Hiroshima and Nagasaki."

49 F. W. Putnam, "Report to President Benjamin Ide Wheeler," 22 typed pages, plus list of additions to museum since July 1, 1906, submitted June 23, 1908, Records of the UC Berkeley Department of Anthropology, Bancroft Library Archives CU-23, Box 2.

50 University of California Museum of Anthropology, *Report to President Robert Gordon Sproul for the Year Ending June 30, 1939*; University of California Robert H. Lowie Museum of Anthropology, *Biennial Report for the Year Ending June 30, 1989*. Infographic by Danielle Elliott.

51 Luby, "Administrative Update," 9.

52 University of California Phoebe A. Hearst Museum of Anthropology, *Annual Report for the Year Ending June 30, 1992*, 2.

53 Luby, "Administrative Update," 6, emphasis added.

54 Luby, "Administrative Update," 7, 9.

55 PAHMA, Museum Portal.

56 Samuel Redman, "The Hearst Museum of Anthropology, the New Deal, and a Reassessment of the 'Dark Age' of the Museum in the United States." *Museum Anthropology* 34, no. 1 (March 2011): 48–49.

57 See, for example, Hearst Portal 1-50699, 1-240248.3, and 1-108395.

58 There are many catalogue entries that include information on human remains but are not categorized this way. See, for example, Hearst Portal 1-33471, 1-6403, 1-32032, 1-168035, 1-35732, 1-86362, 1-138730, 1-34480, 1-133419.13, 1-41961 a-e, 1-17782.

59 Personal communication from Lauren Kroiz, director of the Hearst Museum, April 15, 2021.

60 Hearst Portal L-13028.

61 Hearst Portal 12-4681.

62 Hearst Portal 1-14629, 1-30900, 1-33440.1, 1-34873, 12-4735(0).

63 Hearst Portal 1-133419.13, 1-133438.1.

64 Hearst Portal L-13028.

65 Hearst Portal 1-11380, 1-145306, 1-3090. 1-133471, 12-7674.1, L-13813.

66 Hearst Portal 1-14976, 12-2136.2.

67 Hearst Portal 1-6151.

68 Hearst Portal 1-86362.

69 Edna Fisher, "Identification of Faunal Elements from CA-Ala-309, CA-Ala-307, and other Shell Mounds, 1922-1925," PAHMA AA #17.

70 University of California, "Code of Conduct," adopted by the Regents of the University of California, May 2005.

71 US Department of Interior, National Park Service, "Managing Archaeological Collections," accessed March 23, 2021, https://www.nps.gov/archeology/collections/index.htm; US Department of the Interior, Departmental Manual, *Museum Property Handbook* vols. 1 and 2, accessed March 23, 2021, https://www.doi.gov/sites/doi.gov/files/migrated/museum/policy/upload/mphi-1.pdf.

72 Gordon W. Hewes and Llewellyn Loud, "Field Notes for the Excavation at CA-CCo-138, CCol-1, CA-SJo-68, and others, 1938," PAHMA Manuscript #12.

73 Max Uhle, "The Emeryville Shellmound, 1902," PAHMA AA #20.

74 Nels Nelson and Alfred Wepfer, "Emeryville Mound, #309, Ala-309, 1906," PAHMA AA #348.

75 Joseph Petersen, "Excavations in West Berkeley Shell Mound (Ala-307), 1904," PAHMA AA #33.

76 Ernest Volk, "Explorations in the Delaware Valley, 1904," PAHMA Manuscript # 2.

77 Llewellyn Loud, "Carquinez Mound (CA-Sol-236), 1912," PAHMA AA #364.

78 Llewellyn Loud, "Walnut Creek Mounds (CA-CCO-240), 1913," PAHMA AA #365.

79 Waldo Wedel, "Archaeological Notes on the Howell's Point Site, 1935," PAHMA AA #18.

80 Robert F. Heizer, "Notes on the Excavation at CA-SJo-142, 1937–1938," PAHMA AA #69.

81 Philip M. Jones, "Survey of the Tulare Valley Mounds, Buttonwillow and Adobe Holes, Kern County, 1901," PAHMA Manuscript #42.

82 National Park Service, Department of the Interior, "Notice of Inventory Completion: University of California, Berkeley," *Federal Register* 84, no. 79 (April 24, 2019): 17191–17192.

83 *Annual Report of the President of the University on behalf of the Regents to His Excellency the Governor of the State, 1918–1919* (Berkeley: University of California Press, 1919), 6.

84 See, for example, "Boning in History," *Alameda Times-Star* (August 7, 1931); "Boys Find Old Indian Skulls, *Oakland Post Enquirer* (August 3, 1931), PAHMA AA #33.

85 Donald W. Lathrap and William J. Wallace, "Burial and Feature Records from Ala-307, West Berkeley Mound, 1954," PAHMA AA #179.

86 UC Robert H. Lowie Museum of Anthropology, *Annual Report for the Year Ending June 30, 1964*; *Annual Report for the Year Ending June 30, 1967*; *Annual Report for the Year Ending June 30, 1970*; *Annual Report for the Year Ending June 30, 1973*; *Annual Report for the Year Ending June 30, 1971*; *Annual Report for the Year Ending June 30, 1981*; *Annual Report for the Year Ending June 30, 1987*.

87 University of California Museum of Anthropology, *Report to President Robert Gordon Sproul for the Year Ending June 30, 1942*; University of California Robert H. Lowie Museum of Anthropology, *Report to Chancellor Glenn T. Seaborg for the Year Ending June 30, 1960*.

88 Llewellyn Loud and Jesse Peter, "Sonoma Valley Sites, 1920," PAHMA AA #373; newspaper accounts in 1931 are filed in Joseph Peterson, "Excavations in West Berkeley Shell Mound (Ala-307), 1904," PAHMA AA #33.

89 Jerome Hamilton, "Some Historic Facts about the Ancient Shell Mounds of San Mateo, 1936," PAHMA AA #182; E. Von der Porten, "Fort Ross, California, Sites Investigated by Santa Rosa Junior College, 1961," PAHMA AA #336; Jean Moss and Ruth Mead, "Salvage Report on CA-CCo-311, 1967," PAHMA Manuscript #32.

90 Quoted by Frederic Golden, "Some Bones of Contention," *Time* (December 21, 1981).

91 Putnam, *The Department of Anthropology of the University of California*, 39.

92 Waldo W. Wedel, "Personal Journals . . . , 1935–1936," PAHMA AA #382.

93 Thomas T. Waterman, "Catalogue of the J. McCord Stilson Collection, September 1914," PAHMA AA #198; "Swedish Savant Discovers Relics of Prehistoric Indians of California Near Lodi," *San Francisco Chronicle* (October 12, 1926), PAHMA AA #36. For another example of this kind of collaboration, see Robert F. Heizer, "Notes on the Drescher Site (CA-Sac-109), 1937," PAHMA AA# 64.

94 Redman, "The Hearst Museum of Anthropology," 47.

95 Lt. Cmdr. Stewart Bryant, "Notes on the Indian Shell Mounds, Point Reyes Quadrangle, August 1934," PAHMA AA #25.

96 Robert F. Heizer and Ernst N. Johnson, "Archaeology Notes on the Maltby Site (CA-CCo-250), 1937–1940," PAHMA AA #50; Robert F. Heizer, "Original Field Notes CA-CCo-137, 1947," PAHMA AA # 101; Albert Mohr and David D. Fredrickson, "Appraisal of the Archaeological Resources of Black Butte

Reservoir . . . 1948," PAHMA AA #202; Albert B. Elsasser and Robert F. Heizer, "Notes on the Gunther Island Site, CA-Hum-67, 1964," PAHMA AA #90.

97 Letter from Mrs. Mary J Gates to John C. Merriam, April 10, 1910, filed in John C. Merriam et al., "Archaeological Notes on the Castro Mound, CA-SCL-1, 1910," PAHMA AA #47; Harold A. Estep, "The Indians of Pelican Island, 1933," PAHMA Manuscript #38; John W. Winterbourne, "Report on Sunny Hills Ranch Site No. 1, 1939," PAHMA AA #462.

98 J. B. Lillard, "Notes February 1934," filed in Robert Heizer and Franklin Fenega, "Excavation at CA-Sac-127, 1941," PAHMA AA #42.

99 Thomas R. Hester, "Robert Fleming Heizer, 1915–1979," *American Antiquity* 47, no. 1 (1982), 99–107.

100 University of California Museum of Anthropology, *Report to President Robert Gordon Sproul for the Year Ending June 30, 1942.*

101 UC Museum of Anthropology, *Report to President Robert Gordon Sproul for the Year Ending June 30, 1948.*

102 Hearst Museum Portal #12-652.

103 Letter from William C. Huff to Heizer (December 10, 1959), UCB Anthropology Archives, CU-23, Box 73.

104 American Alliance of Museums, "AAM Code of Ethics of Museums," 1993, amended 2000, https://www.aam-us.org/programs/ethics -standards-and-professional-practices/code-of-ethics-for-museums/.

105 Letter from Kroeber to W. F. Chamlee, December 2, 1932, UCB Anthropology Archives CU-23, Box 41.

106 Mary Sheldon Barnes, "Some Primitive Californians," *Popular Science Monthly* 50 (February 1987).

107 Max Uhle, "The Emeryville Shellmound, 1902," PAHMA AA #20.

108 Edna Fisher, "Shell Deposits of the Monterey Peninsula," PAHMA AA #17.

109 Robert F. Heizer and Franklin Fenega "Archaeological Notes on CA-Col-3, 1938," PAHMA AA #57; Robert F. Heizer, "Notes on the Miller Mound (CA-Col-1), 1936," PAHMA AA #94.

110 John C. Merriam, Arnold R. Pilling, and Franklin Fenega, "Archaeological Notes on the Castro Mound, CA-SCL-1, 1946," PAHMA AA #47.

111 Donald W. Lathrap and William J. Wallace, "Burial and Feature Records from Ala-307, West Berkeley Mound, 1950–1958," PAHMA AA #179.

112 "Miscellaneous Information, Correspondence and Archaeological Data on Northwestern California Sites," no date, PAHMA AA #398; Tracy Garcia, *Colonial Encounters with the Past: Paul Schumacher, the Smithsonian Institution, and the Origins of Pacific Coast Archaeology* (University of Oregon: Master's Thesis, Spring 2010).

113 Nels Nelson, "Archaeological Reconnaissance Notes, the California Coast from the Russian River to the Golden Gate, June 1909," PAHMA AA #385.

114 Llewellyn L. Loud, "Walnut Creek Mounds #419–428, CA-Cco-240), 1913," PAHMA AA #365.

115 Jeremiah B. Lillard, "Notes on the Archaeology of Santa Barbara County, 1937," PAHMA AA #2.

116 Thomas Waterman, "Yurok Marriages," unpublished typed and handwritten manuscript, c. 1909-1928, Trinidad, CA: Trinidad Historical Museum; Robert E. Greengo, "Report on Field Trip, July–August 1950," PAHMA AA #72; Harry K. Roberts, *Walking in Beauty: Growing Up With The Yurok Indians* (Trinidad, California: The Press at Indian Art, 2011), 54.

117 Livingstone Stone, *Report of Operation During 1874 at the US Salmon Hatching Establishment on the McCloud River, California* (April 1875), Washington, DC: 43rd Congress, 2nd session, Senate Miscellaneous Document #108.

118 Sherrie Smith-Ferri, "The Human Faces of Pomo Indian Basketry," introduction to Samuel A. Barrett, *Pomo Indian Basketry* (Berkeley: Phoebe Hearst Museum of Anthropology, 1996), 1; S. A. Barrett, "The Ethno-Geography of the Pomo and Neighboring Indians," *University of California Publications in American Archaeology and Ethnology* 6, no. 1.

119 Interview with Tom Renick, June 28, 2012; Sherrie Smith-Ferri, *"You'll Have Lots of Work When the Indians Are Done Picking Hops*: A. O. Carpenter's Native American Photographs," in Marvin A. Schenk, Karen Holmes, and Sherrie Smih-Ferri, eds., *Aurelius O. Carpenter: Photographer of the Mendocino Frontier* (Ukiah, CA: Grace Hudson Museum and Sun House, 2006), 99.

120 Interview with Sherrie Smith-Ferri, February 13, 2012; Alfred P. Parsell, "The Ukiah Valleys and Its Indian Population," in Rebecca Snetselaar, ed., *Stories and Scholarship From the Social Science Field Laboratory, Ukiah, California, 1939–1948* (Mendocino: Mendocino County Museum, 2002), 7.

121 Quoted in Khal Schneider, "Making Indian Land in the Allotment Era: Northern California's Indian Rancherias," *The Western Historical Quarterly* 41, no. 4 (Winter 2010): 439.

122 Letter from John L. McNab to Benjamin Ide Wheeler, 5 July 1906, UCB Anthropology Archives, CU-23, Box 14.

123 C. E. Kelsey, "Robbing Indian Graves," report sent to Commissioner of Indian Affairs, August 20, 1910, United States Indian Service Archives, RG 75 CCF Ukiah Report, #50087-1910-General Services-175, 11E3 4/26/4 Box 562.

124 Correspondence between Barrett and Kroeber, and McNab and Kroeber, July–August 1906, UCB Anthropology Archives, CU-23, Box 14.

125 Platt, "The Yokayo vs. The University of California," 9–14.

126 Letter from H. W. Cole to Cecile Clarke, February 9, 1931, Cecile Clarke

Papers, Clarke Historical Museum, Eureka, California.

127   Axel R. Lindgren, "Introduction" to Robert F. Heizer and John E. Mills, eds., *The Four Ages of Tsurai: A Documentary History of the Indian Village on Trinidad Bay* (1952) (Trinidad, CA: Trinidad Museum Society, 1991).

128   E. F. Benedict, "The Yuroks: Their Origin, Legends and Culture," *Del Norte Triplicate* (April 8, 1949).

129   Robert F. Heizer and Albert B. Elsasser, "Archaeology of HUM-67, the Gunther Island Site in Humboldt Bay, Northwestern California," *Reports of the University of California Archaeological Survey* 62 (1964): 15, footnote 3.

130   Vine Deloria Jr., *Custer Died For Your Sins: An Indian Manifesto* (New York: Macmillan, 1969), 100.

131   For this discussion of NICPA, I draw upon Platt, *Grave Matters.*

132   Interview with Joy Sundberg, November 3, 2009.

133   Interview with Michael Moratto, July 16, 2008.

134   The museum reported a gift of "human osteological material" from Santa Cruz and "eleven boxes of archaeological material" from San Bernardino in 1987. UC Robert H. Lowie Museum of Anthropology, *Biennial Report for the Year Ending June 30, 1987*; Inouye quoted in Jack F. Trope and Walter R. Echo-Hawk, "NAGPRA," in *Repatriation Reader: Who Owns Native American Remains?* ed. Devon A. Mihesuah (Lincoln: University of Nebraska Press, 2000), 139.

135   Luby, "Administrative Update on Compliance with the Native American Graves Protection and Repatriation Act: January 1, 1999, through December 31, 2000."

136   *United Nations Declaration on the Rights of Indigenous Peoples*, G.A. Res. 61/295, UN Doc. A/RES/61/295 (October 2, 2007).

137   The 2021 figure is based on personal communication from Lauren Kroiz, director of the Hearst Museum, February 17, 2021.

138   Kroeber, *The Languages of the Coast of California*; Gifford, *California Anthropometry.*

Eight: Misanthropology

1   John McGroarty, *California: Its History and Romance* (Los Angeles: Grafton, 1911), 42.

2   Former US senator and media pundit quoted in Jesus Jiménez, "CNN Drops Rick Santorum After Dismissive Comments about Native Americans," *New York Times* (May 22, 2021).

3 William White, *Our California: History–Social Science for California* (Glenview, Illinois: Pearson Scott Foresman, 2006).

4 Barbara A. Davis, *Edward S. Curtis: The Life and Times of a Shadow Catcher* (San Francisco: Chronicle Books, 1985), 70; Stephen Powers, *Tribes of California* (Berkeley: University of California Press, 1976), 404.

5 Carey McWilliams, *California, The Great Exception* (Berkeley: University of California Press, 1998), 58–59.

6 Carey McWilliams, *Southern California: An Island on the Land* (Santa Barbara: Peregrine Smith, 1973); David M. Wrobel and Michael C. Steiner, eds., *Many Wests: Place, Culture, and Regional Identity* (Lawrence: University of Kansas Press, 1997); William Deverell, *Whitewashed Adobe: The Rise of Los Angeles and the Remaking of its Mexican Past* (Berkeley: University of California Press, 2004).

7 See for example Louise Heaven (aka Lucia Norman), *A Youth's History of California* (San Francisco: A. Roman, 1867).

8 See, for example, John S. Hittel, *Hittel's Hand-Book of Pacific Coast Travel* (San Francisco: A. L. Bancroft and Co., 1885); D. L. Thornbury, *California's Redwood Wonderland: Humboldt County* (San Francisco: Sunset Press, 1923).

9 Gerald D. Nash, "California and Its Historians: An Appraisal of Histories of the State," *Pacific Historical Review* 50, no. 4 (November 1981): 387–413.

10 Samuel, *Theatres of Memory*.

11 Hubert Howe Bancroft, *The Wild Tribes*, vol. 1 of *The Native Race* (San Francisco: A. L. Bancroft and Co., 1883), 301.

12 Herbert Bolton, "Forward" to Phil Townsend Hanna, *California through Four Centuries: A Handbook of Memorable Historical Dates* (New York: Farrar and Rinehart, 1935), vii.

13 David P. Barrows, *Berbers and Blacks: Impressions of Morocco, Timbuktu and the Western Sudan* (New York: The Century Co., 1927).

14 Samuel J. Holmes, *The Negro's Struggle for Survival: A Study in Human Ecology* (Berkeley: University of California Press 1937), 4.

15 For examples of popular authors who cited Berkeley anthropologists and historians in their books, see Gertrude Atherton, *California, An Intimate History* (New York: Harper and Brothers, 1914); Rockwell D. Hunt, *New California The Golden* (Sacramento: California State Department of Education, 1937); Enola Flower, *A Child's History of California* (Caldwell, Idaho: The Caxton Printers, Ltd., 1941); Rockwell D. Hunt, *Fifteen Decisive Events of California History* (Los Angeles: Historical Society of Southern California, 1959); Irmagarde Richards, *Our California Home* (Sacramento: California State Printing Office, 1933); Frank C. Carpenter, *North America* (New York: American Book Company,1915); James J. Jones and Lee

McDonald, *Voices of the Golden State* (San Francisco: Leswing Communications, 1971); Andrew F. Rolle, *California A History* (New York: Thomas Y. Crowell, 1963, 1967).

16 The term is used by W. G. Sebald to describe people who thought of themselves as neutral during the Nazi era. Quoted in Schwartz, *The Emergence of Memory*, 67.

17 Gifford, *California Anthropometry*, 224. According to information published in the anthropology museum's annual reports, Gifford gave 134 lectures to 8,900 students in 1912–1913; 106 lectures in 1914–1915; 112 lectures to 6,171 visitors in 1915–1916; 174 lectures in 1916–1917; 134 lectures to 11,000 students in 1917–1918; and 72 lectures in 1918–1919.

18 On Hittell's lectures at Berkeley, see *Annual Report of the Secretary to the Board of Regents of the University of California for Year Ending June 30, 1893* (Sacramento: A. J. Johnston, 1893), 33; Theodore H. Hittell, *History of California* (San Francisco: N. J. Stone and Company, 1898), 728–730.

19 Flyer for "Illustrated Lectures in History and Geography for Classes from the Public Schools, Provided by the University of California Museum of Anthropology, 1912–1913," UC Berkeley, Bancroft Library, UC Regents Records, Box 81, #11, Anthropology; Hunt, *California the Golden*.

20 Herbert E. Bolton, "The Mission as a Frontier Institution in the Spanish-American Colonies," *American Historical Review* 23, no. 1 (October 1917): 42–61; Edward D. Castillo, "The Language of Race Hatred," in Bean, *The Ohlone Past and Present*, 271–289.

21 Herbert E. Bolton and Ephraim D. Adams, *California Story* (Boston: Allyn and Bacon, 1922), 80.

22 "Herbert Eugene Bolton, History: Berkeley," *Online Archive of California*, http://texts.cdlib.org/view?docId=hb6r29p0fn&doc.view=frames&chunk.id=div00003&toc.depth=1&toc.id=.

23 George Orwell, "Politics and the English Language," *Horizon* (April 1946); Hugh Trevor-Roper, ed., *Hitler's Table Talk, 1941–1944: His Private Conversations* (New York: Enigma Books, 2000), 621.

24 Mario Ranalletti, "When Death Is Not The End: Toward a Typology of the Treatment of Corpses of 'Disappeared Detainees' in Argentina from 1975 to 1983," in Anstett and Dreyfus, eds, *Destruction and Human Remains*, 146–179; Rémi Korman, "The Tutsi Body in the 1984 Genocide: Ideology, Physical Destruction, and Memory," *ibid.*, 226–242.

25 The Historical Marker Database, "Don Pedro Fages Expedition," https://www.hmdb.org/m.asp?m=42034.

26 Max Oelschlaeger, *The Idea of Wilderness: From Prehistory to the Age of Ecology* (New Haven: Yale University Press, 1991), 24. See, also, Anderson, *Tending the Wild*.

27 Quoted in C. Perry Paterson, "Jurisprudence of Oliver Wendell Holmes," *Minnesota Law Review* 933 (1947).

28 Iqbal, Saima S. "Louis Agassiz, Under a Microscope," 19 March 2021, https://www.thecrimson.com/article/2021/3/18/louis-agassiz-scrut/; *Louis Agassiz and Polygenism,* Center for the History of Medicine at Countway Library, https://collections.countway.harvard.edu/onview/exhibits/show/this-abominable-traffic/agassiz-and-polygenism; Louis Agassiz, "Permanence of Characteristics in Different Human Species," in *A Journey in Brazil by Professor and Mrs. Louis Agassiz* (Boston: Ticknor and Fields, 1869), 492–532.

29 Atherton, *California,* 15.

30 Burnett, "Governor's Annual Message to the Legislature" (January 7, 1851).

31 Theodore H. Hittell, *History of California,* vol. 1, 729.

32 C. D. Willard, "The Padres and The Indians," *Land of Sunshine* (September 1894), 73.

33 Atherton, *California,* 15.

34 Henry K. Norton, *The Story of California: From The Earliest Days to the Present* (Chicago: A.C. McClurg, 1913), 10.

35 Robert Glass Cleland, *California Pageant: The Story of Four Centuries* (New York: Alfred A. Knopf, 1946), 33.

36 Hunt, *Fifteen Decisive Events of California History.*

37 Uhle, "The Emeryville Shellmound, 1902."

38 Barnes, "Some Primitive Californians"; W. W. Kane, "Aborigine of State Had Few Clothes and Looked Like a Gorilla," *Los Angeles Examiner* (May 19, 1923); "Boning in History," *Alameda Times-Star* (August 7, 1931); Jerome Hamilton, "Some Historic Facts about the Ancient Shell Mounds of San Mateo, 1936," PAHMA AA #182.

39 Carey McWilliams, *Brothers Under the Skin* (Boston: Little, Brown and Company, 1944), 50, 67.

40 Rockwell D. Hunt, *California the Golden* (Sacramento: California State Department of Education, 1911), 20.

41 Heaven, *A Youth's History of California,* 21.

42 John S. Hittel, *A History of San Francisco and Incidentally of the State of California* (San Francisco: A. L. Bancroft, 1878), 20.

43 Arthur W. Dunn, *Civics: The Community and the Citizen* (Sacramento: State Board of Education, 1910), 43.

44 Flower, *A Child's History of California,* 22.

45 White, *Our California,* 37.

46 Gray, *History of California,* 338.

47 M. C. Bruner, *California—Its Amazing Story* (Los Angeles: Wetzel Publishing Co., 1949), 8.

48 Durlynn C. Anema et al., *California: Yesterday and Today* (Morristown, NJ: Silver Burdett, 1984), 167.

49 Gifford, "California Indian Physical Types"; Graeber and Wengrow, *The Dawn of Everything*, 496.

50 Stephen Garton, "'Liberty of the Nation': Eugenics in Australia and New Zealand and the Limits of Illiberalism," in Diane B. Paul, John Stenhouse, and Hamish G. Spencer, eds., *Eugenics at the Edges of Empire: New Zealand, Australia, Canada, and South Africa* (Switzerland: Palgrave Macmillan, 2018), 31.

51 John S. Hittell, *A History of San Francisco*, 60.

52 Hanna, *California Through Four Centuries*, viii.

53 Hrdlička, "Contribution to the Physical Anthropology of California," 50, 54.

54 Holmes, *The Negro's Struggle*, 2, 4, 5, 96.

55 Cook, *The Conflict*, 34, 255–263.

56 Barrows, *The Ethno-Botany of the Coahuilla Indians*, 82.

57 Clarence Ruth, "Research Among the Ancient Chumash Village Sites of Northwestern Santa Barbara County, 1936," PAHMA AA #1.

58 Thornton, "Population History," 39.

59 Berkeley, *A Proposal for the Better Supplying of Churches* (1724).

60 Margolin, Introduction to *Life in a California Mission*; Thornton, "Population History," 27.

61 Helen Elliott Bandini, *History of California* (New York: American Book Co., 1908), 89.

62 Carpenter, *North America*, 334–335.

63 Maidee Thomas Nelson, *California, Land of Promise* (Caldwell, Idaho: Caxton Printers, 1962), 96.

64 Bolton, "The Mission as a Frontier Institution."

65 Holmes, *The Negro's Struggle*, 4–6.

66 Harry Ellington Brook, "Olden Times in Southern California," *Land of Sunshine* (July 1894): 29–31.

67 Harr Wagner and Mark Keppel, *California History* (San Francisco: Harr Wagner Publishing Co., 1922), 69–70.

68 Robert Glass Cleland, *From Wilderness to Empire: A History of California, 1542–1900* (New York: Alfred A. Knopf, 1944), 287–288.

69 Joseph LeConte, *The Race Problem in the South*, Lecture and discussion before Brooklyn Ethical Association, May 1892 (New York: D. Appleton and Company, 1892), 367.

70 Jacqueline Fear-Segal, *White Man's Club: Schools, Race, and the Struggle of Indian Acculturation* (Lincoln: University of Nebraska Press, 2007), 223; David Wallace Adams, *Education for Extinction: American Indians and the Boarding School Experience, 1875–1928* (Lawrence: University Press of Kansas, 1994); Shaunna Oteka McCovey, "Resilience and Responsibility: Surviving the New Genocide," in *Eating Fire, Tasting Blood: An Anthology of the American Indian Holocaust*, ed. Marijo Moore (Philadelphia: Running Press, 2006), 289; Lewis Meriam, *The Problem of Indian Administration: Report of a Survey Made at Request of Honorable Hubert Work, Secretary of the Interior* (Baltimore: The Johns Hopkins Press, 1928), 329, 330, 332.

71 Adams, *Education for Extinction*; Fear-Segal, *White Man's Club*; Cathleen Cahill, *Federal Fathers and Mothers: A Social History of the United States Indian Service, 1869–1933* (Chapel Hill: University of North Carolina Press, 2011); Nabokov, *Native American Testimony*, 216–217.

72 Quoted in Adams, *Education for Extinction*, 231.

73 Cahill, *Federal Fathers and Mothers*; Margaret D. Jacobs, *White Mother to a Dark Race: Settler Colonialism, Maternalism, and the Removal of Indigenous Children in the American West and Australia, 1880–1940* (Lincoln: University of Nebraska Press, 2009); Susan Bernardin et al., *Trading Gazes: Euro-American Women Photographers and Native Americans, 1880–1940* (Newark: Rutgers University Press, 2003).

74 Stern, *Eugenic Nation*; Linda Villarosa, *Under the Skin: The Hidden Toll of Racism on American Lives and on the Health of Our Nation* (New York: Doubleday, 2022). The actual number of forced sterilizations in the United States in the twentieth century can only be estimated. Personal communication from Alexandra Minna Stern, June 12, 2022.

75 Alexandra Minna Stern and Tony Platt, "Sterilization Abuse in State Prisons: Time to Break With California's Long Eugenic Patterns," *Huffington Post* (July 23, 2013), http://www.huffingtonpost.com/alex-stern/sterilization-california-prisons_b_3631287.html.

Nine: Sorrow Songs

1 W. E. B. Du Bois, *The Souls of Black Folk*, introduced by Arnold Rampersad (New York: Alfred A. Knopf, 1993), 88–89, 206.

2 "Disquisition by E. W. Scripps, An Hour with a University President," March 21, 1909. E. W. Scripps Papers, Ohio University Libraries Digital Archival Collections, https://media.library.ohio.edu/digital/collection/scripps/id/3806/.

3   Stern, *Eugenic Nation*, 123.

4   Charles Rasmussen and Rick Tilman, *Jacques Loeb: His Science and Social Activism and Their Philosophical Foundations* (Philadelphia: American Philosophical Society, 1998); Jacques Loeb, "Heredity and Racial Inferiority, *Crisis* 8 (June 1914); Letter from Jacques Loeb to W. E. B. Du Bois, May 14, 1914, reprinted in Herbert Aptheker, ed., *The Correspondence of W. E. B. Du Bois, vol. 1, 1877–1934* (Amherst: University of Massachusetts Press, 1973), 195–196; Jacques Loeb, "Biology and War," *Science* (January 26, 1917).

5   Personal communication to author, March 25, 2022.

6   LeConte, *The Race Problem in the South*, 361.

7   Laura Briggs, *Reproducing Empire: Race, Sex, Science and US Imperialism in Puerto Rico* (Berkeley: University of California Press, 2002); Paul et al., *Eugenics at the Edges of Empire*; David Mitchell and Sharon Snyder, "The Eugenic Atlantic: Race, Disability, and the Making of an International Eugenic Science, 1800–1945," *Disability and Society* 18, no. 7 (2003): 843–864. On contemporary eugenics, see the work of the Center for Genetics and Society, https://www.geneticsandsociety.org/about-us.

8   See, for example, Paul Popenoe and Roswell Hill Johnson, *Applied Eugenics* (New York: Macmillan, 1926).

9   Nellie Bowles, "'Replacement Theory,' a Racist, Sexist Doctrine, Spreads in Far-Right Circles," *New York Times* (March 18, 2019).

10 Stern, *Eugenic Nation*.

11 Teresa Watanabe, "UC Berkeley Is Disavowing Its Eugenics Research Fund After Bioethicist and Other Faculty Call It Out," *Los Angeles Times* (October 26, 2020).

12 Stadtman, *The University of California*, 107; Agassiz, "Permanence of Characteristics."

13 Hrdlička, "Contribution to the Physical Anthropology of California, 51–52, 54.

14 Samuel J. Holmes, *The Negro's Struggle for Survival: A Study in Human Ecology*. Berkeley: UC Press, 1937, 220.

15 *A Decade of Progress in Eugenics: Scientific Papers of the Third International Congress of Eugenics* (Baltimore: The Williams and Wilkins Company, 1934).

16 For background on the Human Betterment Foundation, see Stern, *Eugenic Nation* and Tony Platt, *Bloodlines: Recovering Hitler's Nuremberg Laws, From Patton's Trophy to Public Memorial* (Boulder: Paradigm Publishers, 2006).

17 Charles M. Goethe, "Eugenic Pamphlet no. 12," quoted in Platt, *Bloodlines*, 60.

18 Tony Platt, "Engaging the Past: Charles M. Goethe, American Eugenics, and Sacramento State University," *Social Justice* 32, no. 2 (2005): 17–33.

19 "A History of UCSF," https://history.library.ucsf.edu/evans.html. See, also, Stadtman, *The University of California*, 209.

20 Platt, *Bloodlines*, 55–58. Little remains of the internal records of the HBF, but participation in board meetings is recorded in E. S. Gosney Papers and Records of the Human Betterment Foundation, The Caltech Archives, California Institute of Technology. Personal communication from Peter Callopy, University Archivist, Caltech, September 17, 2020.

21 Holmes, *The Negro's Struggle*, 222–223.

22 Stern, *Eugenic Nation*, 89–90.

23 Samuel J. Holmes, *The Eugenic Predicament* (New York: Harcourt, Brace, 1933), 122–123.

24 Samuel J. Holmes, "Effect of Migration on the Natural Increase of the Negro," in Harry F. Perkins, ed., *A Decade of Progress: The Third International Congress of Eugenics* (Baltimore: The Williams and Wilkins Company, 1934), 122–123.

25 Nisbet, *Teachers and Scholars*, 133.

26 Holmes, *The Eugenic Predicament*, 123.

27 Arthur R. Jensen, "How Much Can We Boost IQ and Scholastic Achievement?" *Harvard Educational Review* 39, no. 1 (Winter 1969): 2–5, 81–82, 117, https://arthurjensen.net/wp-content/uploads/2014/06/How-Much-Can-We-Boost-IQ-and-Scholastic-Achievement-OCR.pdf.

28 Richard J. Herrnstein and Charles Murray. *The Bell Curve: Intelligence and Class Structure in American Life* (New York: The Free Press, 1994), 551.

29 *The Autobiography of Joseph LeConte*, edited by William Dallam Armes (New York: D. Appleton and Co., 1903), 13, 144–153, 230–231.

30 See a petition to Berkeley's Building Name Review Committee in support of the unnaming of Moses Hall on the grounds of Moses's advocacy of white supremacy: https://chancellor.berkeley.edu/task-forces/building-name-review-committee/moses-hall.

31 https://chancellor.berkeley.edu/task-forces/building-name-review-committee/building-name-review-barrows-hall; https://prabook.com/web/david.barrows/3765274; Kenton J. Clymer, "Humanitarian Imperialism: David Prescott Barrows and the White Man's Burden in the Philippines," *Pacific Historical Review* 45, no. 4 (1976): 495–517.

32 Aimé Césaire, *Discourse on Colonialism* (New York: Monthly Review Press, 1955); Michel Foucault, *Society Must Be Defended: Lectures at the Collège de France, 1975–6* (London: Allen Lane, 2003).

33 Julian Go, "The Imperial Origins of American Policing: Militarization and Imperial Feedback in the Early 20th Century," *American Journal of Sociology* 125, no. 5 (March 2020). See, also, Stern, *Eugenic Nation*, 115–118.

34 Quoted in Stern, *Eugenic Nation*, 116; August Vollmer, *The Criminal* (Brooklyn: Foundation Press, 1949).

35 Minutes of Department of Anthropology Executive Committee, September 1, 1903, Bancroft Library, UC Regents Records, Box 33, Anthropology 2A, 1901–1904.

36 Frederick L. Hoffman, *Race Traits and Tendencies of the American Negro* (New York: The Macmillan Company, 1896), 236; William H. Thomas, *The American Negro, What He Was, What He Is, and What He May Become* (New York: The Macmillan Company, 1901), 179; Joseph A. Tillinghast, *The Negro in Africa and America* (New York: The Macmillan Company, 1902), 160.

37 Howard W. Odum, *Social and Mental Traits of The Negro: Research in Conditions of the Negro Race in Southern Towns* (New York: Columbia University Press, 1910), 171; A. L. Kroeber and T. T. Waterman, *Source Book on Anthropology* (Berkeley: University of California Press, 1920), 554.

38 "Eugenics a Snare," *Clunes Guardian and Gazette* (April 24, 1914); "Eugenics a Joke," *Marybrough Chronicle* (March 6, 1914); "Eugenics Condemned," *Tribune* (Melbourne, May 16), 1914; "Eugenics is a Joke, Declares Professor," *Miami News* (March 4, 1914).

39 Kroeber and Waterman, *Source Book on Anthropology*, 553.

40 Alfred L. Kroeber, *Anthropology* (New York: Harcourt, Brace and Company, 1923), 7–8, 59, 85; see, also, A. L Kroeber, "18 Professions," *American Anthropologist* (1915): 283–288, https://archive.org/details/jstor-660348/page/n1/mode/2up.

41 Kroeber, *Anthropology*, 3.

42 Kroeber and Waterman, *Source Book*, 553.

43 Kroeber, "The Indians of California," *Transactions of the Commonwealth Club of California* 4 (December 1909): 430–437.

44 Kroeber, *Anthropology*, 2–3.

45 "Eugenics a Joke," *Marybrough Chronicle* (March 6, 1914).

46 Kroeber, *Anthropology*, 58, 59, 61, 86.

47 Kroeber, *Anthropology*, 504–505.

48 King, *Gods of the Upper Air*, 204–205.

49 A. L. Kroeber, "Thomas Talbot Waterman," *American Anthropologist* 39 (1937): 527–529.

50 T. T. Waterman, "The Subdivisions of the Human Race and Their Distribution," *American Anthropologist* 26 (1924): 474–490.

51 W. E. B. Du Bois, *The Philadelphia Negro: A Social Study* (1899), introduced by Elijah Anderson (Philadelphia: University of Pennsylvania Press, 1996), 385–387.

52 Waterman, "The Subdivisions," 483.

53 Du Bois, *The Souls*, 206–207.

54 W. E. B. Du Bois, "Preface" to *The Negro* (New York: Holt, 1915).

55 Kroeber, *Anthropology*, 505; Du Bois, "The Negro in the United States," *The Negro*.

56 Du Bois, *The Souls*, 37, 88–89.

Ten: Making History

1 "Campus Conversations: UC Berkeley Chancellor Carol Christ," December 18, 2019, https://www.youtube.com/watch?v=kHsFIn_REhc.

2 Nisbet, *Teachers and Scholars*, 23.

3 Leslie King-Hammond, "A Conversation with Fred Wilson," in Corrin, ed., *Mining The Museum*, 32.

4 Carol Hyman, "UC Berkeley's Greek Theatre Turns 100 Years Old This Month," *UC Berkeley News* (September 11, 2003), ww.berkeley.edu/news /media/releases/2003/09/11_greek.shtml.

5 Winling, *Building the Ivory Tower*, 119.

6 Quoted in Hyman, "UC Berkeley's Greek Theatre."

7 Charles Griswold's term "recollective architecture" is cited in Edward T. Linenthal, *Preserving Memory: The Struggle to Create America's Holocaust Museum* (New York: Viking, 1995), 72.

8 "Campanile," https://campanile.berkeley.edu/.

9 Pacific Coast Architecture Database (PCAD), "University of California, Berkeley, Charles Franklin Doe Memorial Library," http://pcad.lib .washington.edu/building/1694/.

10 Nisbet, *Teachers and Scholars*, 26. When Memorial Stadium was reopened after its renovation in 2012, it became a memorial to "all Californians who have lost their lives in war."

11 Gretchen Kell, "A Splendid Esplanade: Major Overhaul for Campanile's Grounds," *Berkeley News* (September 2, 2014), https://news.berkeley .edu/2014/09/02/a-splendid-esplanade-major-overhaul-beneath-campanile/.

12 Andrew Ruppenstein, "Don Pedro Fages Expedition," *The Historical Marker Database*, https://www.hmdb.org/m.asp?m=42034.

13 "The Faculty Club," https://www.berkeleyfacultyclub.com/club/history. The club's original design was created by Bernard Maybeck and implemented by John Galen Howard. It was included in the National Register of Historic Places in 1982.

14 Quoted in William Warren Ferrier, *Ninety Years of Education in California, 1846–1936* (Berkeley: Sather Gate Book Store, 1937), 182.

15 George Berkeley, "On the Prospect of Planting Arts and Learning in America" (1728), https://www.bartleby.com/270/13/15.html.

16 Dolores Hayden, *The Power of Place: Urban Landscapes as Public History* (Cambridge: MIT Press, 1995), 43, 46, 247.

17 Helfand, *The University of California, Berkeley*, 4, 230.

18 Here I draw upon an analysis of nationalism developed by Eric Hobsbawm and Terence Ranger, eds., *The Invention of Tradition* (Cambridge: Cambridge University Press, 1983); E. J. Hobsbawm, *Nations and Nationalism Since 1780: Programme, Myth, Reality* (Cambridge: Cambridge University Press, 1990); Benedict Anderson, *Imagined Communities: Reflections on the Origin and Spread of Nationalism* (London: Verso, 1991); and Homi K. Bhabha, ed., *Nation and Narration* (London: Routledge, 1990).

19 https://www.berkeley.edu/.

20 https://www.berkeley.edu/about/history-discoveries.

21 Eric Hobsbawm, "Introduction: Inventing Traditions," in Hobsbawm and Ranger, *The Invention of Tradition*, 1.

22 Public Affairs, UC Berkeley, "California Memorial Stadium," November 10, 2005, https://www.berkeley.edu/news/media/releases/2005/11/10_stadium_history.shtml; Buckley, *Geoarchaeological Testing Report for the University of California*.

23 John Mitchell, Congressional Medal of Honor Society, https://www.cmohs.org/recipients/john-mitchell; US Army, Indian War Campaigns, https://www.army.mil/medalofhonor/citations3.html; Kell, "A Splendid Esplanade."

24 George Berkeley, *A Proposal for the Better Supplying of Churches in Our Foreign Plantations: And for Converting the Savage Americans to Christianity, by a College to Be Erected in the Summer Islands, Otherwise Called the Isles of Bermuda* (London: H. Woodfall, 1725).

25 Visited October 25, 2021.

26 Phoebe A. Hearst Museum of Anthropology website, accessed July 1, 2020, https://hearstmuseum.berkeley.edu/collection/north-america/.

27 Orin Starn, *Ishi's Brain: In Search of America's Last "Wild" Indian* (New York: W. W. Norton and Co., 2005); Platt, *Grave Matters*, 40–41, 73-75, 164–165.

28 O'Neill, *An Account of the Birth and Growth of the Faculty Club*, 1; Paltridge, *A History of the Faculty Club*, 3.

29 Elena Kadvany, "First Ohlone Restaurant Opens," *San Francisco Chronicle* (September 11, 2022); https://www.makamham.com/cafeohlone.

30 https://www.berkeley.edu/about/history-discoveries.

31 Harvey Helfand, "Walking Central Campus' Classical Core." *University of California, Berkeley: An Architectural Tour* (Princeton Architectural Press, 2002), 53.

32 Mark Yudof, "For 150 Years, UC Science and Agriculture Transform California," *California Agriculture*, 66, no. 2 (2012), https://escholarship.org/uc/item/9gw5b2hq.

33 Matthew Shaer, "The Sordid History of Mount Rushmore," *Smithsonian Magazine* (October 2016); John Taliaferro, *Great White Fathers: The Story of the Obsessive Quest to Create Mount Rushmore* (New York: PublicAffairs, 2002), 186.

34 "The University of California Land Grab," 15.

35 https://botanicalgarden.berkeley.edu/the-garden; M. Kat Anderson, *Tending The Wild: Native American Knowledge and the Management of California's Natural Resources* (Berkeley: University of California Press, 2005), 1.

36 http://www.savio.org/speeches_and_interviews.html.

37 Internal FBI memo from D. J. Brennan, Jr. to W. C. Sullivan (January 27, 1965), discussed in Seth Rosenfeld, *Subversives: The FBI's War on Student Radicals, and Reagan's Rise to Power* (New York: Farrar, Straus and Giroux, 2012).

38 Governor's Commission on the Los Angeles Riots, *Violence in the City—An End or a Beginning?* (Los Angeles: College Book Store, 1965).

39 The memorial was designed by Mark Brest van Kempen, the winner of a competition organized by the Berkeley Art Project. "The Invisible Monument to Free Speech," podcast, April 15, 2011, https://99percentinvisible.org/episode/episode-22-the-invisible-monument-to-free-speech/.

40 Telephone interview with Steve Silberstein, July 9, 2021.

41 https://www.sfgate.com/news/article/SYMBOLIC-STEPS-UC-Berkeley-names-legendary-2819919.php.

42 Monument Lab, *National Monument Audit* (The Andrew W. Mellon Foundation, 2021).

43 "Loafers Guide to the UC Berkeley Campus," University of California Berkeley Facilities, p. 26, https://facilities.berkeley.edu/sites/default/files/loafers_guide_to_the_u.c._berkeley_campus_pt._1.pdf, accessed December 14, 2020.

44 Monument Lab, *National Monument Audit*, 21–22.

45 Alan J. Taylor, "Unstable Motives: Propaganda, Politics and the Late Work of Alexander Calder," *American Art* 26, no. 1 (2012): 25–47.

46 Personal communication from Stephanie Reeves, BAMPFA Associate Registrar for Exhibitions, (June 29, 2021).

47 Personal communication from Charles Cannon, Associate Dean, Law School, UC Berkeley (October 25, 2021).

Epilogue: Reckoning

1 Leslie King-Hammond, "A Conversation with Fred Wilson," in Lisa G. Corrin, ed., *Mining The Museum: An Installation by Fred Wilson* (New York: The New Press, 1994), 33.

2 Ginger Lewis, UC Berkeley track team, 1976, visited October 2021.

3 Office of the Chancellor, "About the Building Name Review Committee," https://chancellor.berkeley.edu/building-name-review-committee/about.

4 In response to a student-led initiative, the university unnamed the LeConte building in November 2020, but as of December 2022 a plaque and oak tree, first planted to honor the LeConte brothers in 1898, still stood.

5 Kavya Gupta, "Members of Berkeley Community Condemn Plaque Honoring Allegedly Racist LeConte Brothers," *The Daily Californian* (January 30, 2022), https://www.dailycal.org/2022/01/30/members-of-berkeley-community -condemn-plaque-honoring-allegedly-racist-leconte-brothers/.

6 Chancellor Carol Christ, "Unnaming LeConte and Barrows Hall," message to campus community, November 18, 2020.

7 "Harriet Nathan, Interview with Albert H. Bowker (1991), University History Series, Online Archive of California, http://oac.cdlib.org/ark:/13030 /hb1p3001qq/?brand=oac4.

8 Daryl E. Lembke, "801 UC ARRESTS: Berkeley Rebellion Broken Up," *Los Angeles Times* (December 4, 1964).

9 Michael Harris, "Black Professors Still a Rarity at UC and Stanford," *San Francisco Chronicle* (June 2, 1986).

10 Wallace Turner, "12 Riot Deputies Indicted for Actions at Berkeley," *New York Times* (February 3, 1970).

11 Tom Dalzell, *The Battle for People's Park, Berkeley 1969* (Berkeley: Heyday, 2019), 264, 316.

12 Baldwin, "Public University, Private Developer"; Winling, *Building the Ivory Tower*, 145–146.

13 "3,000 Protest Crim School Closing," *The Black Panther* (June 8, 1974).

14 Tony Platt, *Beyond These Walls: Rethinking Crime and Punishment in the United States* (New York: St. Martin's Press, 2018), 257–264.

15 Memorandum from Berkeley Chancellor Albert H. Bowker to University Budget Committee, May 1, 1972. Author's personal copy.

16 Chris A. Smith, "Economic Leverage: UC Students Fought Tooth and Nail to Divest from South Africa," *California* (2014), https://alumni.berkeley .edu/california-magazine/fall-2014-radicals/economic-leverage-uc-students -fought-tooth-and-nail-divest/.

17 *UC Berkeley Tribal Forum Report.*

18 California Assembly Bill No. 2836 (September 27, 2018); Alexander Teodorescu, "Gov. Jerry Brown Signs Bill to Facilitate Repatriation of Native American Remains at UC Campuses," *Daily Californian* (October 10, 2018); Nanette Asimov, "UC Berkeley Struggles with How To Return Native American Remains," *San Francisco Chronicle* (September 30, 2018).

19 Executive Dept. State of Calif. Gov. Gavin Newsom, Exec. Order N-15-19 (June 18, 2019).

20 University of California, *Interim Policy NAGPRA*, Cover Letter (July 24, 2020), https://www.ucop.edu/research-policy-analysis-coordination /policies-guidance/curation-and-repatriation/nagpra-letter-pjn-7-24-2020.pdf.

21 Andrew Garrett, Melissa Stoner, Susan Edwards, Jeffery MacKie-Mason, Nicole Myers-Lim, Benjamin W. Porter, Elaine C. Tennant, and Verna Bowie, *Native American Collections in Archives, Libraries, and Museums at the University of California, Berkeley*, Office of the Vice Chancellor for Research, University of California, Berkeley (March 15, 2019).

22 Chancellor Carol Christ, "Talking Points," Native American Cultural Affiliation and Repatriation Work Session, Berkeley, unpublished memo (January 31, 2020). Author's personal copy.

23 Alaa Elassar, "UC Berkeley is Repatriating Cultural Artifacts, Including Ancestral Remains, to Indigenous Tribes," *CNN* (October 17, 2022), https:// www.cnn.com/2022/10/17/us/uc-berkeley-indigenous-repatriate-cultural -artifacts-reaj/index.html?utm_source=facebook&utm_medium=news_tab.

24 Sogorea Te' Land Trust, "What is Rematriation?" https://sogoreate -landtrust.org/what-is-rematriation/.

25 Logan Jaffe, Mary Hudetz, Ash Ngu (ProPublica), and Graham Lee Brewer (NBC News), "America's Biggest Museums Fail to Return Native Human Remains," *ProPublica* (January 11, 2023), https://www.propublica.org/article /repatriation-nagpra-museums-human-remains.

26 Maile Arvin, *Possessing Polynesians: The Science of Settler Colonial Whiteness in Hawai'i and Oceania* (Durham: Duke University Press, 2019).

27 For the work of the Brand Management Team in the Office of Business Contracts and Brand Protection, see https://bcbp.berkeley.edu/ and https:// brand.berkeley.edu/brand-protection/.

28 Kévorkian, "Earth, Fire, and Water," in Anstett and Dreyfus, *Destruction and Human Remains*, 89–116; Max Bergholz, "As If Nothing Ever Happened: Massacres, Missing Corpses, and Silence in the Bosnian Community," *ibid.*, 15–45.

29 Deloria, "Defiance," 80.

30 UC President Michael Drake, quoted in Royster, "This Land," 41. For the university's similarly problematic land acknowledgement, see https://cejce .berkeley.edu/nasd.

31 Joseph Pierce, "Your Land Acknowledgment Is Not Enough," *Hyperallergic*
    (October 12, 2022), https://hyperallergic.com/769024/your-land
    -acknowledgment-is-not-enough/.

32 Jack Guy, "Pope Apologizes for 'Deplorable Evil' of Indigenous Abuse in
    Canadian Catholic Residential Schools," CNN (July 25, 2022), https://www
    .cnn.com/2022/07/25/americas/pope-francis-canada-speech-intl/index.html;
    Damian Costello, "Pope Francis' Visit to Canada is a Time to Embrace an
    Indigenous Future," *National Catholic Reporter* (July 18, 2022), https://www
    .ncronline.org/news/opinion/pope-francis-visit-canada-time-embrace
    -indigenous-future; Robin Wall Kimmerer, *Braiding Sweetgrass: Indigenous
    Wisdom, Scientific Knowledge, and the Teachings of Plants* (Minneapolis:
    Milkweed Editions, 2015).

33 Neighborhood Unitarian Universalist Church, "Truth and Reconciliation Re-
    port" (December 2020); Donna Perkins, "What's In A Name" (June 5, 2022).
    Author's personal copies.

34 California Forced Sterilization Reparations Coalition, "Creating Meaning-
    ful and Accessible Plaques and Markers to Recognize Sterilization Survi-
    vors and Eugenics in California," (July 2022), https://docs.google.com
    /document/d/1MEIiF4XdZYX9FQGo9gnRzkxbIE-Fo8tO95GkKxFAt-Y
    /edit; Gitanjali Mahapatra and Nate Perez, "LA County-UDSC Medical
    Center Unveils Artwork Apologizing to Women Forcibly Sterilized There,"
    KPCC Los Angeles (July 12, 2022), https://laist.com/news/la-county
    -usc-medical-center-unveils-artwork-apologizing-to-women-forcibly
    -sterilized-there; Hilda L. Solis, "New Artwork Unveiled to Recognize
    Practice of Coerced Sterilization at LAC+USC Medical Center" (July 11,
    2022), https://hildalsolis.org/new-artwork-unveiled-to-recognize
    -practice-of-coerced-sterilization-at-lacusc-medical-center/.

35 Presidential Advisory Commission on Holocaust Assets in the United States,
    Report to the President, 2, 17.

36 "Princeton History Project: History and Slavery," https://slavery.princeton
    .edu/stories/princeton-and-slavery-holding-the-center; "Yale, Slavery and
    Abolition," http://www.yaleslavery.org/YSA.pdf; "Georgetown University:
    Slavery, Memory and Reconciliation," http://slavery.georgetown.edu/;
    Craig Steven Wilder, *Ebony and Ivy: Race, Slavery, and the Troubled
    History of America's Universities*, New York: Bloomsbury Publishing, 2013;
    Andrew Delbanco, "Endowed by Slavery," *New York Review of Books* (June
    23, 2022): 59–62.

37 As of November 2022, Berkeley has committed some funds to speed up the
    process of repatriation that should have happened more than thirty years
    ago, and given the Hearst Museum the go-ahead to raise its own funds for
    mak-'amham/Cafe Ohlone. After a year, says the administration, the café
    needs to be self-supporting. The University of California announced in April
    2022 that it would waive in-state tuition fees for California residents who are

members of federally recognized tribes. Fifty-five California tribes, comprising around eighty thousand people (including most Bay Area tribes), are not federally recognized. Elena Kadvany, "Ohlone Café at UC Berkeley a Hopeful Step in Healing History," *San Francisco Chronicle* (April 23, 2022); Danielle Echeverria, "Free Tuition for Native Americans," *San Francisco Chronicle* (April 27, 2022). Stephanie Saul, "Top Colleges Where Affirmative Action Was Banned Say It's Needed," *New York Times* (August 27, 2022).

38 Michael S. Tilden, "Native American Graves Protection and Repatriation Act," California State Auditor Report no. 2021-047, November 2022.

39 Royster, "This Land," 41.

40 Walt Lara Sr., "Closing Statement," in Kishan Lara-Cooper and Walter J. Lara Sr., *Ka'm-t'em: A Journey toward Healing* (Pechanga, CA: Great Oak Press, 2019), 311.

41 Jennifer Raff, *Origin: A Genetic History of the Americas* (New York: Twelve, 2022), 268.

42 Severson et al., "Ancient and Modern Genomics of the Ohlone Indigenous Population of California."

43 For parallel ideas, see Adom Getachew, "The Slow Road to Real 'Decolonization,'" *New York Times* (August 2, 2020); Pankaj Mishra, "Grand Illusions," *The New York Review of Books* (November 19, 2020): 31–32.

44 Judge Abby Abinanti, "A Letter to Justice O'Connor," *UCLA Indigenous Peoples' Journal of Law, Culture, and Resistance* 1 (2004): 1, 18.

Acknowledgments

1 Quoted in Lois Beckett, "Mike Davis, California's 'Prophet of Doom,' on Activism in a Dying World: 'Despair is Useless,'" *The Guardian* (August 31, 2022).

Sources *and* Bibliography

A Note on Sources

This book is based on two years of archival research (2020–2022), primarily at the Bancroft Library, University of California, Berkeley. I also draw upon previous research for *Grave Matters: The Controversy over Excavating California's Buried Indigenous Past* (Heyday 2011 and 2021); for a paper ("Bitter Legacies: A War of Extermination, Grave Looting, and Culture Wars in the American West") presented at a conference on "Corpses of Mass Violence and Genocide" in Manchester, England, September 2013; for a case study of Indigenous resistance to predatory archaeology ("The Yokayo vs. the University of California: An Untold Story of Repatriation," *News from Native California* 26, no. 2, winter 2012–2013); and for an article on culture wars ("Last Stands: History, Memory, and the California Story," *Boom California*, October 25, 2018).

Archives and Collections

A. L. Kroeber Papers (1869–1972), Bancroft Library, University of California, Berkeley.

Annual Reports to the University of California Board of Regents (1872–1908), Bancroft Library, University of California, Berkeley.

Annual Reports (1942–1992), Phoebe A. Hearst Museum of Anthropology, University of California, Berkeley.

Archaeological Archives, Phoebe A. Hearst Museum of Anthropology, University of California, Berkeley.

Cecile Clarke Papers, Clarke Historical Museum, Eureka, California.

Director Records, Peabody Museum, Harvard University.

Division of Archaeology, Smithsonian National Museum of Natural History.

E. S. Gosney Papers and Records of the Human Betterment Foundation, The Caltech Archives, California Institute of Technology.

Ethnographic Collection, American Museum of Natural History, Department of Anthropology.

Sources and Bibliography

E. W. Scripps Papers, Ohio University Libraries Digital Archival Collections.

George and Phoebe Apperson Hearst Papers, Bancroft Library, University of California, Berkeley.

Inventory of Vancouver Expedition Collection, British Museum, London.

Northwest Information Center, California Historical Resources, Information System, Sonoma State University, California.

Phoebe A. Hearst Museum of Anthropology, Hearst Museum Portal, https://portal.hearstmuseum.berkeley.edu/.

Records of the Regents of the University of California (1868–1933), Bancroft Library, University of California, Berkeley.

Records of the University of California Department of Anthropology, Bancroft Library, University of California, Berkeley.

Reports of the Department of Anthropology of the University of California, Bancroft Library, University of California, Berkeley.

The Centre for Anthropology, Department of Africa, Oceania, and the Americas, British Museum, London.

Books

Adams, David Wallace. *Education for Extinction: American Indians and the Boarding School Experience, 1875–1928*. Lawrence: University Press of Kansas, 1994.

Agassiz, Louis. "Permanence of Characteristics in Different Human Species," in *A Journey in Brazil by Professor and Mrs. Louis Agassiz*. Boston: Ticknor and Fields, 1869.

Akins, Damon B. and William J. Bauer Jr. *We Are the Land: A History of Native California*. Berkeley: University of California Press, 2021.

Anderson, Benedict. *Imagined Communities: Reflections on the Origin and Spread of Nationalism*. London: Verso, 1991.

Anderson, M. Kat. *Tending The Wild: Native American Knowledge and the Management of California's Natural Resources*. Berkeley: University of California Press, 2005.

Anema, Durlynn C. et al. *California: Yesterday and Today*. Morristown, NJ: Silver Burdett, 1984.

Anstett, Elisabeth and Jean-Marc Dreyfus, eds. *Destruction and Human Remains: Disposal and Concealment in Genocide and Mass Violence*. Manchester: Manchester University Press, 2014.

Aptheker, Herbert, ed. *The Correspondence of W. E. B. Du Bois, vol. 1, 1877–1934*. Amherst: University of Massachusetts Press, 1973.

Ariès, Philippe. *Western Attitudes toward Death from the Middle Ages to the Present*. Baltimore: Johns Hopkins University Press, 1974.

Armes, William Dallam, ed. *The Autobiography of Joseph LeConte*. New York: D. Appleton and Co., 1903.

Arvin, Maile. *Possessing Polynesians: The Science of Settler Colonial Whiteness in Hawai'i and Oceania*. Durham: Duke University Press, 2019.

Atherton, Gertrude. *California, An Intimate History*. New York: Harper and Brothers, 1914.

Baldy, Cutcha Risling. *We Are Dancing for You: Native Feminisms and the Revitalization of Women's Coming-of-Age Ceremonies*. Seattle: University of Washington Press, 2018.

Bancroft, Hubert Howe. *The Wild Tribes*, vol. 1 of *The Native Race*. San Francisco: A. L. Bancroft & Co., 1883.

———. *California Inter Pocula*. San Francisco: The History Company, 1888.

Bandini, Helen Elliott. *History of California*. New York: American Book Co., 1908.

Barker, Pat. *Another World*. New York: Farrar, Straus and Giroux, 1998.

Barrett, Samuel A. *Pomo Indian Basketry*. Berkeley: Phoebe Hearst Museum of Anthropology, 1996.

Barrows, David Prescott. *The Ethno-Botany of the Coahuilla Indians of Southern California*. Chicago: The University of Chicago Press, Ph.D. dissertation, 1900.

———. *Berbers and Blacks: Impressions of Morocco, Timbuktu and the Western Sudan*. New York: The Century Co., 1927.

Bauer, William J., Jr. *California through Native Eyes: Reclaiming History*. Seattle: University of Washington Press, 2016.

Bauman, Zygmunt. *Modernity and the Holocaust*. Ithaca: Cornell University Press, 2000.

Baumgardner, Frank H., III. *Killing for Land in Early California: Indian Blood at Round Valley, 1856–1863*. New York: Algora Publishing, 2006.

Bean, Lowell John, ed. *The Ohlone Past and Present: Native Americans of the San Francisco Bay Region*. Menlo Park, CA: Ballena Press, 1994.

Bender, Thomas. *A Nation among Nations: America's Place in World History*. New York: Hill and Wang, 2006.

Berkeley, George. *A Proposal for the Better Supplying of Churches in Our Foreign Plantations: And for Converting the Savage Americans to Christianity, by a College to Be Erected in the Summer Islands, Otherwise Called the Isles of Bermuda*. London: H. Woodfall, 1725.

Bernardin, Susan et al. *Trading Gazes: Euro-American Women Photographers and Native Americans, 1880–1940*. Newark: Rutgers University Press, 2003.

Bernstein, Matthew. *George Hearst: Silver King of the Gilded Age*. Norman: University of Oklahoma Press, 2021.

Bhabha, Homi K., ed. *Nation and Narration*. London: Routledge, 1990.

Bieder, Robert E. *Science Encounters the Indian: The Early Years of American Ethnology*. Norman: University of Oklahoma Press, 1989.

Bird, Kai and Martin J. Sherwin. *American Prometheus: The Triumph and Tragedy of J. Robert Oppenheimer*. New York: Alfred A. Knopf, 2005.

Blackburn, Thomas C. and Travis Hudson. *Time's Flotsam: Overseas Collections of California Material Culture*. Menlo Park: Ballena Press, 1990.

Bolton, Herbert E. and Ephraim D. Adams. *California Story*. Boston: Allyn and Bacon, 1922.

Bourdieu, Pierre and Alain Darbel. *The Love of Art: European Art Museums and Their Public*. Stanford: Stanford University Press, 1990.

Brechin, Gray. *Imperial San Francisco: Urban Power, Earthly Ruin*. Berkeley: University of California Press, 1999.

Briceño, Mario Sifuentes. *Cerro de Pasco: The Greatest Investment of the XXth Century*. Peru: Ludens Communicaciones, 2017.

Briggs, Laura. *Reproducing Empire: Race, Sex, Science and US Imperialism in Puerto Rico*. Berkeley: University of California Press, 2002.

Bruner, M. C. *California—Its Amazing Story*. Los Angeles: Wetzel Publishing Co., 1949.

Buckley, Thomas. *Standing Ground: Yurok Indian Spirituality, 1850–1990*. Berkeley: University of California Press, 2002.

Cahill, Cathleen. *Federal Fathers and Mothers: A Social History of the United States Indian Service, 1869–1933*. Chapel Hill: University of North Carolina Press, 2011.

Carpenter, Frank C. *North America*. New York: American Book Company, 1915.

Carrigan, William D. and Clive Webb. *Forgotten Dead: Mob Violence against Mexicans in the United States, 1848–1928*. New York: Oxford University Press, 2013.

Caughey, John Walton. *California*. New York: Prentice-Hall, 1940.

Césaire, Aimé. *Discourse on Colonialism*. New York: Monthly Review Press, 1955.

Cleland, Robert Glass. *From Wilderness to Empire: A History of California, 1542–1900*. New York: Alfred A. Knopf, 1944.

———. *California Pageant: The Story of Four Centuries*. New York: Alfred A. Knopf, 1946.

Cole, Douglas. *Captured Heritage: The Scramble for Northwest Artifacts*. Norman: University of Oklahoma Press, 1995.

Cook, Sherburne. *The Conflict between the California Indian and White Civilization*. Berkeley: University of California Press, 1943.

Corrin, Lisa G., ed. *Mining The Museum: An Installation by Fred Wilson*. New York: The New Press, 1994.

Dalzell, Tom. *The Battle for People's Park, Berkeley 1969*. Berkeley: Heyday, 2019.

Davis, Barbara A. *Edward S. Curtis: The Life and Times of a Shadow Catcher*. San Francisco: Chronicle Books, 1985.

Dawson, Grace S. *California: The Story of Our Southwest Corner*. New York: Macmillan, 1939.

Deloria, Philip J. *Playing Indian*. New Haven: Yale University Press, 1998.

Deloria, Vine, Jr. *Custer Died For Your Sins: An Indian Manifesto*. New York: Macmillan, 1969.

Deverell, William. *Whitewashed Adobe: The Rise of Los Angeles and the Remaking of Its Mexican Past*. Berkeley: University of California Press, 2004.

De Zulen, Dora Mayer. *The Conduct of the Cerro de Pasco Mining Company*. Lima, Peru: El Progresso, 1913.

Du Bois, W. E. B. *The Philadelphia Negro: A Social Study* (1899), introduced by Elijah Anderson. Philadelphia: University of Pennsylvania Press, 1996.

———. *The Souls of Black Folk* (1903), introduced by Arnold Rampersad. New York: Alfred A. Knopf, 1993.

———. *The Negro.* New York: Holt, 1915.

———. *Black Reconstruction in America: An Essay toward a History of the Part Black Folk Played in the Attempt to Reconstruct Democracy in America 1860–1880.* New York: Atheneum, 1973. First published 1935.

Duncan, Robert. *The H. D. Book.* Buffalo: Frontier Press, 1984.

Dunlap, John F. *The Hearst Saga: The Way It "Really" Was.* Self-published, 2002.

Dunn, Arthur W. *Civics: The Community and the Citizen.* Sacramento: State Board of Education, 1910.

Eckstein, Arthur M. *Bad Moon Rising: How the Weather Underground Beat the FBI and Lost the Revolution.* New Haven: Yale University Press, 2016.

Fabian, Ann. *The Skull Collectors: Race, Science and America's Unburied Dead.* Chicago: University of Chicago Press, 2010.

Fear-Segal, Jacqueline. *White Man's Club: Schools, Race, and the Struggle of Indian Acculturation.* Lincoln: University of Nebraska Press, 2007.

Ferrier, William Warren. *Ninety Years of Education in California, 1846–1936.* Berkeley: Sather Gate Book Store, 1937.

Flower, Enola. *A Child's History of California.* Caldwell, Idaho: The Caxton Printers, Ltd., 1941.

Foucault, Michel. *Society Must Be Defended: Lectures at the Collège de France, 1975–6.* London: Allen Lane, 2003.

Franklin, H. Bruce ed. *Prison Writing in 20th-Century America.* New York: Penguin Books, 1998.

George, Henry. *Progress and Poverty: An Inquiry into the Cause of Industrial Depression and the Increase of Want with Increase of Wealth.* New York: D. Appleton and Co., 1881.

Governor's Commission on the Los Angeles Riots. *Violence in the City—An End or a Beginning?* Los Angeles: College Book Store, 1965.

Graeber, David and David Wengrow. *The Dawn of Everything: A New History of Humanity.* New York: Farrar, Straus and Giroux, 2021.

Gray, A. A. *History of California from 1542.* Boston: D. C. Heath, 1934.

Haines, Michael R. and Richard H. Steckel, eds. *A Population History of North America.* Cambridge: Cambridge University Press, 2000.

Hales, Peter Bacon. *Atomic Spaces: Living on the Manhattan Project.* Urbana: University of Illinois Press, 1997.

Handler, Richard, ed. *Central Sites, Peripheral Visions: Cultural and Institutional Crossings in the History of Anthropology.* Madison: University of Wisconsin Press, 2006.

Hanna, Phil Townsend. *California through Four Centuries: A Handbook of Memorable Historical Dates.* New York: Farrar and Rinehart, 1935.

Hartman, Saidiya V. *Scenes of Subjection: Terror, Slavery, and Self-Making in Nineteenth-Century America.* New York: Oxford University Press, 1997.

Hayden, Dolores. *The Power of Place: Urban Landscapes as Public History.* Cambridge: MIT Press, 1995.

Heaven, Louise (aka Lucia Norman). *A Youth's History of California.* San Francisco: A. Roman, 1867.

Heizer, Robert F., ed., *An Anthropological Expedition, or Get It Through Your Head, or Yours for the Revolution.* Berkeley: University of California Department of Anthropology, 1970.

———. *They Were Only Diggers: A Collection of Articles from California Newspapers, 1851–1886.* Ramona, CA: Ballena Press, 1974.

———. *Handbook of North American Indians, California,* vol. 8. Washington, DC: Smithsonian Institution, 1978.

Heizer, Robert F. and John E. Mills, eds. *The Four Ages of Tsurai: A Documentary History of the Indian Village on Trinidad Bay* (1952). Trinidad, CA: Trinidad Museum Society, 1991.

Heizer, Robert F. and M. A. Whipple, eds. *The California Indians: A Source Book.* Berkeley: University of California Press, 1971.

Helfand, Harvey. *University of California, Berkeley: An Architectural Tour and Photographs.* New York: Princeton Architectural Press, 2002.

Helmer, John. *Drugs and Minority Oppression.* New York: Seabury, 1975.

Herrnstein, Richard J. and Charles Murray. *The Bell Curve: Intelligence and Class Structure in American Life.* New York: The Free Press, 1994.

Hittel, John S. *A History of San Francisco and Incidentally of the State of California.* San Francisco: A. L. Bancroft, 1878.

———. *Hittel's Hand-Book of Pacific Coast Travel.* San Francisco: A. L. Bancroft and Co., 1885.

Hittell, Theodore H. *History of California.* San Francisco: N. J. Stone and Company, 1898.

Hobsbawm, Eric J. *Nations and Nationalism Since 1780: Programme, Myth, Reality.* Cambridge: Cambridge University Press, 1990.

Hobsbawm, Eric J. and Terence Ranger, eds. *The Invention of Tradition.* Cambridge: Cambridge University Press, 1983.

Hoffman, Eva. *After Such Knowledge: Memory, History, and the Legacy of the Holocaust.* New York: PublicAffairs, 2004.

Hoffman, Frederick L. *Race Traits and Tendencies of the American Negro.* New York: The Macmillan Company, 1896.

Hrdlička, Aleš. *Directions for Collecting Information and Specimens for Physical Anthropology.* Washington, DC: Smithsonian Institution, 1904.

Holmes, Samuel J. *The Eugenic Predicament.* New York: Harcourt, Brace, 1933.

————. *The Negro's Struggle for Survival: A Study in Human Ecology*. Berkeley: University of California Press, 1937.

Hunt, Rockwell D. *California the Golden*. Sacramento: California State Department of Education, 1911.

————. *New California the Golden*. Sacramento: California State Department of Education, 1937.

————. *Fifteen Decisive Events of California History*. Los Angeles: Historical Society of Southern California, 1959.

Hurtado, Albert L. *Indian Survival on the California Frontier*. New Haven: Yale University Press, 1988.

Jacobs, Margaret D. *White Mother to a Dark Race: Settler Colonialism, Maternalism, and the Removal of Indigenous Children in the American West and Australia, 1880–1940*. Lincoln: University of Nebraska Press, 2009.

Jefferson, Thomas. *Writings*. New York: The Library of America, 1984.

Jones, James J. and Lee McDonald. *Voices of the Golden State*. San Francisco: Leswing Communications, 1971.

Kerr, Clark. *The Uses of the University*. Cambridge: Harvard University Press, 1963.

Kimmerer, Robin Wall. *Braiding Sweetgrass: Indigenous Wisdom, Scientific Knowledge, and the Teachings of Plants*. Minneapolis: Milkweed Editions, 2015.

King, Charles. *Gods of the Upper Air: How a Circle of Renegade Anthropologists Reinvented Race, Sex, and Gender in the Twentieth Century*. New York: Doubleday, 2019.

Koonz, Claudia. *The Nazi Conscience*. Cambridge: The Belknap Press, 2003.

Kroeber, Alfred L. *Anthropology*. New York: Harcourt, Brace & Co., 1923.

————. *Handbook of the Indians of California*, Bulletin #78. Washington, DC: Smithsonian Institution, 1925.

————. *Yurok Myths*. Berkeley: University of California Press, 1976.

Kroeber, Alfred L. and Robert F. Heizer. *Continuity of Indian Population in California from 1770/1848 to 1959*. Berkeley: University of California Archaeological Research Facility, 1970.

Kroeber, Alfred L. and T. T. Waterman. *Source Book on Anthropology*. Berkeley: University of California Press, 1920.

Kroeber, Theodora. *Alfred Kroeber: A Personal Configuration*. Berkeley: University of California Press, 1979.

Kroeber, Theodora and Robert F. Heizer. *Almost Ancestors: The First Californians*. San Francisco: The Sierra Club, 1968.

Lara-Cooper, Kishan and Walter J. Lara Sr., eds. *Ka'm-t'em: A Journey toward Healing*. Pechanga, CA: Great Oak Press, 2019.

LeConte, Joseph. *The Race Problem in the South*. New York: D. Appleton and Company, 1892.

Linenthal, Edward T. *Preserving Memory: The Struggle to Create America's Holocaust Museum*. New York: Viking, 1995.

Linenthal, Edward T. and Tom Engelhardt, eds. *History Wars: The Enola Gay and Other Battles for the American Past*. New York: Henry Holt and Company, 1996.

London, Jack. *Martin Eden* (1909). New York: Modern Library, 2002.

Los Alamos Historical Society. *Los Alamos 1943–1945: Beginning of An Era*. Los Alamos: Los Alamos Historical Society, 2007.

Lundberg, Ferdinand. *Imperial Hearst: A Social Biography*. New York: The Modern Library, 1936.

Madley, Benjamin. *An American Genocide: The United States and the California Indian Catastrophe, 1846–1873*. New Haven: Yale University Press, 2016.

Margolin, Malcolm. *The Ohlone Way: Indian Life in the San Francisco–Monterey Bay Area*. Berkeley: Heyday Books, 1978.

Margolin, Malcolm, ed. *Life in a California Mission: The Journals of Jean François de la Pérouse*. Berkeley: Heyday Books, 1989.

McGroarty, John. *California: Its History and Romance*. Los Angeles: Grafton, 1911.

McNamara, Robert S. *In Retrospect: The Tragedy and Lessons of Vietnam*. With Brian VanDeMark. New York: Times Books, 1995.

McWilliams, Carey. *Brothers under the Skin*. Boston: Little, Brown and Company, 1944.

———. *California: The Great Exception*. Berkeley: University of California Press, 1998.

Meriam, Lewis. *The Problem of Indian Administration: Report of a Survey Made at Request of Honorable Hubert Work, Secretary of the Interior*. Baltimore: The Johns Hopkins Press, 1928.

Meyer, Carl. *Bound for Sacramento: Travel Pictures of a Returned Wanderer*. Translated by Ruth Frey Axe. Claremont: Saunders Studio Press, 1938.

Mihesuah, Devon A., ed. *Repatriation Reader: Who Owns American Indian Remains?* Lincoln: University of Nebraska Press, 2000.

Miller, Michael V. and Susan Gilmore, eds. *Revolution at Berkeley: The Crisis in American Education*. New York: The Dial Press, 1965.

Milner, Clyde A. et al., eds. *The Oxford History of the American West*. New York: Oxford University Press, 1994.

Monument Lab. *National Monument Audit*. The Andrew W. Mellon Foundation, 2021.

Moore, Marijo, ed. *Eating Fire, Tasting Blood: An Anthology of the American Indian Holocaust*. Philadelphia: Running Press, 2006.

Nabokov, Peter ed. *Native American Testimony: A Chronicle of Indian–White Relations from Prophecy to the Present, 1492–1992*. New York: Viking Penguin, 1991.

National Action/Research on the Military-Industrial Complex (NARMIC). *Police on the Homefront: A Collection of Essays*. Philadelphia: American Friends Service Committee, 1971.

Nelson, Byron Jr. *Our Home Forever: The Hupa Indians of Northern California*. Salt Lake City: Howe Brothers, 1978.

Nelson, Maidee Thomas. *California, Land of Promise*. Caldwell, Idaho: Caxton Printers, 1962.

Nickliss, Alexandra M. *Phoebe Apperson Hearst: A Life of Power and Politics*. Lincoln: University of Nebraska Press, 2018.

Nokes, R. Gregory. *The Troubled Life of Peter Burnett, Oregon Pioneer and First Governor of California*. Corvallis: Oregon State University Press, 2018.

Nisbet, Robert. *Teachers and Scholars: A Memoir of Berkeley in Depression and War*. New Brunswick: Transaction Publishers, 1992.

Norton, Henry K. *The Story of California: From the Earliest Days to the Present*. Chicago: A.C. McClurg, 1913.

Odum, Howard W. *Social and Mental Traits of the Negro: Research in Conditions of the Negro Race in Southern Towns*. New York: Columbia University Press, 1910.

Oelschlaeger, Max. *The Idea of Wilderness: From Prehistory to the Age of Ecology*. New Haven: Yale University Press, 1991.

Okihiro, Gary Y. *Margins and Mainstreams: Asians in American History and Culture*. Seattle: University of Washington Press, 1994.

O'Leary, Cecilia. *To Die For: The Paradox of American Patriotism*. Princeton: Princeton University Press, 1999.

O'Neill, Edmond. *An Account of the Birth and Growth of the Faculty Club of the University of California*. Berkeley: privately printed, 1933.

Paltridge, James Gilbert. *A History of the Faculty Club at Berkeley*. Berkeley: University of California, The Faculty Club, 1990.

Pelfrey, Patricia A. *A Brief History of the University of California*. Berkeley: The University of California, 2004.

Paul, Diane B., John Stenhouse, and Hamish G. Spencer, eds. *Eugenics at the Edges of Empire: New Zealand, Australia, Canada, and South Africa*. Switzerland: Palgrave Macmillan, 2018.

Perkins, Harry F., ed. *A Decade of Progress: The Third International Congress of Eugenics*. Baltimore: The Williams and Wilkins Company, 1934.

Piatote, Beth. *The Beadworkers: Stories*. Berkeley: Counterpoint, 2019.

Platt, Tony, with Cecilia O'Leary. *Bloodlines: Recovering Hitler's Nuremberg Laws, from Patton's Trophy to Public Memorial*. Boulder: Paradigm Publishers, 2006.

Platt, Tony. *Grave Matters: The Controversy Over Excavating California's Buried Indigenous Past*. 2nd ed. Berkeley: Heyday, 2021.

———. *Beyond These Walls: Rethinking Crime and Punishment in the United States*. New York: St. Martin's Press, 2018.

Popenoe, Paul and Roswell Hill Johnson. *Applied Eugenics*. New York: The Macmillan Company, 1918.

Powers, Stephen. *Tribes of California*. Berkeley: University of California Press, 1976.

Raff, Jennifer. *Origin: A Genetic History of the Americas*. New York: Twelve, 2022.

Rasmussen, Charles and Rick Tilman. *Jacques Loeb: His Science and Social Activism and Their Philosophical Foundations*. Philadelphia: American Philosophical Society, 1998.

Rawls, James. *Indians of California: The Changing Image*. Norman: University of Oklahoma Press, 1984.

Richards, Irmagarde. *Our California Home*. Sacramento: California State Printing Office, 1933.

Ridge, John, ed. *Ore Deposits of the Park City District with a Contribution on the Mayflower Lode, in Ore Deposits of the United States, 1933–1967*. New York: The American Institute of Mining, Metallurgical, and Petroleum Engineers, 1968.

Roach, Joseph. *Cities of the Dead: Circum-Atlantic Performance*. New York: Columbia University Press, 1996.

Roberts, Harry K. *Walking in Beauty: Growing Up With The Yurok Indians*. Trinidad, California: The Press at Indian Art, 2011.

Robinson, Judith. *The Hearsts: An American Dynasty*. New York: Avon Books, 1991.

Rolle, Andrew F. *California A History*. New York: Thomas Y. Crowell, 1967.

Rolph-Trouillot, Michel. *Silencing the Past: Power and the Production of History*. Boston: Beacon Press, 1995.

Rosenfeld, Seth. *Subversives: The FBI's War on Student Radicals, and Reagan's Rise to Power*. New York: Farrar, Straus and Giroux, 2012.

Rothman, Hal K. *On Rims and Ridges: The Los Alamos Area Since 1880*. Lincoln: University of Nebraska Press, 1997.

Royce, Josiah. *California: From the Conquest in 1846 to the Second Vigilance Committee in San Francisco, A Study in American Character*. Boston: Houghton Mifflin Company, 1886.

Rydell, Robert W. *All the World's a Fair: Visions of Empire at American International Expositions, 1876–1916*. Chicago: University of Chicago Press, 1984.

Samuel, Raphael. *Theatres of Memory*, vol. 1 of *Past and Present in Contemporary Culture*. London: Verso, 1994.

Schenk, Marvin A., Karen Holmes, and Sherrie Smith-Ferri, eds. *Aurelius O. Carpenter: Photographer of the Mendocino Frontier*. Ukiah, CA: Grace Hudson Museum and Sun House, 2006.

Schrecker, Ellen W. *No Ivory Tower: McCarthyism and the Universities*. New York: Oxford University Press, 1986.

Sitting Bull: The Collected Speeches. United States: Coyote Books, 1998.

Slotkin, Richard. *The Fatal Environment: The Myth of the Frontier in the Age of Industrialization, 1800–1890*. Wesleyan University Press, 1986.

Snetselaar, Rebecca, ed. *Stories and Scholarship From the Social Science Field Laboratory, Ukiah, California, 1939–1948*. Mendocino: Mendocino County Museum, 2002.

Spott, Robert and A. L. Kroeber, *Yurok Narratives*. Berkeley: University of California Press, 1942.

Spruce, Duane Blue, ed. *Spirit of a Native Place: Building the National Museum of the American Indian*. Washington, DC: National Geographic Society and National Museum of the American Indian, 2004.

Stadtman, Verne A., ed. *The Centennial Record of the University of California, 1868–1968.* University of California, 1967.

———. *The University of California, 1868–1968.* New York: McGraw-Hill Book Company, 1970.

Starn, Orin. *Ishi's Brain: In Search of America's Last "Wild" Indian.* New York: W. W. Norton and Co., 2005.

Stern, Alexandra Minna. *Eugenic Nation: Faults and Frontiers of Better Breeding in Modern America.* Berkeley: University of California Press, 2005.

Stewart, George R. *The Year of the Oath: The Fight for Academic Freedom at the University of California.* New York: Doubleday, 1950.

Taliaferro, John. *Great White Fathers: The Story of the Obsessive Quest to Create Mount Rushmore.* New York: PublicAffairs, 2002.

Taylor, Alexander S., *The Indianology of California.* Fresno: Three Rocks Research, 2015.

Tharp, Twyla. *The Creative Habit: Learn It and Use It for Life.* New York: Simon and Schuster, 2003.

Thomas, William H. *The American Negro: What He Was, What He Is, and What He May Become.* New York: The Macmillan Company, 1901.

Thompson, Lucy. *To the American Indian: Reminiscences of a Yurok Woman* (1916). Berkeley: Heyday, 1991.

Thornbury, D. L. *California's Redwood Wonderland: Humboldt County.* San Francisco: Sunset Press, 1923.

Tillinghast, Joseph A. *The Negro in Africa and America.* New York: The Macmillan Company, 1902.

Tilly, Charles. *Coercion, Capital, and European States, A. D. 990–1992.* New York: Wiley-Blackwell, 1993.

Trevor-Roper, Hugh, ed. *Hitler's Table Talk, 1941–1944: His Private Conversations.* New York: Enigma Books, 2000.

Truettner, William H., ed. *The West as America: Reinterpreting Images of the Frontier, 1820–1920.* Washington, DC: National Museum of American Art, 1991.

Uchida, Yoshiko. *Desert Exile: The Uprooting of a Japanese American Family.* Seattle: University of Washington Press, 1982.

Vancouver, George. *A Voyage of Discovery to the North Pacific Ocean and Round the World, 1791–1795.* London: G. C. and J. Robinson, 1798.

Villarosa, Linda. *Under the Skin: The Hidden Toll of Racism on American Lives and on the Health of Our Nation.* New York: Doubleday, 2022.

Virilio, Paul et al., eds. *Native Land: Stop Eject.* Arles, France: Actes Sud, 2009.

Vollmer, August. *The Criminal.* Brooklyn: Foundation Press, 1949.

Wagner, Harr and Mark Keppel. *California History.* San Francisco: Harr Wagner Publishing Co., 1922.

White, William. *Our California: History–Social Science for California*. Glenview, Illinois: Pearson Scott Foresman, 2006.

Wilder, Craig Steven. *Ebony and Ivy: Race, Slavery, and the Troubled History of America's Universities*. New York: Bloomsbury Publishing, 2013.

Winks, Robin W. *Frederick Billings: A Life*. Berkeley: University of California Press, 1991.

Winling, LaDale C. *Building the Ivory Tower: Universities and Metropolitan Development in the Twentieth Century*. Philadelphia: University of Pennsylvania Press, 2018.

Wrobel, David M. and Michael C. Steiner, eds. *Many Wests: Place, Culture, and Regional Identity*. Lawrence: University of Kansas Press, 1997.

Journals and Magazines

Abinanti, Abby. "A Letter to Justice O'Connor." *The Indigenous Peoples' Journal of Law, Culture, and Resistance* 1, no. 1, (April 2004): 1–5, 10–21.

Barnes, Mary Sheldon. "Some Primitive Californians." *Popular Science Monthly* 50 (February 1897): 486–495.

Bolton, Herbert E. "The Mission as a Frontier Institution in the Spanish-American Colonies." *American Historical Review* 23, no. 1 (October 1917): 42–61.

Benedict, Burton. "Anthropology and the Lowie Museum," *Museum Anthropology* 15, no. 4 (November 1991): 26–29.

Brook, Harry Ellington. "Olden Times in Southern California." *Land of Sunshine* (July 1894).

Brown, Donald R. "Jonathan Baldwin Turner and the Land-Grant Idea." *Journal of the Illinois State Historical Society* 55, no. 4 (Winter 1962): 370–384.

Cahalan, Margaret. "Trends in Incarceration in the United States since 1880: A Summary of Reported Rates and the Distribution of Offenses." *Crime and Delinquency* 25, no. 1, (January 1979): 9–41.

Clymer, Kenton J. "Humanitarian Imperialism: David Prescott Barrows and the White Man's Burden in the Philippines." *Pacific Historical Review* 45, no. 4 (1976): 495–517.

De Waal, Alex. "Lab Leaks." *London Review of Books* (December 2, 2021): 28.

Delbanco, Andrew. "Endowed by Slavery." *New York Review of Books* (June 23, 2022): 59–62.

Deloria, Philip J. "Defiance." *The New Yorker* (November 2, 2020): 76–80.

Douglass, John Aubrey. "Creating a Fourth Branch of State Government: The University of California and the Constitutional Convention of 1879." *History of Education Quarterly* 32, no. 1 (Spring 1992): 31–72.

Dore, Christopher D. et al. "Why Here? Settlement, Geoarchaeology, and Paleoenvironment at the West Berkeley Site (CA-Ala-307)." *Proceedings of the Society for California Archaeology* 17 (2004): 27–33.

Edwards, Tai S. and Paul Kelton. "Germs, Genocides, and America's Indigenous Peoples." *Journal of American History* (June 2020): 52–76.

Ehrlich, Gretel. "Chronicles of Ice," *Orion Magazine* (November 1, 2004): https://orion magazine.org/article/chronicles-of-ice/.

Go, Julian. "The Imperial Origins of American Policing: Militarization and Imperial Feedback in the Early 20th Century." *American Journal of Sociology* 125, no. 5 (March 2020): 1193–1254.

Hartman, Saidiya. "Venus in Two Acts." *Small Axe* 12, no. 2 (June 2008): 1–14.

Heizer, Robert F. "A Question of Ethics in Archaeology—One Archaeologist's View." *Journal of California Anthropology* 1 and 2 (1974): 145-151.

Hester, Thomas R. "Robert Fleming Heizer, 1915–1979: A Biographical Memoir." *National Academy of Sciences* (1996).

Holy, Alexandra New. "The Heart of Everything That Is: Paha Sapa, Treaties, and Lakota Identity." *Oklahoma City University Law Review* 23 (1998): 349–350.

Hrdlička, Aleš. "Eugenics and Its Natural Limitations in Man." *Science* 42, no. 1085 (October 1915): 546.

Jacknis, Ira. "A Museum Prehistory: Phoebe Hearst and the Founding of the Museum of Anthropology, 1891–1901." *Chronicle of the University of California* 4 (2000): 47–77.

———. "The First Boasian: Alfred Kroeber and Franz Boas, 1896–1905." *American Anthropologist* 104, no. 2 (2002): 520–532.

Jaffe, Logan et al. "America's Biggest Museums Fail to Return Native Human Remains." *ProPublica* (January 11, 2023): https://www.propublica.org/article /repatriation-nagpra-museums-human-remains.

Jensen, Arthur R. "How Much Can We Boost IQ and Scholastic Achievement?" *Harvard Educational Review* 39, no. 1 (Winter 1969): 1–123.

Krisberg, Barry. "Teaching Radical Criminology." *Crime and Social Justice* 1 (1974), 64–66.

Loeb, Jacques. "Heredity and Racial Inferiority." *Crisis* 8 (June 1914).

———. "Biology and War," *Science* 45, no. 1152 (January 26, 1917).

Kroeber, Alfred L. "Progress in Anthropology at the University of California." *American Anthropologist* 8, no. 3 (July–September 1906): 483–492.

———. "The Indians of California." *Transactions of the Commonwealth Club of California* 4 (December 1909): 430–437.

———. "The Languages of the Coast of California North of San Francisco." *University of California Publications in American Archaeology and Ethnology* 9, no. 3 (1911): 273–435.

———. "18 Professions." *American Anthropologist* (1915): 283–288.

———. "Two Papers on the Aboriginal Ethnography of California." *Reports of the University of California Archaeological Survey* 56, no. 1 (March 1962).

Lee, Robert and Tristan Ahtone. "Land-Grab Universities: Expropriated Indigenous Land is the Foundation of the Land-Grant University System." *High Country News* (March 30, 2020): 32–45.

Loud, Llewellyn L. "Ethnogeography and Archaeology of the Wiyot Territory." *University of California Publications in American Archaeology and Ethnology* 14, no. 3 (December 1918).

Mecklin, John. "The Energy Department's Fusion Breakthrough: It's Not Really about Generating Electricity." *Bulletin of the Atomic Scientists* (December 16, 2022).

Mishra, Pankaj. "Grand Illusions." *The New York Review of Books* (November 19, 2020): 31–32.

Mitchell, David and Sharon Snyder. "The Eugenic Atlantic: Race, Disability, and the Making of an International Eugenic Science, 1800–1945." *Disability and Society* 18, no. 7 (2003), 843–864.

Nash, Gerald D. "California and Its Historians: An Appraisal of Histories of the State." *Pacific Historical Review* 50, no. 4 (November 1981): 387–413.

Nash, Margaret A. "Entangled Pasts: Land-Grant Colleges and American Indian Dispossession." *History of Education Quarterly* 59, no. 4 (2019): 1–31.

Nelson, Nels C. "Shellmounds of the San Francisco Bay Region." *University of California Publications in American Archaeology and Ethnology* 7, no. 4 (December 1909).

Orwell, George. "Politics and the English Language," *Horizon* (April 1946).

Pape, Elise and Holger Stoecker. "Human Remains from Namibia in German Collections," *Human Remains and Violence* 4, no. 2 (2018): 1–4.

Platt, Tony. "Engaging the Past: Charles M. Goethe, American Eugenics, and Sacramento State University." *Social Justice* 32, no. 2 (2005): 17–33.

———. "The Yokayo vs. The University of California." *News from Native California* 26, no. 2 (2012–2013): 9–14.

Preston, Douglas J. "Skeletons in Our Museums' Closets." *Harper's* (February 1989): 66–75.

Putnam, Frederic Ward. "A Problem in American Anthropology." *Science* 10, no. 243 (August 25, 1899): 225–236.

Read, Charles H. "An Account of a Collection of Ethnographical Specimens Formed During Vancouver's Voyage in the Pacific Ocean, 1790–1795." *The Journal of the Archaeological Institute of Great Britain and Ireland* 21 (1892): 99–108.

Redman, Samuel. "The Hearst Museum of Anthropology, the New Deal, and a Reassessment of the 'Dark Age' of the Museum in the United States." *Museum Anthropology* 34, no. 1 (March 2011): 48-49.

Rowe, John Howland. "Max Uhle, 1856–1944: A Memoir of the Father of Peruvian Archaeology," *University of California Publications in American Archaeology and Ethnology* 46, no. 1 (1954).

———. "Alfred Louis Kroeber, 1876–1960." *American Antiquity* 27, no. 3 (January 1962), 395–415.

Royster, Hayden. "This Land Is Their Land." *California* 133, no. 2 (Summer 2022): 32–41.

Schneider, Khal. "Making Indian Land in the Allotment Era: Northern California's Indian Rancherias." *The Western Historical Quarterly* 41, no. 4 (Winter 2010): 429–450.

Sebald, W. G. "An Attempt at Restitution: A Memory of a German City." *The New Yorker* (December 20, 2004).

Severson, Alissa L. et al. "Ancient and Modern Genomics of the Ohlone Indigenous Population of California." *Proceedings of the National Academy of Sciences* 119, no. 13 (March 2022): https://doi.org/10.1073/pnas.211153311.

Shaer, Matthew. "The Sordid History of Mount Rushmore." *Smithsonian Magazine* (October 2016).

Simon, John Y. "The Politics of the Morrill Act." *Agricultural History* 37, no. 2 (1963): 103-111.

Spott, Robert. "Address." *Transactions of the Commonwealth Club of California* 21, no. 3 (1926): 133-135.

Stern, Alexandra Minna, and Tony Platt. "Sterilization Abuse in State Prisons: Time to Break With California's Long Eugenic Patterns," *Huffington Post* (July 23, 2013).

Takagi, Paul. "Growing Up a Japanese Boy in Sacramento County," *Social Justice* 26, no. 2 (1999): 135–149.

Takagi, Paul and Tony Platt. "Behind the Gilded Ghetto: An Analysis of Race, Class, and Crime in Chinatown." *Crime and Social Justice* 9 (Spring–Summer, 1978): 2–25.

Taylor, Alan J. "Unstable Motives: Propaganda, Politics, and the Late Work of Alexander Calder." *American Art* 26, no. 1 (2012): 25-47.

Tee, Gary J. "The Elusive C. D. Voy." *Journal of the Historical Studies Group* 39 (September 2010): 17–50.

"The Lost Island of Sandoval County," *The Atom* 1, no. 1 (January 1964): https://www.lanl.gov/library//find/lanl-publications-atom.php.

Thomas, Janice. "Strawberry Canyon, 'A Mountain Gorge.'" *Berkeley Landmarks* (September 2005): http://berkeleyheritage.com/berkeley_landmarks/strawbcanyon.html.

Uhle, Max. "The Emeryville Shellmound." *University of California Publications in American Archaeology and Ethnology* 7, no. 1 (1907).

"University of California, A Photographic Essay." *Life* (October 25, 1948).

Walker, Alice. "The Civil Rights Movement: What Good Was It?" *American Scholar* (Autumn 1967): 554.

Waterman, Thomas T. "The Subdivisions of the Human Race and Their Distribution." *American Anthropologist* 26 (1924): 474–490.

Wellerstein, Alex. "Counting the Dead at Hiroshima and Nagasaki," *Bulletin of the Atomic Scientists* (August 4, 2020).

Willard, C. D. "The Padres and The Indians." *Land of Sunshine* (September 1894): 73.

Yudof, Mark. "For 150 years, UC Science and Agriculture Transform California." *California Agriculture* 66, no. 2 (2012): https://escholarship.org/uc/item/9gw5b2hq.

Government and Legal Documents

Executive Dept., State of Calif, Gov. Gavin Newsom, Exec. Order N-15-19 (June 18, 2019).

National Park Service, Department of the Interior. "Notice of Inventory Completion: University of California, Berkeley." *Federal Register* 84, no. 79 (April 24, 2019): 17191–17192.

Presidential Advisory Commission on Holocaust Assets in the United States. *Plunder and Restitution: The US and Holocaust Victims' Assets*. Washington, DC: US Government Printing Office, 2000.

Stone, Livingstone. *Report of Operation During 1874 at the US Salmon Hatching Establishment on the McCloud River, California* (April 1875). Washington, DC: 43rd Congress, 2nd session, Senate Miscellaneous Document #108.

United Nations General Assembly. *United Nations Declaration on the Rights of Indigenous Peoples*, General Assembly Resolution 61/295, UN Doc. A/RES/61/295 (October 2, 2007).

United States Atomic Energy Commission. "In The Matter of J. Robert Oppenheimer," Washington, DC, transcript (April 16, 1954).

US Department of Interior, National Park Service. "Managing Archaeological Collections," https://www.nps.gov/archeology/collections/index.htm.

US Department of the Interior. Departmental Manual, *Museum Property Handbook* vols. 1 and 2, https://www.doi.gov/sites/doi.gov/files/migrated/museum/policy/upload/mphi-1.pdf.

Wheeler, George M. *Report upon United States Geographical Surveys West of the One Hundredth Meridian*, vol. 7, "Archaeology." Washington, DC: US Government Printing Office, 1879.

Manuscripts and Unpublished Reports

Buckley, David et al. William Self Associates. "Geoarchaeological Testing Report for the University of California, Berkeley, Student Athlete Performance Center, Alameda County, California." December 2008.

Christ, Carol, Chancellor. "Talking Points." Unpublished memo from a Native American Cultural Affiliation and Repatriation Work Session, Berkeley, January 31, 2020.

Charbonneau, Robert. "Strawberry Creek Management Plan, UC Berkeley." December 1, 1987. https://creeks.berkeley.edu/sites/default/files/publications/scmp1987_chapter3.pdf.

Garrett, Andrew, Melissa Stoner, Susan Edwards, Jeffery MacKie-Mason, Nicole Myers-Lim, Benjamin W. Porter, Elaine C. Tennant, and Verna Bowie. "Native American Collections in Archives, Libraries, and Museums at the University of California, Berkeley." Office of the Vice Chancellor for Research, University of California, Berkeley. March 15, 2019.

Kielusiak, Carol. "Archaeological Survey of 70 Acres of Land and Recordation and Evaluation of Four Historic Resources at the E. O. Lawrence Berkeley National Laboratory." Northwestern Information Center S-028039, 19-2224 Sonoma State University. February 2000.

Kroiz, Lauren. "Report for Strategic Planning Conversation." Unpublished memo, September 1, 2020.

Luby, Edward M., Special Assistant to the UC Berkeley Vice Chancellor for Research and Director, NAGPRA Unit. "Administrative Update on Compliance with the Native American Graves Protection and Repatriation Act (NAGPRA): January 1, 1999, through December 31, 2000."

Reavis, Amy and Nora Wallace. "Entitled to Our Land: The Settler Colonial Origins of the University of California." *California Law Review* 13, forthcoming 2023.

Roop, William. "Archaeological Reconnaissance of the Proposed Biological Sciences Construction and Alterations Project, University of California at Berkeley." Northwestern Information Center S-005625, 19-2224 Sonoma State University. September 28, 1982.

————. "Archaeological Survey of Underdeveloped Lands and Proposed Building Locations within the Lawrence Berkeley Laboratory, University of California Berkeley." Northwestern Information Center S-008719, 19-2224 Sonoma State University. July 29, 1986.

Werry, Margaret. "Moving Objects (on the Performance of the Dead)." Paper presented at Conference of International Federation of Theatre Research, 2013.

Index

281

About *the* Author

Tony Platt is a Distinguished Affiliated Scholar at the Center for the Study of Law and Society at the University of California, Berkeley. The author of twelve books dealing with issues of race, inequality, and social justice in American history—including *Grave Matters: The Controversy over Excavating California's Buried Indigenous Past* (2011 and 2021) and *Beyond These Walls: Rethinking Crime and Punishment in the United States* (2018)—he previously taught at the University of Chicago, UC Berkeley, San Jose State University, and Sacramento State University. His experience as a political activist with the Coalition to Protect Yurok Cultural Legacies at O-pyúweg (Big Lagoon, California) and Berkeley's Truth and Justice Project shaped this book.